# SOUTH

Also by Merlin Coverley

*London Writing*
*Psychogeography*
*Occult London*
*Utopia*
*The Art of Wandering*

# SOUTH

MERLIN COVERLEY

OLDCASTLE BOOKS

First published in 2016 by
Oldcastle Books Ltd,
PO Box 394, Harpenden,
AL5 1XJ
oldcastlebooks.com

Editor: Nick Rennison

A CIP catalogue record for this book is available from the British Library

ISBNs
978-1-84344-725-2 (print)
978-1-84344-726-9 (epub)
978-1-84344-727-6 (kindle)
978-1-84344-728-3 (pdf)

2 4 6 8 10 9 7 5 3 1

Typeset by Avocet Typeset, Somerton, Somerset in 11.5pt Bembo
Printed and bound by CPI Group (UK) Ltd, Croydon, CR0 4YY

*'I shall go further south – feel I want to go further and further south – don't know why.'*

DH Lawrence[*]

# Contents

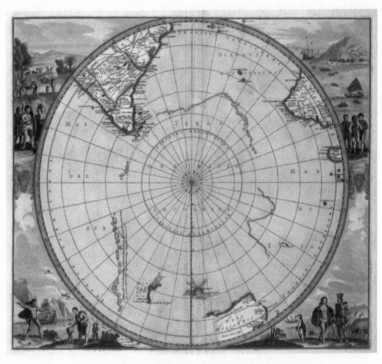

*Map of the South Pole* by unknown artist (17th Century)

# Introduction: The Idea of South

*Every person is born with his own north or south, whether he is born into an external one as well – is of little consequence.*

Jean Paul[1]

*Our sense that north is 'up' and south is 'down' is purely an artefact of map-making conventions in the northern hemisphere.*

Gyrus[2]

In 1989 the landscape artist, Andy Goldsworthy, constructed four circular arches from snow bricks, positioning them to face one another across the arctic axis at the North Pole. Goldsworthy named his sculpture 'Touching North', an ambiguous title for a work which demonstrates how the directions of the compass may effectively be rendered meaningless: emerge through any of the four arches and one finds oneself heading south.[3] Goldsworthy's work reminds us not only of the ease with which our man-made attribution of the cardinal directions may be overridden, but also of the way in which the meanings of these axial points are implied by one another. For there can be no north without south, as the OED entry for 'South' confirms: 'Towards, or in the direction of, that part of the earth or heavens which is directly opposite to the North.'[4] Such a definition suggests an equality between such designations, the one informed by the other, and vice versa. Yet within the family of cardinal points, some directions are clearly more equal than others. For 'Touching North' is also indicative of the unstated but nevertheless unequal relationship which governs our understanding of north

# MERLIN COVERLEY

and south, the one implicit within the other yet somehow ancillary to it.

The fact that most early civilisations are now believed to have developed to the north of the equator goes some way to explaining the privileged position the north has since acquired as the summit of the world. The enduring power of such a worldview is demonstrated by the fact that even civilisations such as that of the Mayans in the southern hemisphere regarded the North Pole as the 'top' of the world, despite the fact that at their latitude it is barely fifteen degrees above the horizon. While at an even more southerly latitude of some 13.5 degrees south of the equator, the indigenous population of the Incan capital of Cuzco in Peru also regarded the 'upper' part of their city as that which lay to the north, despite the North Pole lying well below the horizon, a fact which has since been attributed to the influence of the southward migration of Stone Age colonists.[5] Even in medieval Europe, maps such as those found in the *Etymologies* of Isidore of Seville (c.560–636) located the cardinal point in the south not at the South Pole, as one might imagine, but rather on the equator, perpetuating a view of the world established in the early classical era in which the *meridies*, or Roman cardinal point for the south, signified the southern boundary of the known world, then located within the equatorial region.[6] Historical representations of the south, as well as the mythology in which they are embedded, will be explored elsewhere in this book. But in seeking the origin of the dominant position which the north has come to hold over its southern counterpart, it is useful to note the comments of the author, John T Irwin, who has outlined the evolution of this disparity:

> Just as there is a privileged pole in each of the oppositions associated with bodily directionality (i.e., front over rear, right over left), so there is also a privileged pole in each of the oppositions associated with geographic directionality. [...] In the definitions of *right* and *left* and of *east* and *west*,

it is stipulated that one be "facing north"; while in the definitions of *north* and *south* the condition is that one be "facing the sunset" (west). This preference for north over south and west over east as the directions one faces in order to define the other cardinal points and the sides of the body can perhaps be explained in terms of practical navigation. The privileging of the north probably results in part from the fact that on a day-to-day basis the North Star is a more reliable approximate indicator of true north than the rising sun is of true east or the setting sun of true west, while the privileging of the west may well be a function of the fact that in the modern world the sun's setting is an event likely to be observed by more people on a given day than the sun's rising. Yet in the privileging of one pole of a differential opposition over another, there is always a cultural bias at work, and certainly the favored status of north and west in these definitions results in part from their being the directions most closely associated with both the geographic location and the historical designation of that culture represented by the dictionary, the modern, scientific culture of that industrialized portion of the northern hemisphere traditionally referred to as the West.[7]

As Irwin's comments suggest, both west and north, whether as a consequence of astronomical considerations or through cultural bias, have come to be seen as the privileged cardinal points, as well as the global designators of wealth and political power. As for the Orient (from the Latin *oriens*), this has long since been equated with the spiritual radiance of the rising sun, with the churches of the Christian faith orientated to the east; this is widely held to be 'the pre-eminent sacred direction, the point by which to orient oneself, to place oneself in this world with regard to the divine.'[8] If then, these three points of the compass can so readily be assigned a role, albeit a symbolic one, what of the remaining cardinal point, the south? In what manner should this direction, this region of the globe, be portrayed? This book will attempt to provide an answer to this question, by exploring some of the world's 'souths' and the many different ways in which they are represented.

One such way, of course, is via the convenient but monolithic shorthand of the Global South, the 'collective name for the industrially and economically less advanced countries of the world, typically situated to the south of the industrialised nations.'[9] Yet if this is a region which has, however unfairly, become perceived as one synonymous with poverty and deprivation, it is also one which has often been depicted historically, from a Western perspective at least, as an 'empty' region, a blank slate which has been repeatedly overwritten by the mapmakers and mythologists of the northern hemisphere.

There are many ways in which the cardinal points may be brought to life, and many symbols which may be attributed to them, from colours to mythological creatures; from times of the day to seasons of the year; from winds and weather to gender and bodily form. In Cesare Ripa's iconographical compendium, *Iconologia* (1593), for example, they are personified in the following manner: the east is a 'pretty youth, with golden locks'; holding flowers in his right hand ready to blossom, he represents the morning and the rising sun. The west, by contrast, is an old man holding a bunch of poppies in his left hand; his is the representation of the setting sun at the close of day. The north is depicted by a man in the prime of life, fair-haired, blue-eyed and of a 'ruddy complexion'; suited in white armour, his hand clasping his sword, 'his habit of body denotes the *quality* of the cold climate that makes men have a good stomach, and quick digestion'; his posture, as he stands tall against a backdrop of cloud and snow, reflects 'the *bravery* of the *northern* people'. While in the south we see a young black man illuminated by the noon-day sun above his head; in his right hand, arrows, representing the sun's penetrating rays, in his left, a lotus branch, symbolising water.[10] One does not require a keen understanding of Ripa's complex symbolic vocabulary to identify the dominant figure here.

Alongside such symbolic representations, another way in which the four corners of the earth have commonly been characterised is through the attribution of human temperament: hard-working or lazy; cunning or stupid; short-tempered or placid. This is the manner in which one group or region has traditionally portrayed its neighbour. Such is the case in Wu Che'êng-ên's Chinese folk-tale, translated into English as *Monkey,* or *Journey to the West,* in which we encounter this passage:

> One day when Buddha had been preaching to the Bodhisattvas and Arhats, he said at the end of his sermon, 'I have been noticing that there is a lot of difference in the inhabitants of the Four Continents of the universe. Those in the Eastern Continent are respectful, peaceable and cheerful; those of the Northern are somewhat prone to take life, but they are so dumb, lethargic and stupid that they don't do much harm. In our Western Continent, there is no greed or slaughter; we nurture our humours and hide our magic, and although we have no supreme illuminates everyone is safe against the assaults of the age. But in Jumbudvīpa, the Southern Continent, they are greedy, lustful, murderous, and quarrelsome. I wonder whether a knowledge of the True Scriptures would not cause some improvement in them?'[11]

This less than flattering portrait of the inhabitants of the 'Southern Continent' is by no means peculiar to China in the sixteenth century. Indeed, at around much the same time in Europe, the Reformation was helping to forge a similar outlook, as new religious divisions between north and south emerged, and ignorance and suspicion gradually hardened into lasting prejudice.[12] Once established in the popular imagination, such prejudices have proven surprisingly enduring, and thus more than three hundred years later, we find John Ruskin's description of European architectural styles betraying precisely the same chauvinism towards the south:

> There is, first, the habit of hard and rapid working; the industry of the tribes of the North, quickened by the coldness of the climate, and giving an expression of sharp energy to all they do, as opposed to the languor of the Southern tribes, however much of fire there may be in the heart of that languor, for lava itself may flow languidly. [...] Strength of will, independence of character, resoluteness of purpose, impatience of undue control, and that general tendency to set the individual reason against authority, and the individual deed against destiny, which, in the Northern tribes, has opposed itself throughout all ages, to the languid submission, in the Southern, of thought to tradition, and purpose to fatality, are all more or less traceable in the rigid lines, vigorous and various masses, and daringly projecting and independent structure of the Northern Gothic ornament: while the opposite feelings are in like manner legible in the graceful and softly guided waves and wreathed bands, in which Southern decoration is constantly disposed; in its tendency to lose its independence, and fuse itself into the surface of the masses upon which it is traced; and in the expression seen so often, in the arrangement of those masses themselves, of an abandonment of their strength to an inevitable necessity, or a listless repose.[13]

Of course, ideas such as these are replicated not only at a continental level, but within individual countries and individual cities; they reflect an outlook which is often dependent upon little more than which side of this, frequently imaginary, border one happens to inhabit, originate from, or identify with. In this light, one may compare the comments of Ruskin, above, with those of Antonio Gramsci, whose polemical essay, 'Some Aspects of the Southern Question'

(1926), explores the effects of a similarly entrenched north-south axis within the borders of his own twentieth-century Italy. Here Gramsci reveals how such designations may be employed not only to highlight or caricature cultural differences but also in support of rather more pernicious ideological purposes:

> It is well-known what kind of ideology has been disseminated in myriad ways among the masses in the North, by the propagandists of the bourgeoisie: the South is the ball and chain which prevents the social development of Italy from progressing more rapidly; the Southerners are biologically inferior beings, semi-barbarians or total barbarians, by natural destiny; if the South is backward, the fault does not lie with the capitalist system or with any other historical cause, but with Nature, which has made the Southerners lazy, incapable, criminal and barbaric – only tempering this harsh fate with the purely individual explosion of a few great geniuses, like isolated palm-trees in an arid and barren desert.[14]

Such divisions are equally visible in the UK, where the North-South divide remains a social and economic reality bolstered by similarly extravagant perceptions of the relative strengths and weaknesses of the populations on either side. This national disparity, both real and imagined, continues to be the subject of endless discussion, but amidst the multifarious voices which have been raised in celebration or denigration of their chosen side in this partisan and often parochial debate, there is one which is worthy of particular attention: 'One must have a proper moral sense about the points of the compass,' writes WH Auden, 'North must seem the "good" direction, the way towards heroic adventures, South the way to ignoble ease and decadence.'[15] According to his biographer, Rupert Davenport-Hines, Auden developed his acute and lasting association with northernness as a young boy, through the powerful influence of his father's love of Nordic history, encouraging him to construct 'a world of private associations around latitudes and longitudes: his artistic, moral and sensual criteria were all related to his personalised reordering of the planet.'[16] Many writers, as we shall see, have expressed a similarly devout association with their favoured point of the compass; it is those of a more southerly disposition that I shall be discussing here. But few of them have been able to articulate such feelings with the degree of precision which Auden displays:

> My feelings have been orientated by the compass as far back as I can remember [...] To this day Crewe Junction marks the wildly exciting frontier where the alien South ends and the North, my world, begins.
>
> For reasons which will be, perhaps, more obvious to psychologists than to me, North and South are the foci of two sharply contrasted clusters of images and emotions [...] North – cold, wind, precipices, glaciers, caves, heroic conquest of dangerous obstacles, whales, hot meat and vegetables, concentration and production, privacy. South – heat, light, drought, calm, agricultural plains, trees, rotarian crowds, the life of ignoble ease, spiders, fruits and desserts, the waste of time, publicity. West and East are relatively neutral. West is more favourable, i.e., more northern, but conjures up the unheroic image of retired couples holding hands in the sunset; East is definitely southern and means dried figs and scorpions.[17]

Auden attributes his outlook to two formative factors, Puritanism and introversion, arguing that it is these traits which identify one as a 'cold weather man', temperamentally unsuited to what he catalogues as the lush vegetation, heat, noise and crowds to be found in the south.[18] Written in 1947, Auden's words may still be seen as the definitive statement of 'northernness' as it is recognised in the UK, a moral position as much as it is one of temperament, contrasting the north, in all its hardy, austere simplicity, with the effete delinquency of the south. Almost seventy years later, however, and little appears to have changed. For Auden's vision of the North continues to hold sway, a position which has only been reinforced by the startling array of publications to have appeared in recent years devoted to an analysis of all things northern.[19] While at first glance such a septentrional obsession may appear a peculiarly English phenomenon, it is in fact one whose influence extends far beyond the borders of this country, including much of the wider world within its embrace. This is the prevailing current against which this book was written.

What Auden's comments confirm, however, as do those of Ruskin and Gramsci before him, is that the parameters of one's own north and south have far less to do with any cartographical convention than with one's own sensibility; for just as the south is both a direction and a destination, so too is it a state of mind, an internal compass bearing through which one orientates one's place in the world. That this is the case should become evident to any reader of this book, which was written from the perspective of a northern European, albeit one living in the south of a southern city. As a consequence, many of the souths that I shall be exploring in these pages are to be found in the northern hemisphere, while many of the literary representations of the southern hemisphere I shall be discussing were written by authors from Europe and North America; and as for the polar south, this is a region which has for much of its brief human history been viewed as little more than a southern outpost of the north. Of course, there are omissions too: the islands of the South Pacific, long since the site of the most exotic of all the many northern utopian dreams, find a place here; while Australia, the Great Southern Land itself, does not. Borges' Buenos Aires is included as a representative of the 'magic south' of the Americas; Africa and Asia are absent. My home city, London, is discussed; but at the expense of the remainder of southern England which it overshadows. These choices are themselves a consequence of my own sense of the south, a sense shaped both by the north and through northern perceptions of the south.

Throughout this book I have used the idea of the south in a number of different ways: as a nascent tourist destination, from the Grand Tour in southern Europe to the development of the 'Southland' in the southern United States; as a personal trajectory that has impelled individuals southward in search of creative renewal, from Goethe and Nietzsche to Gauguin and Lawrence; as the destination of choice, often the final destination, for those simply following their feet, from naturalists such as von Humboldt and John Muir to the heroes of southern polar exploration; as the ever-changing goal of colonial ambition and political expediency, from the voyages of Cook and de Bougainville to the emergence of the Nuclear South in French Polynesia and elsewhere; and finally as the location for some highly esoteric ideas, from Hollow Earth theories to myths of Nazi survival. In doing so, I have brought together historical testimony, theoretical speculation and literary representation, in an attempt to establish a composite image of what the term 'South' has come to mean, and to highlight some of the extraordinary array of ideas and visions its usage continues to provoke.

## Epigraph

★   DH Lawrence in a letter to Cecily Lambert Minchin, 18 November 1919, quoted in Owen, p. 159.

## Notes

1. Jean Paul [Johann Paul Friedrich Richter] quoted in Bertram, p. 213.
2. Gyrus, p. 203.

3. Gyrus, p. 237.
4. *Oxford English Dictionary* (Second Edition), prepared by JA Simpson & ESC Weiner, Oxford: Clarendon Press, 1989, Vol. XVI, pp. 67–69.
5. Gyrus, pp. 91–2.
6. Wortham, p. 65.
7. Irwin, pp. 161–2. For a discussion of the cognitive origins of this 'vertical orientation' between north and south and its consequences, see Murray, 'Verticality and its Underbelly' (2009).
8. Gyrus, pp. 101–102.
9. *Oxford English Dictionary* (Second Edition), prepared by JA Simpson & ESC Weiner, Oxford: Clarendon Press, 1989, Vol. XVI, pp. 67–69.
10. Ripa, p. 77. See also Davidson, pp. 38–39.
11. Che'êng-ên, p. 88.
12. Davidson writes (p. 38):

In Europe the map of relations between north and south was catastrophically redrawn at the Reformation: a new set of divisions appeared and, from the sixteenth century, travel between north and south was gravely restricted. In the south the proverbial evil of the north was equated with the writings of Luther, the armies of Gustavus Adolphus – *ab aquilone omne malum*. In the north, the black legend began to grow of the backwardness and decadence of the south.

13. Ruskin, pp. 106–7.
14. Gramsci, p. 173.
15. WH Auden, 'England, Six Unexpected Days', *American Vogue*, 15 May 1954, quoted in Davidson, p.99.
16. Davenport-Hines, p. 16.
17. WH Auden, 'I like it Cold', *House & Garden*, December 1947, in *The Complete Works*, p. 335.
18. Auden, p. 335.
19. For example: Simon Armitage, *All Points North* (1998); Peter Davidson, *The Idea of North* (2005); Stuart Maconie, *Pies and Prejudice: In Search of the North* (2008); Martin Wainwright, *True North: In Praise of England's Better Half* (2009); John Bulmer, *The North* (2012); Paul Morley, *The North: And Almost Everything in It,* (2013) and Gyrus, *North*, (2014).

*Goethe in the Roman Campagna* by Johann Heinrich Wilhelm Tischbein (1787)
STÄDEL–MUSEUM FRANKFURT

# 1

## Goethe's Law

*All dwellers in the Teutonic north, looking out at the winter sky, are subject to spasms of nearly irresistible pull, when the entire Italian peninsula from Trieste to Agrigento begins to function like a lodestone. The magnetism is backed by an unseen choir, there are roulades of mandolin strings in the air; ghostly whiffs of lemon blossom beckon the victims south and across the Alpine passes. It is Goethe's Law and is ineluctable as Newton's or Boyle's.*

Patrick Leigh Fermor[1]

*The Mediterranean is the model for the concept* south, *and it is a rare Briton whose pulses do not race at mention of that compass direction.*

Paul Fussell[2]

There are many ways to characterise the division between the north and the south in Europe. It may be done by highlighting differences in landscape and climate, the sea and the sun of the Mediterranean south contrasted with the colder more mountainous terrain of the north. Equally one may identify a fault line between the peoples of the north and south, their customs, language, religion and morality; the stereotypically easy-going existence of the Catholic south, for example, is often contrasted with what is frequently perceived (usually by those who live there) to be the more industrious lifestyles of their Protestant counterparts in the north. Architectural styles, diet, and a preference for beer or wine, the ways in

which we confirm this continental divide seem endless; but
what is more difficult to identify with any degree of precision
is the point at which one world gives way to another. For
we carry our own sense of north and south within us, an
internal compass which regulates our worldview and which
impresses our personal and imaginary vision onto the world
around us. In his essay 'Ordered South' (1874), Robert Louis
Stevenson, a writer whose life, perhaps more than any other,
followed an unerring southerly course, has described the
sensations that this moment of transition entails:

> Moreover, there is still before the invalid the shock of
> wonder and delight with which he will learn that he
> has passed the indefinable line that separates South from
> North. And this is an uncertain moment; for sometimes the
> consciousness is forced upon him early, on the occasion of
> some slight association, a colour, a flower, or a scent; and
> sometimes not until, one fine morning, he wakes up with
> the southern sunshine peeping through the persiennes,
> and the southern patois confusedly audible below the
> windows. Whether it come early or late, however, this
> pleasure will not end with the anticipation, as do so many
> others of the same family. It will leave him wider awake
> than it found him, and give a new significance to all he
> may see for many days to come. There is something in
> the mere name of the South that carries enthusiasm along
> with it. At the sound of the word, he pricks up his ears;
> he becomes as anxious to seek out beauties and to get by
> heart the permanent lines and character of the landscape,
> as if he had been told that it was all his own – an estate
> out of which he had been kept unjustly, and which he was
> now to receive in free and full possession. Even those who
> have never been there before feel as if they had been; and
> everybody goes comparing, and seeking for the familiar,
> and finding it with such ecstasies of recognition, that
> one would think they were coming home after a weary
> absence, instead of travelling hourly farther abroad.[3]

Stevenson was 'ordered' south to the French Riviera on health grounds, but the experience he relates above was by no means unique to him, for by 1874, young men across Europe had been performing a similarly southward migration for more than two centuries. Of course, the motivations behind such excursions changed over the intervening years, as the Grand Tourists of the seventeenth and eighteenth centuries gave way to the invalids and sun-worshippers of the nineteenth and twentieth. Today the growth of mass tourism has transformed the coastal landscapes of southern Europe, creating a seemingly endless series of anonymous beachside communities, supported by a transient population of predominantly northern European holidaymakers. These changes, some gradual, others much less so, have been witnessed and recorded by an array of writers and travellers, from Goethe to Nietzsche; DH Lawrence to Laurie Lee; Norman Lewis to JG Ballard. Such a disparate series of observations and impressions, of different regions and at different periods, might at first glance appear to hold little in common, but on closer inspection all these accounts, regardless of time and place, demonstrate the endurance of our fluctuating, but apparently boundless, fascination with the south.

## The Grand Tour

According to the historian, Ian Littlewood, the first recorded usage of the term 'Grand Tour' is in Richard Lassels' travel narrative, *The Voyage of Italy* (1670), although twenty years earlier the diarist John Evelyn had described a traveller on a journey through Europe 'making the tour as they call it.'[4] The ideas behind the Grand Tour, however, the custom of travelling through continental Europe which was undertaken, largely by aristocratic young men (young women would have to wait another 200 years or so), between the mid-seventeenth and mid-nineteenth centuries, have their roots in Enlightenment thought. Indeed, the very name, Enlightenment (in French, *Les Lumières*) is, as Adam Gopnik notes, suggestive of the metaphors of warmth, light and sunshine which were employed to illustrate the illumination of dark superstition through reason, and which had the inevitable, yet irrational, consequence of promoting the idea of distinct national cultures as reflections of their own particular climates.[5] With its newfound emphasis upon the senses and physical stimuli as the source of all knowledge, Enlightenment thinking saw the environment and the natural world take on a new relevance and as a result the idea of travel developed a role as a crucial part of a young man's education. Thus from around the latter half of the seventeenth century, young men of a principally wealthy, predominantly northern European Protestant background began to head southward through continental Europe in search of the classical antiquities and Renaissance treasures of the south. Over time a well-trodden circuit was established through France and Switzerland before crossing the Alps into northern Italy. From there the intrepid traveller, accompanied, according to wealth and status, by a retinue of guides and servants would head southwards via Turin to Florence, before turning north to Padua and on to Venice, the cultural highpoint of the Tour. The ruins of ancient Rome came next, and finally Naples. For many this marked the southernmost extent of the Grand Tour, but for the more adventurous the Greek ruins on Sicily, or even Greece itself, awaited, before the return journey home, often via Germany and the Netherlands.

Describing the Tour as a rite of passage, the historian, John Pemble, writes: 'On the threshold of the South he [the Grand Tourist] experienced an apotheosis. He passed from the circumference to the centre of things, and his thoughts dwelt on roots, origins, essentials and ultimate affinities'.[6] Lasting anywhere from a few months to several years, the Tour was certainly presented, perhaps even intended, as primarily an educational experience, one that provided an opportunity to expose oneself to the splendours of the classical world, while permitting the ruling classes to mix with aristocratic European society before returning home suitably elevated, both morally and spiritually. This in any event was the official version. In reality, however, the scholarly and artistic elements of the Tour paint only half the picture, and the unofficial version has less to do with cultural enrichment and more to do with sexual adventure.[7] That this was the case was not lost on the public left at home who often viewed the Tour and the motives of those who chose to experience it with great suspicion. If, however, the sexual element was a central feature of the Grand Tour from the outset, it is hardly surprising that such motivations remain unspoken in the numerous contemporary accounts of such travellers' adventures, in which the cultural element is always in the foreground. For, as Littlewood notes, as a record of their observations, 'letters home commonly tell of the churches visited, not the brothels.'[8]

The first wave of eighteenth-century Grand Tourists envisaged a role for themselves as that of the 'cultural connoisseur', whose goal was 'to pick his way through Europe gathering information and artefacts, developing his understanding of social institutions, refining his manners along with his appreciation of the arts.'[9] But in the following century this rather rigidly interpreted view of cultural acquisition gradually gave way to a sense that the Grand Tourist was engaged upon a quest for personal fulfilment. In his popular guidebook, *The Grand Tour* (1749), the scholar and antiquarian, Thomas Nugent, summarises the purpose first envisaged for the Tour: 'to enrich the mind with knowledge, to rectify the judgement, to remove the prejudices of education, to compose the outward manners, and in a word to form the complete gentleman.'[10] Such worthy notions are, however, somewhat at odds with other rather less rarefied descriptions, such as the depiction of the traveller to be found in the following lines from Alexander Pope's *The Dunciad* (1743):

… he saunter'd Europe round,
And gather'd ev'ry Vice on Christian Ground;
Saw ev'ry Court, heard ev'ry King declare
His royal Sense, of Op'ra's or the Fair;
The Stews and Palace equally explor'd,
Intrigu'd with glory, and with spirit whor'd;[11]

The glaring disparity between such accounts simply confirms the existence of the Tour in both its official and unofficial guises, as well as acknowledging the unavoidable fact that the public, including, of course, the families of those whose sons had embarked upon the tour, were well aware of the twofold nature of the experiences awaiting them in southern Europe. In short, if not officially recognised, sexual liaisons were not only to be expected but to a degree actively encouraged as an important element of a young man's education. Such an education inevitably gave rise to some unwelcome consequences and sexually transmitted disease came to be regarded as an occupational hazard; while the doctor who would have been responsible for administering an uncomfortable course of mercury treatment was seen as 'an essential member of the supporting cast.' Such considerations would have been further amplified by an awareness of the fact that 'one of the main functions of the Grand Tourist when he got home was to breed sons to continue the family line.'[12]

If there was an awareness of the potential threat posed by what was widely seen as a degenerate and pervasive southern morality, then such a threat was seen as part of the implicit challenge presented by opposing ways of life to the established order at home. In the case of the Grand Tour, populated as it was almost solely by aristocratic and wealthy young individuals, any fear of potentially revolutionary sentiments being exported homeward was mitigated by the fact that few of these highly privileged individuals were likely to question a system which promoted their own interests.[13] In terms of personal behaviour, however, in even offering up the opportunity to compare one's own way of life with another which, in the south at least, appeared to be characterised by a sexual freedom unparalleled in the countries of the north, the Grand Tour 'had opened another door to moral truancy.'[14]

Throughout the eighteenth and nineteenth centuries, there was one country, more than any other, which encapsulated, in the minds of northern Europeans at least, this twofold sense of the official and unofficial aspects of the Tour: Italy. The cultural axis of European travel as well as the notorious home to 'every kind of sexual iniquity', Italy remained throughout this period the primary attraction and principal lure of the Grand Tour. 'No other country', writes Littlewood, 'has been so long and so consistently associated with erotic freedom. From the Renaissance until well into the twentieth century its identity for British travellers was shaped by a reputation for transgressive pleasure that stretched back to the more colourful Roman emperors.'[15] While sodomy was regarded as the sexual act most peculiarly associated with Italy, its broader reputation for sensuality and decadence was as well-known to would-be visitors from the north as was its warm climate and its repository of classical treasures, and such a national perception went some way to maintaining the pivotal role that the country, and in particular Venice and the south, enjoyed within the standard European itinerary of the day. Of course, such an itinerary changed over time, subject to fluctuating intellectual and cultural (as well as sexual) fashions, but perceptions of just what constituted the 'South' and quite where it began and ended, were shaped most clearly by the political and social realities of the period. Thus throughout the eighteenth century, with the Turks continuing to control Europe east of Vienna, and in conflict with the Christian countries of the Mediterranean, the contours of southern European travel became rigidly delineated and the favoured route of the Grand Tour was fixed accordingly. Greece was effectively ruled out, with the consequence that the remnants of the classical Greek world still available for perusal in southern

Europe were now to be found predominantly in Rome, southern Italy, and on the former Greek colony of Sicily.[16] It was here, on the extreme southern boundary of the European continent, that the idea of the 'South' was crystallised in the minds of those northern Europeans who had first made its 'discovery'; and it was through their travels that perceptions of the region would be shaped for future generations.

## Goethe's *Italian Journey*

On 28 August 1786, Johann Wolfgang von Goethe (1749–1832) was on holiday in Carlsbad celebrating his thirty-seventh birthday. In the eyes of the public he was an enviable figure: as the author of *Götz von Berlichingen* and *Werther* he had been famous since his early twenties; as a Privy Councillor in the government administration at Weimar he had gained both respect and responsibility; in addition he had a long-term mistress in the form of Charlotte von Stein, an aristocratic member of the Weimar Court. Outwardly, then, all looked well; in reality, however, Goethe was frustrated, overworked and disillusioned. He was under pressure to produce a new work that would establish the promise of his youthful reputation; he felt suffocated by his life at the Weimar court and by his huge administrative responsibilities; and he was embroiled in an unsatisfactory and frustratingly platonic relationship with a woman eleven years his senior. In short, Goethe was a walking mid-life crisis and the time was ripe for him to make his escape.[17]

Goethe's father, Johann Casper Goethe, had visited Italy in 1740, at the time an unusual journey to make for a German Protestant who was not an aristocrat. His journey was a highly influential one, however, for as a result of this trip he came to idealise the country, passing on his journal to his son and encouraging him to make his own pilgrimage south. Yet despite several opportunities, Goethe had thus far resisted the temptation to do so, getting as far as Switzerland and within sight of Italy in 1775 before choosing to return home.

By 1786, however, his father was dead and when it came
to turning his back on his life in Weimar there was really
only one destination that Goethe had in mind. In the end,
his journey appears to have been spontaneous rather than
planned, and on 3 September 1786, in the middle of the night,
he made his getaway: 'On 3 September at 3 in the morning
I crept out of Carlsbad, they wouldn't have let me go if I
hadn't. They could tell I wanted to get away [...] but I wasn't
going to be stopped, for it was time.'[18] Leaving his travelling
companions under the impression that he was taking a short
excursion into the mountains, Goethe jumped into a coach
and without a servant and travelling light and incognito – he
assumed the name of Möller – he headed swiftly southward
through Bavaria and Austria before crossing into Italy and
moving on to Rome. And it was here, some eight weeks
after his initial flight and by now having acquired another
identity – this time that of a painter called Filippo Miller –
that Goethe finally wrote home to disclose his whereabouts.
An account of this headlong rush south can be found in his
diary of this period (available in English as *The Flight to Italy*),
but it is not through this document that Goethe's journey has
since been celebrated, but instead it is the account he was to
write some twenty-five years after these events, in which he
was to describe both this journey and the following two-year
period he spent travelling through Italy, a period in which he
shed his old self altogether to emerge a quite different person.

The *Italian Journey* was the work of an old man recalling
his youthful, or at least younger self; published over 13
years, by the time the third and final part was completed
in 1829, Goethe was almost 80 years old. As such, it is a
book which is notable not only for what it contains but
also for what it omits. Written in three parts covering the
period from September 1786 to April 1788, the first section
recalls the events outlined above on the road to Rome; the
second recounts the continuation of his journey southwards
to Naples and Sicily between February and June of 1787;
while the third and much belated final part covers his second

stay in Rome between June 1787 and April of the following year. Within these three parts, three major themes coexist. Firstly, an observation of nature; amongst many other things, Goethe was a naturalist, geographer, and meteorologist, and the *Italian Journey* abounds with detailed observations of landscape and climate, the latter setting the tone for future accounts of southern European journeys in which the climate is favourably compared with that of the north. The second theme records Goethe's commentary on the progress of the composition of his collected works. Thirdly, and most memorably, Goethe recalls his encounters with the cultural antiquities of the Renaissance.[19] In short, and in terms of the discussion of the Grand Tour above, if Goethe's *Italian Journey* is to be read as a guide to one man's experiences and impressions of eighteenth-century Italy, then it should be seen very much as the 'official' version.

While Goethe's account demonstrates the transformative effects of his southern journey upon him personally, it is also painstaking in its attempts to offer an analysis of the differing characteristics of the peoples of southern and northern Europe. But where Goethe's account differs from so many of his contemporaries, and indeed many of his successors, is in his refusal to equate the obvious poverty and discomfort he sees and experiences with some kind of spiritual or moral inferiority. For example, he is reluctant to endorse the widespread belief that laziness is an endemic characteristic of the south, writing: 'Now that I am better acquainted with the conditions in the south, I suspect that this was the biased view of a person from the north, where anyone who is not feverishly at work all day is regarded as a loafer. [...] I asked friends where I could meet all these innumerable idlers, but they couldn't show me any either.'[20] While elsewhere, despite acknowledging the merits of the northern character, he warns against any attempt to pass judgement on the south through the prism of one's own, northern, perspective:

No doubt their national environment, which has remained unchanged for millennia, has conditioned the character of the northern nations, so admirable in so many respects. But we must not judge the nations of the south, which Heaven has treated so benevolently, by our standards. [...] It is false [...] to think of these people as miserable; their principle of going without was favoured by a climate which gave them all the necessities of life. Here, a poor man, whom, in our country, we think of as wretched, can satisfy his essential needs and at the same time enjoy the world to the full [...] A Cynic philosopher would, I am certain, consider life in our country intolerable; on the other hand, Nature invited him, so to speak, to live in the south. Here the ragged man is not naked, nor poor he who has no provision for the morrow. [...] This explains a good many things: it explains, for instance, why, in most kinds of skilled labour, their artisans are technically far behind those of the northern countries, why factories do not succeed, why, with the exception of lawyers and doctors, there is little learning or culture considering the size of the population, why no painter of the Neapolitan school has ever been profound or become great, why the clergy are happiest when they are doing nothing, and why most of the great prefer to spend their money on luxury, dissipation and sensual pleasures. [...] To return to the common people again. They are like children who, when one gives them a job to do, treat it as a job but at the same time as an opportunity for having some fun.[21]

By the standards of the day, Goethe's journey was a highly unorthodox one. 'I am going to travel quite alone', he writes, 'under another name, and I have great hopes for this venture, odd as it seems.'[22] Travelling alone, without letters of introduction, with no servant or private transport, and in local dress, Goethe's experience of Italy was quite different from that of the normal retinue of Grand Tourists who tended to travel with all the insulation that money and class could provide. As a result, the *Italian Journey* was revelatory in depicting a view of the country that had never been seen before. By 1786, Goethe was already following in the footsteps of many of his countrymen, amongst them the writers Winckelmann and Lessing, but where his account differs from theirs is in the degree to which he felt able, indeed willing, to cast off his former identity (as his use of assumed names suggests) and to embrace everything that this new life presented to him: 'I feel as if I was born and brought up here, and am now coming back from a whaling voyage to Greenland.'[23] Goethe had, in his own terms, experienced a kind of 'rebirth' in the south, a sense of renewal marked by a return to his youthful self, and nowhere was he to feel this sense of a new life more acutely than in Naples: 'Naples is a paradise', he wrote, 'everyone lives in a kind of intoxicated self-forgetfulness, myself included. I seem to be a quite different person, whom I hardly recognise.'[24] The precise nature of this paradisiacal existence is uncertain as Goethe later destroyed the letters and diaries relating to his stay there. But what Goethe intimates here is the existence of the other, 'unofficial' aspect of his travels which, despite not appearing in the pages of the *Italian Journey* are no less real than those which he chose to describe.

The principal charm of the *Italian Journey* is Goethe's seemingly inexhaustible enthusiasm for almost every aspect of his Italian experience: climate; landscape; local customs and meetings with local people; art and architecture; alongside an awareness of the profound changes he is undergoing. Yet despite his repeated references to a sense of rebirth and renewal, the precise content of such changes and the experiences which have provoked them seem strangely undeveloped and at odds with the detailed appreciations to be found elsewhere in his journal. It is as if the eye which he turns so acutely upon the external world is unable to ascertain the contours of his own changing psyche. A more likely explanation, however, is, as many commentators have concluded, that the reason that some parts of his journal, most notably the final section concerning his second stay in Rome, are so markedly less vivid than the remainder, is precisely because it is at these points that the divergence between the 'official' and 'unofficial' aspects of his journey is at its most stark.[25] For if one can truly characterise Goethe's time in Italy as a period of renewal, then this renewal was not simply the spiritual and creative renewal outlined in his journal, but also a sexual renewal, wholly absent from his account.

Goethe's sexual life, or lack of it, during his time in Rome has since been the subject of endless conjecture and debate, and while answers to such questions, or even the questions themselves, are conspicuous by their absence from the *Italian Journey*, they were later to form the basis of his series of poems, the *Roman Elegies*. Previously known as the *Erotica Romana*, Goethe's frank celebration of his Roman sexual awakening were considered so revealing that many were suppressed, and the volume was only published in its entirety in 1914. Here Goethe recalls his meeting with the Italian waitress 'Faustina', the identity of whom has also been the source of much speculation. Was this fictional figure simply that, a figment of Goethe's fevered imagination? Could this be the figure whose absence shadows the pages of Goethe's Roman sojourn in the *Italian Journey*? Or was she simply the literary representation of Goethe's mistress, and later wife, Christiana Vulpius? This seems less likely, however, as they were not to meet until after his return to Germany. Whatever the answer, what is undeniable is that the Goethe who departed Germany in 1786 was a wholly different man to the Goethe who was to return home two years later. These two years were to prove the happiest of Goethe's life, and they were to sustain him over the long years ahead; later he was to claim that 'he had never again been really happy since leaving Rome.'[26] Apart from a trip to Venice in 1790 he was not to return to Italy again. Goethe's *Italian Journey* was to set the precedent for a journey in which the physical experience of travel becomes a counterpart to a spiritual journey of self-discovery and transformation, shaping a whole new perception of the Mediterranean and the south as not simply a destination but a state of mind. As a result, the journey itself was transformed into a pilgrimage, a quest for a new way of life, free from the moral constraints of the north.

According to the critic, Martine Prange, the name 'Goethe' stands for 'the South, paganism, naturalism, and sensualism', traits which may be contrasted with the more northerly characteristics of 'religious tendency, morality, and Romanticism', symbolised by his countryman, Wagner. 'Goethe versus Wagner', she concludes, 'means health against sickness, the classical poet against the archetype of modernism, the gay scientist against the Romantic artist.'[27] More than any other book, Goethe's *Italian Journey* established the image of Italy in the German imagination and foregrounded the divisions which it revealed between north and south. In doing so, however, it not only exposed two countries, two climates and two landscapes, but two wholly opposed philosophies, two worldviews. If, then, Goethe can be said to have blazed a trail for his countrymen to follow, it was one such successor, the 'Gay Scientist' himself, Friedrich Nietzsche, who was to place this polarity between north and south at the heart of his work.

## Nietzsche's Discovery of the South

If 1786 was the year in which Goethe was to finally escape southwards, the year 1879 marks a similar turning point in the life of Friedrich Nietzsche (1844–1900), as he too turned his back on his northern existence and began life anew in the south. Having been appointed to the Chair of Classical Philology at the University of Basel in 1869 at the remarkable age of 24, in 1879, Nietzsche, by then aged 35 and in poor health, resigned his position and embarked on a ten-year odyssey of itinerant travel through southern Europe, living as an 'independent' philosopher, a decade of prolific writing that was to see the publication of *The Birth of Tragedy* (1882) and *Thus Spoke Zarathustra* (1883–5).

Like Goethe before him, Nietzsche's flight south was also prompted by poor health, a large workload, and the need for renewal. But in comparison to Goethe, a figure whom he was to hold in high esteem, Nietzsche's departure was rather less abrupt, his resignation in 1879 merely a delayed response to his first experience of Italy some three years before. For in 1876 the then 32-year-old Nietzsche had first set foot on Italian soil in Genoa, a city whose very name, as the critic Martina Kolb notes, was to carry a portent of his future: 'The city's name has two possible etymologies: *ianua* (door, gate), and *genu* (knee, turn). They suggest beautifully the new beginning or turning point in his life that Nietzsche was about to embark on.'[28] Nietzsche was to travel widely in Italy, and while he was often critical of what he found there – Rome, for example, he despised – it was this corner of Italy, Genoa and the Ligurian coast, to which he was to return most frequently and which came to symbolise all which he felt was best about the south. Apart from Genoa, Nietzsche spent the winter of 1876–7 in Sorrento and he also visited Capri. He was later to claim that Sorrento allowed him to shake off the 'moss' that had accumulated over the previous nine years, while his visit to a cave housing a relief portraying Mithras, the Persian sun god, has been seen as crucial in explaining the pivotal role the sun was later to assume in his symbolic pantheon. One commentator has since posed the question, 'What did Nietzsche do on Capri?'; his answer being that, like Goethe before him, he was 'aroused to sensuality' by his experiences of the south, or rather 'the South of the South', as Nietzsche describes Capri, provoking him to place the body, from this point on, at the centre of his work.[29]

From 1880 until his breakdown in 1889 (he was to live in the care of his mother and sister until his death in 1900), Nietzsche led a nomadic existence. He was effectively stateless, having given up his Prussian citizenship on his appointment to the Professorship in Basel, and he soon fell into the habit of spending his winters on the Mediterranean, principally in Genoa and Nice, a city he regarded as being essentially Italian in character. His first extended Genoese stay was between November 1880 and April 1881, and he returned in October 1881, staying until the spring of 1882. Nietzsche came to adore Genoa's 'verticality and terraced topography, as well as its location right on the Mediterranean Sea, and its port, parks, and palaces'; crucially, however, it was Genoa's climate, its sunshine and clear skies, which attracted Nietzsche so powerfully, resulting in his conviction that one's atmosphere and the air one breathes has a strong bearing on one's thought and writing.[30] It was in Genoa that Nietzsche was first to describe himself as 'ein Südländer, dem Glauben nach', or 'a man of the south in spirit', and he saw in the city and the Genoese a 'time-honoured will to life, egotism, conquest, and survival' that were soon to become the hallmarks of his philosophical ideal.[31]

Having assumed the life of the wanderer in exile, Nietzsche's travels may appear to conform to those of the Grand Tourist, much in the same vein as Goethe's a century before. But where Goethe may be seen as the detached observer, storing up experiences with which to sustain himself after his return home, Nietzsche's journey south was more of a one-way ticket, and having burned his bridges in Basel, he was to immerse himself in his new southern existence. In Genoa he felt himself to be Genoese and in each new place he settled, rather than adopting the position of an onlooker, he assumed the role of a native inhabitant. Living simply, if not ascetically, Nietzsche can in no way be seen as a tourist, and certainly not a 'grand' one. Although he was to reread Goethe's *Italian Journey* while in Genoa, it was not a city that Goethe himself visited, and Nietzsche's own southern European odyssey was to bypass the more traditional route of the Grand Tour. Where he does follow more closely in his precursor's footsteps, however, is in replicating the sense of liberation that Goethe was to celebrate so fervently. For Nietzsche too articulates this same sense of rebirth and renewal, a newfound freedom through self-sufficiency and self-expression, a freedom 'based on sacrificing a home for the sake of nomadic, poetic wandering, for a cultivation of strength and stamina, life and joy, courage and energy.'[32]

It was in Genoa in the summer of 1882 that the first edition of *The Gay Science* was published, the single volume in which he refers most directly to his 'discovery of the South.' Here, Nietzsche was to come closest to articulating a southern philosophy, a philosophy inspired by 'a better, lighter, more southern, sunnier world'; a world wholly at odds with a vision of the north characterised by shame and suspicion: 'Is it because there is no sense of shame and everything vulgar appears as poised and self-assured as anything noble, lovely, and passionate in the same sort of music or novel?', he asks, 'That seems to me to be the moral of this story and the peculiarity of Southern humanity.'[33] At the heart of Nietzsche's portrayal of the opposition between north and south, lies his disdainful view of Christianity, an opposition grounded in the contrasting worldviews of the Protestant and Catholic Churches:

> The entire Roman church rests upon a southern suspicion about the nature of man, and this is always misunderstood in the north. The European south has inherited this suspicion from the depths of the Orient, from primeval and mysterious Asia [...] the north has always been more good-natured and shallower than the south. [...] The edifice of the church at any rate rests on a southern freedom and enlightenment of the spirit as well as a southern suspicion of nature, man and spirit; it rests on an altogether different knowledge of man and experience of man than is to be found in the north.[34]

Nietzsche's celebration of the south can often reach a frenzied pitch, but his affirmation of the south should not be read purely as a repudiation of the north, but should instead be seen as part of an attempt to establish a synthesis between the two. For while Nietzsche experienced his life in the south as a 'recovery' from what he regarded as a 'Romantic disease', German culture, so too was he aware that without his northern background he would have been unable to gain the necessary distance from which to form his appreciation of southern virtue. Nietzsche describes this ideal, in which north and south meet and coalesce, in the form of the 'Good European', the figure who has successfully managed to 'de-Germanise' while integrating the cheerfulness, free-spiritedness, and 'southern lightness' with northern wisdom to attain a reconciliation between these two worldviews.[35] Goethe is one example Nietzsche provides of a Good European, but it is the French who Nietzsche identifies as the nation which has been most successful in integrating these two positions: 'The French character contains a halfway successful synthesis of the north and the south which allows them to comprehend many things and to do things which an Englishman could never understand. Their temperament, periodically turned toward and away from the south [...] protects them against the gruesome northern grey on grey and the sunless concept-spooking and anaemia. [...] They know how to love the south in the north and the north in the south.'[36]

In a later edition of *The Gay Science* Nietzsche was to include a selection of poems, amongst them 'Im Süden', or 'In the South', and it is here that one encounters Nietzsche's clearest encapsulation of the impact of his southern awakening:

> Idylls around me, bleating sheep:
> Accept me, southern innocence!
>
> Step upon step – this heavy stride
> Is German, not life – a disease:
> To lift me up, I asked the breeze,
> And with the birds I learned to glide;
> Southward I flew, across the seas.[37]

Just as the birds migrate south in winter, so too was Nietzsche's southern migration a response to nature's call, a physical, instinctive reaction against the imprisonment of the northern winter and a yearning to experience a new life in the warmer climate of the south. The goal of Nietzsche's southern migration was one of self-development and, according to Martine Prange, this poem 'attests to Nietzsche's thankfulness for Italian culture, without which he would have remained imprisoned in the northern coldness and morality instead of developing a new view of things, undergoing a strange and unique experience of life.' 'Without the south', she concludes, 'he would never have found the weapon of cheerfulness as partner of wisdom. In that case, he would never have experienced the "recovery", which founds *The Gay Science*, as a pinnacle of free-spiritedness and good Europeanism.'[38]

Of all Nietzsche's legions of critics and commentators, perhaps the most insightful, and certainly the most alert to his subject's 'southern' epiphany, is the writer Stefan Zweig. Zweig's analysis of Nietzsche's work is grounded in the contrast between what he sees, on the one hand, as Nietzsche's successful transformation from sickly northerner to luminous southerner, and on the other, the more belated, and consequently less successful, attempt by Goethe to achieve the same goal. Nietzsche, according to Zweig, looked confidently to the future, 'his eyes delighting in the sapphire skies, in the clear and infinite horizons, in the magical sensation of luminosity flooding him through every pore'; while poor Goethe, by contrast, burdened by his concern with 'things dead and buried – classical art, the Roman spirit, the mysteries of plant and stone' was unable to free himself from his obsession with the past. In short, states Zweig, Goethe had simply missed his chance: pushing forty by the time he made his first journey to Italy, 'a hard rind had formed around his character, which was essentially of a methodical and reflective kind […] He had become so firmly crystallized within himself that no element in the world was henceforward capable of completely modifying him.'[39] This distinction seems a harsh one, not least because of the fact that when the respective turning points in their lives were to arrive and they both moved south, Nietzsche was barely two years younger than the aged Goethe that Zweig describes. Yet age is not the only distinguishing factor here, claims Zweig, for alongside his backward gaze into the past, Goethe's nascent transformation was further impeded by his over-reliance on intellect which restricted his experiences of Italy to a purely mental and aesthetic affair, at odds once again with what Zweig characterises as Nietzsche's more vital plunge into a wholly Italian lifestyle. The result was that while 'Goethe was merely fecundated', 'Nietzsche was completely uprooted, transplanted, renewed'.[40] In Italy, continues Zweig, 'Goethe found what he was in search of and very little else.' He had an instructive and enjoyable journey at the end of which he returned 'to the exact point whence he took his departure, carrying in his boxes, his heart, and his brain things precious and delightful for a home, for his home in particular.'[41] Zweig, however, appears to have taken Goethe's *Italian Journey* at face value, apparently unaware that Goethe's account conceals as much as it reveals, and as a result he rather unfairly depicts him as an elderly obsessive trapped in the past. Yet to the same degree that Zweig denigrates Goethe's experiences and downplays their impact, so too does he broaden and elevate Nietzsche's transformation to an apotheosis, his experiences in the south opening his eyes to a whole new world of unlimited possibility:

> Nietzsche expatriates himself and finds his true self [...] The inestimable gift he brought away from the South was the awareness that the whole earth was simultaneously a foreign land and a mother country, where there are no frontiers, but only the endless open horizons on every side and as far as the eye could see. [...] It was not his mind which rose in revolt against the North, against Germany, against his homeland, but his heart, his nerves,

his very fibres. His cry was a cry of delight at having at length "found the climate that suited his soul," at having discovered "freedom." That is why his exultation was so unbounded, that is why he exuberantly shouted: "I gave a leap!" – "I took a leap!" – "I escaped!" – "I have escaped!"[42]

At times the sheer exuberance of Zweig's language can outstrip that of Nietzsche himself, and in those moments when his excitement seems to get the better of him it is hard to think of a critic better matched to his subject. In fact, Zweig does appear to identify precisely what it is that generates Nietzsche's energetic proclamations and which illuminates his overheated prose: the sun. 'It seems to me', writes Zweig, 'that in no other German author was the style of his writing so swiftly and completely renewed. Certainly none other was so flooded with sunshine, or ever became so enfranchised, so essentially southern, so divinely light of foot, so full of a good vintage, so pagan.'[43] Only van Gogh, claims Zweig, is able to approach Nietzsche in providing an example of such a mania for sunlight, his sun-drenched paintings capturing the light which was to flood through Nietzsche's entire being:

These two fanatical lovers of change were intoxicated with light, absorbed light with the vampire lust of passion, gulped down light in rapid and inconceivably large doses. But Nietzsche [...] was, therefore, constantly in search of a superlative in relation to the South in general and to Italy in particular. Not satisfied with light, he desired "super-light." [...] He wanted to be burned by the sun, not merely to be illuminated by it; clarity must have cruel teeth that bite; joviality must develop into a voluptuous orgasm.[44]

Goodness. It is difficult to see here in whom the mania is the greater, Nietzsche or Zweig himself, but in identifying the dominant position that the sun was ultimately to attain

41

in Nietzsche's heliocentric philosophy, Zweig is simply articulating a view that had, by the time of Nietzsche's death in 1900, become increasingly fashionable: that the sun was no longer to be feared or avoided, but embraced and even worshipped as the giver of health and vitality. Luminous, sun-filled, alight, aflame, the adjectives of sun-worship abound in Nietzsche's prose, reflecting his rediscovery of the sun and pointing the way to the wider discovery of the south which was to follow.

## Heliotherapy and the Invention of Sunbathing

The idea of travelling south for the pleasure of the climate, to bask in glorious sunshine and to momentarily forget the frigid northern latitudes, is a relatively recent phenomenon that would, in itself, have motivated few of the travellers en route to southern Europe even a century ago. Indeed, the idea of going abroad purely for pleasure of any sort, is, remarkable as it may seem, itself a largely twentieth-century phenomenon. For as we have seen, despite the realities of the unofficial aspects of the Grand Tour, this was a practice that originated and was presented throughout as primarily a means of cultural advancement, a process devoted to education rather than pleasure. Since then, of course, our understanding of tourism, and the motivations behind it, have undergone a transformation, a decisive movement from the cultural to the sensual, from self-development to self-indulgence, a shift in attitude that is harnessed to one overriding factor: the sun.[45]

In Enlightenment thought the effects of the sun upon character were thought to be almost wholly pernicious. While the sun was to symbolise the role of reason in shining a light into the darkness of ignorance and superstition, the by-product of such illumination, heat, was much less welcome; the sun was seen as 'second only to the Pope' in the responsibility it bore for the perceived lethargy of the southern races.[46] The northern traveller, by contrast, was able to forge ahead, secure in the knowledge that he had originated in a climate 'that nurtured enterprise and freedom, as much as its opposite encouraged indolence and idolatry.'[47] The commonly held view of the Victorians is that they too shared this opprobrium towards the sun and its unwholesome effects on character and morality, and yet contrary to popular belief, the Victorians did not dislike suntanned skin, appreciating its aesthetic appeal, and their refusal to expose themselves to the sun was the consequence not of fashion but of fear, an awareness of the sun's harmful effects that now seems rather less misguided than it once did.[48] For throughout the nineteenth century, strong sunlight was seen as something to be avoided by those who could, or more precisely by those who could afford to: the agricultural workers were left to take their chances and the tanned skin that they were to display as a result only helped to reinforce the class divide and to perpetuate the heliophobia of the ruling classes, in turn ensuring that the prevailing fashion remained one for pale, translucent skin. While the winter sun of southern Europe was acceptable, therefore, to the would-be traveller, the southern summer was to be avoided at all costs as a hellish and pestilent season of sunstroke, fever and contagion. As a consequence, few travellers on the Grand Tour were foolhardy enough to risk Italy in July and August and even in the spring they were to spend much of their time indoors. So it would seem the sun-drenched image of Italy and the Mediterranean that we have today would have been quite alien to the ranks of British and Americans who wintered there, amongst their number Henry James, a critic of whom notes that while his *Italian Hours* (1909) cannot be said to vibrate with what he calls '*meridionale* energy', it is not alone in this respect, for neither can anything else in nineteenth-century English or American literature, as almost all the writers of this period were absent during the summer months.[49]

While the sun seems to have been regarded as having little to offer the healthy, the climate of the southern European winter had long since been seen as beneficial to the sick, and by 1861 *The British Medical Journal* was declaring San Remo, on the Italian Riviera, to be 'the most beautiful and healthiest place with the mildest climate to be found on the Mediterranean coast', claiming that it was ideal for people with a delicate constitution.[50] By 1874, with the Riviera now in reach by railway, a veritable army of consumptives had begun their annual migration to the beneficial climes of France and Italy, with one contemporary observer calculating that 'between seven and eight thousand English invalids [...] annually spend the winter in the south in pursuit of health.'[51] 'The invalids showed us the way', writes the historian of sun-worship, Robert Mighall, and the cohorts of the sick can be said to have acted as trailblazers, their search for a more amenable climate for their weakened northern lungs establishing the routes that the tourists of the future were to follow; so too the British physicians who diagnosed a southern cure can be regarded as the resort developers of their day, their patients 'package tourists *avant la lettre*', swapping their position in the northern ward of the great European sanatorium for one with a more southerly exposure:

The invalid [...] was explicitly encouraged to take things easy. Such indolence went against the official 'national temperament' of the northerner. Whilst the southerner might be considered languid, effeminate and lazy, northerners (and especially, so they believed, the English) had industry and enterprise in their blood and in their climates. Invalids learned to let go of these demands and give themselves over to the *dolce far niente*. [...] Not only did he carve out the geography of modern sun-seeking leisure travel, the English physician also wrote its script. Relax, chill out, do practically nothing, advised the physician, and we willingly swallow the medicine first dispensed a century ago. [...] It is possible to detect a general thawing of northern frigidity in invalid accounts of southern exposure. Simple pleasures, unknown freedoms, were capable of blossoming uniquely at this latitude. [...] The invalid is a sensual experimentalist, whose ailment has allowed him to stumble across a secret pleasure denied to those whose robust health and hauteur steel them against such seductions. Throwing open the window on the northern hospital ward, letting this stimulant flood in to the self-imposed gloom of a heliophobic epoch, must have been an intoxicating experience indeed.[52]

The invalid's trajectory certainly appears to anticipate that of their more hedonistic counterparts a century later, but while today's tourist comes in search of the sun, and the hotter the better, his more frail nineteenth-century forebear retained his habitual and deeply engrained mistrust of the summer sun, pursuing a much milder environment in which to recuperate from his northerly ailments. The south could allow one to maintain an outdoor lifestyle throughout the winter that was impossible in the north, and so provided a means of effecting a cure and prolonging one's life without the need for what was still perceived as an equally dangerous overexposure to the sun.

It was only at the end of the nineteenth century that such deep-rooted anxieties about the sun's baleful influence began to wane, as the scientific community, for so long stridently opposed to solar exposure, began to form the opinion that perhaps there was something to be said for the sun after all.

In 1903, the Dane, Niels Finsen, was awarded the Nobel Prize for his use of artificial sunlight to cure tuberculosis of the skin. But it was not Finsen who was to be remembered for his pioneering use of sunlight as a treatment for such illnesses, but rather his contemporary, the Swiss Doctor Auguste Rollier (1874–1954). For it was later that same year that Rollier was to open the world's first dedicated sun clinic, at Leysin in the Swiss Alps, and it was here, 5,000 feet above sea level, that he began to expose his patients to what he believed were the healing effects of the sun's ultraviolet light. Rollier's experimental treatment relied upon the simple and abundant supplies of pure air and bright sunlight to tackle a variety of diseases, most commonly external forms of tuberculosis, which had hitherto been treated, often unsuccessfully, with surgery. Now, amidst the fresh air and cool mountain conditions, the patient was gradually uncovered and their whitened body exposed to the galvanising effects of the sun's rays:

> You start with the feet, for exactly five minutes, repeated three times daily for about three days. (Isn't this fun?) Next the legs, for similar treatment, followed by the trunk, and finally the head. Full solar immersion takes about five weeks, and only then would they start to treat the critical area. Precise, prescribed, protracted, Rollier's 'insolation' was conducted on the strictest scientific and therapeutic principles. [...] Far from being feared and avoided, sunshine became highly valued. Sunlight was of course free as air, but this new sun, the healing sun, at first belonged to medical science. Rollier insisted that Alpine sunshine and air were of specific quality and an essential part of the cure. [...] A 'healthy' tan meant exactly that: proof that the rays had worked their curative magic. Health appeared to radiate from these rejuvenated bodies, and after a while these rays extended their influence beyond the sanatorium. A new ideal rose with the dawn of the twentieth century. A new age of bronze had arrived.[53]

In his book *Heliotherapy*, first published in France in 1916, Rollier was to provide photographic evidence of the transformative effects of surgical sunning on the skin lesions of his patients. The benefits of Rollier's methods were soon well-known with *Time* magazine that same year claiming: 'the sun cure for tuberculosis and undernourished children is becoming a recognised part of modern treatment for these conditions.'[54] In fact, the British government was to recommend sun cures for victims of the 1918 Spanish flu epidemic, which killed 200,000 people in England alone, with posters at English railway stations declaring 'Sunshine is life – Come to the Riviera.'[55] The first English translation of *Heliotherapy* was to follow in 1923 and by this time sunlight was being advocated not simply as a cure but as a means of preventing illness and of increasing the health of the general population. By the end of the 1920s a solar revolution was taking place in Europe.[56] What had previously been the preserve of the invalid was now available for general consumption, as Victorian attitudes to the sun were effectively reversed: what had once been seen as dangerous was now seen as beneficial to health; what had once been the mark of the working classes – a tanned skin – was now a symbol of fashion and good taste; where once the sun had been thought to corrode morals, the sun and the south became hallmarks of openness and honesty free from the perceived hypocrisies of the past. With the workers enclosed in factories, the 'Great Outdoors' was now once again an acceptable arena for the ruling classes, and those who could afford to headed south to make use of the plentiful sunshine. In the footsteps of the Grand Tourists and later the invalids, now came the sun-worshippers, ready to partake in the latest fashion: sunbathing.

'Between the wars', writes Mighall, 'sunshine didn't just acquire a layer of history, it was history.'[57] Having for so long avoided the sun for health reasons or to resist its deleterious effects on morals, when this barrier was finally broken down, the sun was embraced with a passion and fervour which would have been unimaginable a generation before. The inter-war years in Britain experienced a number of exceptionally warm summers which not only helped to promote this newfound desire for the sun, but also led to a radical change in the meanings denoted by a tanned skin, which acquired the sensual, erotic and libertarian connotations which it has held ever since.[58] In economic terms, however, sunbathing was regulated along more characteristic lines, with those who could afford to escaping abroad to a more amenable climate, while those who remained at home were forced to take their chances with the British summer and to face 'an uncertain two-week annual window to get their "quota".'[59] Once seen as rich in cultural heritage but in little else, southern Europe between the wars became defined increasingly through its access to seemingly unlimited reserves of this newly valued natural resource: sunshine, a resource sadly depleted in the north, and in particularly short supply in Britain. And despite the fact that the seaside resorts of the UK were to enjoy a huge upsurge in visitors keen to bask in the warmish sunlight and to swim in the chilly water, the true sun-worshipper was forced to look further afield.

## Southern Twilight: DH Lawrence in Italy

In what is surely the first work of fiction devoted to this new-found fashion for sunbathing, DH Lawrence's short story 'Sun' was published in 1926 at the height of sun-worship in Europe. The tale of an unhappily married New Yorker who is sent by her doctors to Sicily for the winter to recover from an unspecified illness, and is prescribed a form of heliotherapy which sees her rapidly transformed into a passionate sun-worshipper. Lawrence's story charts the course of this conversion, both physically and psychically, as the sun awakens her dormant sexuality, introducing her to an existence free from the constraints and conformities of her former life.

'"Take her away, into the sun," the doctor said.' And with few preliminaries, Lawrence does exactly as the doctor orders, transporting Julia (minus her husband) from New York to Sicily, from darkness into light: 'It was as if she had never seen the sun rise before. She had never seen the naked sun stand up pure upon the sea-line, shaking the night off himself, like wetness. And he was full and naked. And she wanted to come to him. So the desire sprang secretly in her, to be naked to the sun. She cherished her desire like a secret. She wanted to come together with the sun.'[60] Little analysis is required here to elicit the true meaning of 'Sun', but in case any further explanation is needed, Lawrence continues:

> She knew the sun in all her body, the blue-molten with his white fire edges, throwing off fire. [...] With her knowledge of the sun, and her conviction that the sun was gradually penetrating her to know her, in the cosmic carnal sense of the word, came over her a feeling of detachment from people, and a certain contemptuous intolerance for human beings altogether. [...] It was not just taking sun-baths. It was much more than that. Something deep inside her unfolded and relaxed, and she was given to cosmic influence. By some mysterious will inside her, deeper than her known consciousness and her known will, she was put into connection with the sun, and the stream of the sun flowed through her, round her womb [...] "I am another being," she said to herself, as she looked at her red-gold breasts and thighs.[61]

At first glance, Lawrence's story appears to contain all the ingredients of the prototypical beachside romance, but despite the lustful gaze of a watching Sicilian peasant, Julia's secret, or not so secret, desires remain unfulfilled, and Lawrence's story ends with the arrival of Julia's symbolically pallid husband and the acknowledgement that she cannot escape her previous life.[62] Lawrence's intensely felt but rather overblown equation of sex and sunshine can read a little ludicrously at times, and yet this short story summarises precisely the sort of sun mania that was to become, momentarily at least, so widespread in the southern Europe of the 1920s. For 'Sun' encapsulates not merely the liberation of moral constraint that sunshine was supposed to deliver, but also the impulse to turn away from the cities of the industrialised north to a simpler, and older, way of life awaiting in the south. This was, of course, precisely the direction that Lawrence's own life was to take, and in this sense 'Sun' may be read as a fictional projection of his own beliefs. Yet while he would certainly have endorsed the southward trajectory that Julia follows, Lawrence himself had little time for either sunbathing or the hedonistic lifestyle it symbolises, for he was a puritan by nature with a character quite unsuited to enforced leisure.[63] In fact, in this instance, it is not so much the author, Lawrence, whose personality can be said to inhabit this story, as its publisher, the American expatriate, Harry Crosby. Written in 1925, 'Sun' was not published in unexpurgated form until three years later, under the terms of what must have been a most peculiar contract: 'Crosby paid [Lawrence] a hundred dollars for it in twenty-dollar gold pieces emblazoned with the sun. It was brought out in a deluxe edition by the Black Sun Press, and Crosby, having sent Lawrence two copies in gold boxes, went to elaborate lengths to secure the promised gold coins and have them smuggled out of America and finally delivered to Lawrence in Italy. More than a little mad, Crosby was the most sun-obsessed of the whole sun-obsessed inter-war generation.'[64]

Lawrence's first encounter with the south, indeed his first journey outside England, was made in 1912–13 and the series of travel essays this journey was to inspire form the basis (albeit in a much revised form) of *Twilight in Italy*, first published in 1916. Notoriously unsettled and dissatisfied by temperament, this was an unusually happy period for Lawrence, in his twenties and experiencing Europe for the first time; he was also enjoying an illicit affair with Frieda Weekley, who was later to become his wife. Having travelled through Germany and across the Alps into Italy, Lawrence and Frieda spent almost seven months, from September 1912 to April 1913, on Lake Garda, in a villa overlooking the lake in Villa di Gargnano, and it is this period which forms the final part of *Twilight in Italy*, written to the backdrop of the impending war, and the prospect of twilight descending on Europe.[65] The title of Lawrence's book refers not merely to the twilight of the approaching war, however, but more broadly to the passing of the old agrarian way of life, as the inhabitants of southern Italy increasingly began to eye the possibility of a new life in the industrialised north. It is this polarity, as well as those between light and dark, intellect and sensuality, man and woman, and the possibility of a reconciliation between them, that informs not only *Twilight in Italy*, but his entire body of work.[66] Lawrence and Frieda were to travel no further south than Milan in *Twilight in Italy*, although they were to remedy this in a later book, *Sea and Sardinia* (1921), in which they were to complete their journey southward to the Mediterranean, yet nowhere else in his work was Lawrence to articulate so explicitly his philosophy of the opposing values of north and south, and the wholly different modes of life which they represent:

> When one walks, one must travel west or south. If one turns northward or eastward it is like walking down a cul-de-sac, to the blind end.
>
> So it has been since the Crusaders came home satiated, and the Renaissance saw the western sky as an archway into the future. So it is still. We must go westwards and southwards.
>
> It is a sad and gloomy thing to travel even from Italy into France. But it is a joyful thing to walk south to Italy, south and west. It is so. And there is a certain exaltation in the thought of going west, even to Cornwall, to Ireland. It is as if the magnetic poles were south-west and north-east, for our spirits, with the south-west, under the sunset, as the positive pole. So whilst I walk through Switzerland, though it is a valley of gloom and depression, a light seems to flash out under every footstep, with the joy of progression. [...] It is strange how different the sun-dried, ancient, southern slopes of the world are, from the northern slopes. It is as if the god Pan really had his home among these sun-bleached stones and tough, sun-dark trees. And one knows it all in one's blood, it is pure, sun-dried memory.[67]

The Germany and Italy that Lawrence describes in *Twilight in Italy* represent two opposing worldviews, the scientific and the sensual, and it is the often troubled relationship between the two that he places at the heart of European history. These two poles have been reconciled before, however, and it is to their current division that Lawrence ascribes the chaos that is now consuming Europe: 'It is from the intermingling of the two opposite spirits, two different and opposite streams of blood, that modern Europe has arisen. The fusion of the two opposites brought us the greatness of modern days: just as the hostility of the two brings disaster, now as in the old past.'[68] One consequence of the growing chaos that Lawrence was to witness, was the restless migration of people from across Europe whom he found joining him on his journey southwards, in a foretaste of the upheavals to come. But paradoxically, just at the moment when Lawrence was in search of the old world in the south, a world doomed to extinction, so many of the people he encountered, such as the Italian community in Switzerland, were doing precisely the opposite, in searching for a new world in the north.[69] For Lawrence such mass migrations of people were simply to be regarded as one further symptom of European decline. Yet despite his clear antipathy to what he sees as the disaster of northern industrialisation, particularly in his home country, Lawrence is not promoting the primacy of southern values over those of the north, for he is aware that both ways of life have benefits as well as drawbacks, and a synthesis of the two is necessary if we are to live a fully human existence. The twilight that he encounters in Italy, however, is not the synthesis he is seeking but rather a 'neutral region' in which southern values decline in the face of industrialism to create the worst of both worlds.[70] Lawrence is not advocating southern progress in terms of what is understood in the north as modernisation, but rather through a return to a more primitive outlook expressed through the symbolism of light and darkness. 'In the north', he writes, 'man tends instinctively to imagine, to conceive that the sun is lighted like a candle, in an everlasting darkness, and that one day the candle will go out, the sun will be exhausted, and the everlasting darkness will resume uninterrupted sway. But to the southerner, the sun is so dominant that if every phenomenal body disappeared out of the universe, nothing would remain but bright luminousness, sunniness.'[71] For it is the sun, and the light and heat which it provides, that gives the south its distinctive character, a character which had, until the encroachments of an alien twentieth-century science, remained unchanged since the Renaissance:

> This is the soul of the Italian since the Renaissance. In the sunshine he basks asleep, gathering up a vintage into his veins which in the night-time he will distil into ecstatic sensual delight, the intense, white-cold ecstasy of darkness and moonlight, the raucous, cat-like, destructive enjoyment, the senses conscious and crying out in their consciousness in the pangs of enjoyment, which has consumed the Southern nation, perhaps all the Latin races, since the Renaissance.[72]

In fact, the polarities that Lawrence explores in *Twilight in Italy* and the range of heliocentric expressions he employs to illustrate them, suggest not so much Renaissance thinking as a return to a far older pagan tradition, in which the sun and the diurnal division between night and day, light and darkness are paramount. Indeed, one can go further still in locating the polarity between north and south that Lawrence so obsessively delineates in his work, placing it at the very heart of what it means to be human, as much a question of character and temperament as it is of geography. If this is true, however, the question remains of how these two warring sides to our nature can be reconciled, or whether the conflict between them is elemental and unavoidable. Lawrence's own conclusion is a pessimistic one, for it is his belief that not only are north and south hostile to one another in modern, early twentieth-century life, but that north and south are under threat from a twilight that threatens to engulf them both, as they are devoured by the seemingly inexorable advance of industrial civilisation.[73] Lawrence's gloomy prognosis is also a prophetic one, however, as the spread of globalisation has confirmed. It is also entirely consistent with the period in which he was writing, on the eve of the first truly global industrialised war. Yet his bleak outlook somehow befits a man of his temperament, seemingly at home neither in the south or the north, instead fated to remain perpetually in search of a home that is forever out of reach. For just as Lawrence's journey south across the Alps places him within the tradition of southern exile exemplified by Goethe and Nietzsche, so too does it represent the first southward movement in a life which came to be characterised by a series of such escapes.

For Lawrence was an exile, and not just an exile from his homeland or from the north, but from life itself, and his biography can often read as a futile attempt to stay one step ahead of his own restless pursuit of change. 'Like most of his contemporaries', writes Paul Fussell, 'Lorenzo was in search of the sun. […] But unlike many of his contemporaries he was also in search of virtue, of cosmic order, and of perfect harmony between man and his places.' But he never found what he was searching for, and when he thought he had, 'he soon discovered that he himself had manufactured the ecstasy and laid it over the actuality of a place. He thus repeatedly took off again, embittered and disillusioned. He is always both escaping and seeking.'[74]

Following his first taste of the south, Lawrence and Frieda returned to England, finally settling in the most southerly location available to them, Cornwall. Lawrence's experience of the English south was, however, quite different to that of southern Europe; after the outbreak of war and now married to a wife of 'hostile origin', Lawrence and Frieda found themselves under constant surveillance by the authorities; his works were increasingly censored, while his health deteriorated in the English climate. Poverty and persecution were the hallmarks of their final years in England and in November 1919 they sailed for Italy again, unwittingly embarking on a ten-year odyssey that was to take them through the Mediterranean and on to the Pacific, American southwest, Mexico, and finally back to southern Europe, where Lawrence died, in Vence, in 1930. Seen in retrospect, Lawrence's first southerly migration to Italy was to prefigure the wider trajectory he was to follow for the remainder of his life, a life that can itself be seen as foreshadowing the wider 'British Literary Diaspora', that great flight of writers from England (and also the US) that was to take place in the Twenties and Thirties.[75] In this respect, Lawrence, once again like Goethe and Nietzsche before him, can be seen as a pioneer, not only in literary terms, but also as a traveller, following the southern sun through Europe and across the world, in the process helping to establish an itinerary we have been following ever since.

## Gold Rush: Spain and the Tourist South

In 1934, Laurie Lee, then only 19, left his home in the Cotswolds to walk to London, from where, the following year, he was to continue his journey south. The destination, as he was to recall more than 30 years later in his celebrated memoir, *As I Walked Out One Midsummer Morning* (1969) was less important than the journey itself: 'So where should I go? It was just a question of getting there – France? Italy? Greece? I knew nothing at all about any of them, they were just names with vaguely operatic flavours.'[76] Remembering that he had picked up the Spanish phrase for 'Will you please give me a glass of water?' his decision was made and shortly afterwards he was to embark for Vigo in Galicia. Lee's amble south through Spain, then on the brink of civil war, was as much a journey through time as space, revealing a landscape and way of life in many ways unchanged since medieval times, and one largely untouched by the tourism which had already transformed the coastal regions of Spain's southern

European neighbours. Lee's journey was delightfully spontaneous, wholly without structure or itinerary, yet driven throughout by the same southerly impulse that had first transported him from his village in 1934: 'Where should I go now? It didn't matter. Anywhere south would do. [...] and that was the direction I took.'[77] Supporting himself by playing his violin, a sort of modern-day troubadour, Lee's precarious journey took him to the then deserted beaches of the south, whose small fishing communities were largely oblivious to the twin devastations of war and tourism that were shortly to be unleashed: 'The road to Málaga followed a beautiful but exhausted shore, seemingly forgotten by the world. I remember the names – San Pedro, Estepona, Marbella, and Fuengirola [...] They were salt-fish villages, thin-ribbed, sea-hating, cursing their place in the sun. At that time one could have bought the whole coast for a shilling. Not Emperors could buy it now.'[78]

If Lee's experiences of Spain were to reveal a country largely bypassed by European tourism, it was in the following decade, shortly after the war, that Norman Lewis was to witness the moment when the tourists finally arrived. Once again in a small fishing village unchanged for generations, although in this case on Spain's north-eastern coast, *Voices of the Old Sea* (1984) describes a period of three summers in which Spain was propelled into an alternate, northern European, conception of twentieth-century living: 'By the end of my third season it was clear that Spain's spiritual and cultural isolation was at an end, overwhelmed by the great alien invasion from the north of money and freedoms. Spain became the most visited tourist country in the world, and slowly, as the foreigners poured in, its identity was submerged, its lifestyle altered more in a single decade than in the previous century.'[79] Lewis describes the way in which a village is destroyed, or rather recreated, in order to satisfy a northern European idea of how 'authentic' Spanish life should be conducted. Hence a way of life that had continued largely unchanged for centuries was, in the space of a couple of summers, replaced by a 'Spanish dreamland, a gimcrack Carmen setting in which the realities of poverty and work were tolerable so long as they remained picturesque.'[80] The transformation that Lewis describes here is one that was to be repeated endlessly across southern Europe, before being exported across the globe, a view of the south born in the north and one wholly alien to those whose lives were about to be uprooted. The poignancy of Lewis' book lies in the fact that it was not published until 1984 and so as readers we are fully aware of how this particular story ends, a knowledge that mocks the feeble optimism of these Spanish villagers, unable to view the disruption to their way of life as anything other than a temporary aberration: 'It's a kind of sickness, an infection. In the past we suffered from the plague. Now we suffer from tourists, but like any other sickness it dies out in the end. We have these people for a year, and they corrupt us. Next year things are going to be better – I'm told the bookings are down by fifty per cent. The year after it'll be all over. A thing of the past [...] They'll all go and we'll be back where we were before.'[81] For most travellers Spain was too far south and therefore too distant from the cultural centres of Italy and Greece to feature on the traditional itinerary of the Grand Tour; judged as too hot and inaccessible it was also largely spared the influx of northern Europeans between the wars. In the first half of the nineteenth century, Malaga was briefly fashionable as a health resort while San Sebastián continued as an attractive destination for Spaniards in the summer months until the 1940s.[82] But having been spared the transformation wrought by the first great wave of southern European tourism, as France and Italy became the focus of early sun-seekers, once Spain had been identified as an untapped market for the tourist industry it was to experience a transformation on a scale unheard of in other European destinations. The southern Spanish coast, perhaps forewarned of what was to come by the steady trickle of visitors who began to arrive in the 1920s to escape the northern winter, was to rebrand itself as the Costa del Sol in the 1930s, but it wasn't until the 1950s that summer tourism was invented and northern Europeans began to 'roast themselves on the beach throughout the torrid August days in a way that fills the local inhabitants with concern.'[83] From this point onwards, the trickle was to become a torrent and from the 1950s to the end of the century the number of tourists arriving in Spain was to increase by more than 4000 percent. They were drawn mainly to the Mediterranean coast and the Balearics, and by the 1970s southern Spain had eclipsed the French Riviera to become the prime destination for European sun-seekers, a position it has retained ever since.[84]

Looking back on this unparalleled boom, there now seems to be a sense of inevitability about the dominant role Spain was to assume as a tourist destination, yet according to the writer Giles Tremlett, this process might well have taken place elsewhere were it not for the intervention of a single, unforeseen element: 'The wind of change that blew south with the first package tourists was symbolised by something that, when first seen on a Spanish beach, shocked and delighted people in equal proportions – the bikini.'[85] In the Spain of the 1950s, writes Tremlett, the arrival of northern Europeans to the beaches of the south caused some dismay in the minds of the Catholic clergy, concerned that beaches were fast becoming a moral danger to the nation. At this time the Civil Guard would sometimes order bikini-clad foreign tourists to cover up, but in the ensuing battle between cultural and religious conservatism on the one hand, and the economic potential that such tourists represented on the other, it was money that was victorious. It was in Benidorm, before the war a quiet fishing village, soon however to become the tourist capital of southern Europe, that this battle was first played out, and in 1959, the town's mayor, Pedro Zaragoza Orts, signed a municipal order authorising the wearing of bikinis. The Church responded with the threat of excommunication, and, as support for his position ebbed away, Zaragoza climbed onto his Vespa and went to Madrid to present his case to General Franco. Eight days later his position as mayor was reaffirmed, excommunication proceedings were dropped and the bikini stayed:

> Some see this, at least symbolically, as a defining moment in recent Spanish history. It marked the beginning of a timid sexual revolution and helped take the Catholicism out of National Catholicism. The tourists, more importantly, had the power to outface the Church. They brought not just money, but the seeds of change. They also brought the fresh air of democracy. There was no turning back. [...] Without the bikini there, quite possibly, would have been no modern Benidorm and, in fact, precious little tourism at all. At this stage, had Spain not welcomed it, the nascent package tourism could easily have put its roots down elsewhere in the Mediterranean.[86]

If, then, the Mayor of Benidorm is the Spaniard with the greatest claim to having ushered in this new Golden Age of tourism on Spain's southern coast, his counterpart in the UK, and the person responsible for delivering these bikini-clad tourists, is a man called Vladimir Raitz. It was in 1950 that Raitz founded his travel company, Horizon, on Fleet Street in London and he was soon to transport a group of British tourists to Calvi in Corsica, having for the first time hired an airliner especially for this purpose. By 1953 Raitz had expanded his operation and he took some 1700 tourists on holiday to Spain; by the end of the decade destinations included France, Sardinia and Portugal. So the package holiday was born. In 1951, 1.5 million people went abroad for their holiday; by 1965 this number had risen to 5 million; by 1979 this figure had broken 10 million. Interviewed in 1993, by which time this figure was beyond 12 million, Raitz said, 'I am pleased by what I have achieved. But I am upset by what has happened in some destinations.'[87]

One such destination which, more than any other, is likely to have upset Raitz, is Benidorm, once 'a modest beach-side village, a place of sailors, fishermen and farmers who patiently tended almond, olive, carob and citrus trees', yet fifty years later the symbol of the invasion to which Spain has since been subjected (and to which it has subjected itself). 'A fresh invading horde', writes Tremlett, 'sun-hat and sandal-wearing northern European tourists, has rampaged its way along the coast over this past forty years. The horde has made Benidorm its capital. This time there has been no resistance. The burghers of Benidorm have rolled out a welcome carpet of concrete, tarmacadam and brick. Jointly they have vandalised what was once one of the most beautiful spots on the Spanish coast.'[88] Of course, Benidorm is not alone and is merely one amongst many such towns, all with their own particular customs and histories, which have, as a result of the tourist boom, now found themselves submerged within a larger region, a greater south whose borders extend throughout the entirety of Spain's southern coastline, forming what is in effect an entirely new city, a Spanish megalopolis more than a hundred miles in length, from Nerja in the east to Sotogrande in the west, a city which it is predicted will eventually become the largest in Spain.[89] This then is the tourist south, a standardised and homogenised region, notorious for the ugliness of its architecture and the crowds that dominate its beaches. Cut free from its moorings in any one particular time or place, this is a new kind of space, endlessly replicated around the globe, disorientating in its anonymity and peopled by a transient population with little involvement in the society in which they have chosen to live:

I felt lost. [...] Eventually, I decided that I was not in Spain any more. This was really the outer suburbs of a coastal city in Florida, Australia or any of the white-dominated suburbs along South Africa's Indian Ocean coast. It was, essentially, a new place. It had been invented out of nothing and answered to nothing more than its residents' desire to live a life of leisure. [...] The Brits came to Spain to get away from a country they saw as rotten with crime, immigration, broken communities and a failing health service. They fooled themselves that they were living a Spanish lifestyle, but spoke little or no Spanish and remained in their ghettoes. [...] Again, Spain has become America or, at least, Florida. It is the last refuge of a greying population, come to stretch their northern European pensions, and their final years, in the sunshine and supermarkets of the costas.[90]

Today Spain is estimated to be home to more than one million visitors from the UK, 700,000 of whom are believed to be permanent residents. The vast majority of these are to be found in the *costas* of the south, but can the life they have created there really be as soulless as is commonly supposed? In drawing attention to the perceived vulgarity of this new southern enclave, a general mood of hostility towards what is to be found here now seems to have become a compulsory reaction. 'It is customary at this point', writes Robert Mighall, 'to hold one's nose at the vulgarity, cheapness and ugliness of the hotels, bars and restaurants that crowd this – once charmingly pristine – stretch of coast now sacrificed to other nationalities', other classes' idea of fun. [...] Snobbery is acceptable, even obligatory, here.'[91] The solar gold rush that has swamped the south of Europe, and the south of Spain in particular, has been conducted on such a huge scale, in such a short space of time, and involves such staggering amounts of money, that standardisation and corruption have been the inevitable by-products of this historically unique attempt to establish a utopian existence of endless leisure underwritten by an equally boundless pool of cheap labour. One consequence of such mass commodification of sunshine is that what was once, and relatively briefly, seen as the lifestyle of the exclusive few, has within a generation or two become its opposite, and is now seen as an everyday experience for millions. Mass tourism has been shown to have a distinctly dystopian effect upon the communities on which it is unleashed, but it may also have unwelcome and unpredictable effects upon the tourists themselves, whose withdrawal into ghettos of enforced leisure can have a wholly unforeseen impact on their behaviour.

It is precisely these unwholesome effects that the novelist JG Ballard explores in his novel *Cocaine Nights* (1997) set in the fictional (but all too real) setting of Estrella de Mar on the Costa del Sol:

> In many ways Estrella de Mar was the halcyon county-town England of the mythical 1930s, brought back to life and moved south into the sun [...] As everyone never tired of saying, Estrella de Mar was a true community, with schools for the French and British children, a thriving Anglican church and a local council of elected members which met at the Club Nautico. However modestly, a happier twentieth century had rediscovered itself in this corner of the Costa del Sol.[92]

Ballard's novel depicts an anonymous landscape of beachside developments, retail parks and leisure facilities that provide an escape from an unwanted northern present into a southern recreation of a non-existent northern past. Here, amidst the endless sunshine and seemingly limitless opportunities for leisure, Ballard explores how a community of British expats copes with the unique demands of having almost nothing to do. The answer, of course, is that they become deeply bored, a boredom that they assuage with the usual cocktail of booze, drugs, sleep, television and sunbathing: 'A billion balconies facing the sun [...] The Costa del Sol is the longest afternoon in the world, and they've decided to sleep through it.'[93] Entering this curious world of sun-baked stupefaction, a sinister newcomer uses the lure of violence to rouse the dormant population from their slumber, gradually leading to the unravelling of the community. In Ballard's other dystopian rendering of Mediterranean coastal life, *Super Cannes* (2000), a small community outside Cannes is subjected to a similarly invigorating routine of sex and violence in an attempt to shake off the enervating effects of the sun; in both novels the geography of Europe's southern coastline is presented as an anonymous and self-enclosed world at odds not only with the countries of the north from which its inhabitants are drawn, but even more so with the countries which they now inhabit, effectively creating a world outside conceptions of north and south, and at home in neither. Ballard was himself a regular and enthusiastic visitor to precisely those parts of southern Europe he was to recreate in his fiction, and in an earlier work, *The Atrocity Exhibition* (1969) he outlines his vision of this brave new world:

The curious atmosphere of the Mediterranean beach resorts still awaits its chronicler. One could regard them collectively as a linear city, some 3000 miles long, from Gibraltar to Glyfada beach north of Athens, and 300 yards deep. For three summer months the largest city in the world, population at least 50 million, or perhaps twice that. The usual hierarchies and conventions are absent; in many ways it couldn't be less European, but it works. It has a unique ambience – nothing, in my brief experience, like Venice, California, or Malibu. At present it is Europe's Florida, an endless parade of hotels, marinas and apartment houses, haunted by criminals running hash from North Africa, stealing antiquities or on the lam from Scotland Yard.

Could it ever become Europe's California? Perhaps, but the peculiar geometry of those identical apartment houses seems to diffuse the millenarian spirit. Living there, one is aware of the exact volumes of these generally white apartments and hotel rooms. After the more sombre light of northern Europe, they seem to focus an intense self-consciousness on the occupants. Sex becomes stylised, relationships more oblique. The office workers and secretaries all behave like petty criminals vaguely on the run, so many topless Janet Leighs who have decided not to take that shower and can't remember where they left their lives. The growing numbers of full-time residents seem almost decorticated. My dream is to move there permanently. But perhaps I already have.[94]

Ballard's understanding of the contradictory appeal such beachside communities may hold and the uneasy relationship with reality that they may engender can be found throughout his work, in which the beach itself becomes a recurrent metaphor for a pervasive kind of late twentieth-century lethargy. But it is in his early tale of post-apocalyptic London, *The Drowned World* (1962) that he was first to describe the peculiar, and in this case fatal, allure the south can come to exert. Following the melting of the polar ice caps by solar radiation, Ballard's novel imagines a world in which the territories of the equatorial south have advanced to reclaim much of the north, transforming London into a lurid, semi-tropical wilderness, and stranding most of the Earth's remaining population at the now temperate poles. What distinguishes *The Drowned World* from numerous other ingenious examples of post-apocalyptic worlds, is the fact that rather than retreating in the face of such devastation, Ballard's protagonists find themselves irresistibly drawn southward into the heart of this newly submerged world. And it is here, in the fictional voice of Ballard's principal character, Kerans, that we find a striking reminder of that irresistible urge southward with which so many of the figures I have explored elsewhere in this chapter appear to have been afflicted. For as Ballard's novel ends, Kerans turns his back on what remains of civilisation and turns into the jungle, 'following the lagoons southward through the increasing heat and rain, attacked by alligators and giant bats, a second Adam searching for the forgotten paradises of the reborn sun.'[95] Kerans scrawls a message for those of a similar disposition who choose to follow in his footsteps, and in a curious way, with its echo of Lawrence's equally instinctive advance southward, it seems to offer a suitable conclusion here:

*27th day. Have rested and am moving south. All is well.
Kerans.*[96]


## Notes

1. Leigh Fermor, p. 199. Leigh Fermor's account of his walk across
   Europe has some interesting affinities with Goethe's *Italian
   Journey*, not least the fact that both were written some 30 years
   after the events which they describe; and while both books are
   based upon their respective journals, the inevitable result of
   such a time lag is that their youthful voices (or middle-aged in
   Goethe's case) can often appear subject to the authorial intrusions
   of their older selves.
2. Fussell, p. 131. The gateway to this enchanted realm is, however,
   rather more prosaic: 'The way you got to the south was to go first
   to Victoria Station, an unlikely gateway to faërie, with its dirty
   brick and nasty prole food, but once inside the mythical Blue
   Train stood ready to whisk you all the way to the Riviera.' (p.
   132).
3. Stevenson, 'Ordered South', pp. 244–5.
4. Littlewood, p. 13.
5. Gopnik, p. 17.
6. Pemble, p. 8. Describing the Tour in the late nineteenth century,
   Pemble writes (p. 14): 'No understanding of the lives of the
   Victorian and Edwardian leisured and literary classes can be
   complete without some knowledge of how they travelled to the
   South, where they went in the South, why they went, how their
   experiences shaped their attitude, and how their attitudes shaped
   their experiences.'
7. For a full account of this 'unofficial' version of the Tour see
   Littlewood, pp. 11–28.
8. Littlewood, p. 4.
9. Littlewood, p. 2.
10. Thomas Nugent, *The Grand Tour* (1749), quoted in Littlewood,
    p. 13.
11. Alexander Pope, *The Dunciad* (1743), IV, 311–316, quoted in
    Littlewood, p. 14.
12. Littlewood, pp. 16–17.
13. Littlewood, p. 21.

14. Littlewood, p. 21.

15. Littlewood, p. 24.

16. Saine, Introduction, Goethe, *Collected Works,* p. 2.

17. Reed, Introduction, Goethe, *The Flight to Italy,* p. ix.

18. Goethe, *The Flight to Italy,* p. 4.

19. Saine, Introduction, Goethe, *Collected Works,* p. 4.

20. Goethe, *Italian Journey,* p. 317.

21. Goethe, *Italian Journey,* pp. 320–321.

22. Goethe, *Italian Journey,* p. 14.

23. Goethe, *Italian Journey,* p. 22.

24. Goethe, *Italian Journey,* p. 207.

25. In their introduction to Goethe's *Italian Journey,* WH Auden and Elizabeth Mayer write (p. 16):

> One of the reasons why his account of his time in Rome, particularly of his second stay, is less interesting than the rest of the Italian Journey is that one feels that much is happening to Goethe which is of great importance to him, but which he declines to tell. There is no reason to suppose that Goethe's life in Rome was anything like Byron's in Venice, but it is impossible to believe that it was quite so respectable, or so exclusively devoted to higher things as, in his letters home, for obvious reasons, he makes it sound. The difference between the over-refined, delicate, almost neurasthenic face of the pre-Italian portraits and the masculine, self-assured face in the portraits executed after his return is very striking; the latter is that of a man who has known sexual satisfaction.

26. Saine, Introduction, Goethe, *Collected Works,* p. 3.

27. Prange, p. 240.

28. Kolb, p. 106.

29. Melberg, 'What did Nietzsche do on Capri?' (2007).

30. Kolb, p. 107.

31. Kolb, pp. 107–108.

32. Kolb, p. 115.

33. Nietzsche, *Gay Science,* pp. 162 & 132.

34. Nietzsche, *Gay Science,* p. 254.

35. Prange, p. 209.

36. Nietzsche, *Basic Writings,* pp. 384–5.

37. Nietzsche, *Gay Science,* pp. 355–356.

38. Prange, pp. 246–7.

39. Zweig, *Hölderlin,* p. 496.
40. Zweig, *Hölderlin,* p. 497.
41. Zweig, *Hölderlin,* p. 498.
42. Zweig, *Hölderlin,* pp. 498–500.
43. Zweig, *Hölderlin,* p. 503.
44. Zweig, *Hölderlin,* p. 504.
45. Littlewood, p. 190.
46. Mighall, p. 73.
47. Mighall, p. 73.
48. Littlewood, p. 190.
49. John Auchard, Introduction, James, *Italian Hours,* p. xi.
50. Owen, p. 53.
51. Mighall, p. 76.
52. Mighall, pp. 82–86.
53. Mighall, pp. 39–41.
54. *Time,* 6 August 1923, quoted in Owen, p. 53.
55. Owen, p. 53.
56. John Weightman writes (p. 9): 'Sun-worship as a thorough-going religion is, of course, as old as recorded history [...] But I think we can say that, in Europe, the sun is by way of being a very recent invention. [...] These changes are symptomatic of what we might call the solar revolution which has taken place in Europe during rather less than a hundred years.'
57. Mighall, p. 45.
58. Littlewood writes (p. 194):

    But if the tanned skin of the tourist denotes sensuality, this is not merely because getting a tan is itself a sensual process; just as important is the long tradition that associates dark skin with primitive sexuality. From this point of view, the crass racial assumptions of the nineteenth century have passed on an unrecognised legacy in the cultural significance we give to suntan. [...] To get a tan was, and to some extent still is, to borrow a cultural sign of the savage and the sensual.

59. Mighall, p. 66.
60. Lawrence, 'Sun', p. 245.
61. Lawrence, 'Sun', pp. 248–252.
62. Mighall, pp. 90–91.
63. 'Lawrence was essentially a puritan', writes Littlewood (p. 201), 'and the new religion was essentially about pleasure. He ends up

as high priest of a practice he came to detest precisely because it was the hallmark of the hedonist.'

64. Littlewood, pp. 201–202. See also Paul Fussell (p. 139):

The power of the sun idea to take over entirely a malleable mind can be studied in the case of Harry Crosby, the ultimately mad American who settled in France, naming his residence Le Moulin de Soleil. He established the Black Sun Press and devised a homemade ritual of sun worship in which onanism played some part. On his back he had tattooed a sun (to testify his fidelity to "the Sun God") [...] He seemed to grow madder and madder until he finally murdered his mistress and killed himself.

65. Stefania Michelucci, Introduction, Lawrence, *Twilight in Italy*, pp. xv-xvii.
66. Fussell, p. 149.
67. Lawrence, *Twilight in Italy*, pp. 207 & 219–222.
68. DH Lawrence, *Movements in European History*, Oxford: OUP, 1971, p. 54, quoted in Michaels-Tonks, p. 8.
69. Stefania Michelucci, Introduction, Lawrence, *Twilight in Italy*, p. xxxix.
70. Michaels-Tonks, p. 159.
71. Owen, pp. 163–4.
72. Lawrence, *Twilight in Italy*, p. 116.
73. Stefania Michelucci, Introduction, Lawrence, *Twilight in Italy*, p. xxxii.
74. Fussell, p. 147.
75. Fussell, pp. 11–13.
76. Lee, p. 43. Lee's account recalls that of another trans-European journey, also undertaken on foot, which had begun the previous year. At only 18, Patrick Leigh Fermor was a year younger than Lee when he embarked upon his walk from Holland to Istanbul, a journey he was later to record in *A Time of Gifts* (1977). While his trajectory was broadly from west to east, in contrast to that of Lee's journey south, both accounts share an exuberant sense of freedom, an exuberance that survives the 30-year interval between the events these books describe and their eventual publication.
77. Lee, pp. 87–88.
78. Lee, p. 136.

79. Lewis, *Voices of the Old Sea*, p. 5.
80. Lewis, *Voices of the Old Sea*, p. 153.
81. Lewis, *Voices of the Old Sea*, p. 180.
82. Mighall, p. 99.
83. Tremlett, pp. 111–112.
84. Mighall, p. 100.
85. Tremlett, p. 95.
86. Tremlett, pp. 102–3.
87. Tremlett, p. 107. While Raitz was to pioneer package tourism in the UK, his counterpart on the Continent is Gérard Blitz. In 1950, in the same year that Raitz founded Horizon, Blitz put an advertisement on the Paris metro consisting of an image of the sun and the sea, alongside his telephone number. This was the start of Club Méditerranée. The first Club Med village opened in Majorca, spawning others across the Mediterranean before arriving in Tahiti in 1955. Within four decades Club Med had become the largest holiday resort company in the world. See Littlewood, pp. 208–214.
88. Tremlett, pp. 97–98.
89. Tremlett, p. 117.
90. Tremlett, pp. 120–123.
91. Mighall, pp. 221–222.
92. Ballard, *Cocaine Nights*, p. 66.
93. Ballard, *Cocaine Nights*, pp. 180 & 218.
94. Ballard, *The Atrocity Exhibition*, pp. 99–100.
95. Ballard, *The Drowned World*, p. 175.
96. Ballard, *The Drowned World*, p. 175. Ballard's novel, which sees its protagonist succumb to his fatal but instinctive attraction to the south takes its place within a micro-genre of similarly fatal southerly excursions: as we shall see, Poe's *Narrative of Arthur Gordon Pym of Nantucket* (1838) is one such example, as is Paul Bowles' *The Sheltering Sky* (1949), albeit in strikingly dissimilar terrain. Poetry aside, the life of Arthur Rimbaud also appears to conform to this particular trajectory, with much the same conclusion.

*Where Are You Going?* or *Woman Holding a Fruit* by Paul Gauguin (1893)
HERMITAGE MUSEUM

# 2

# In the South Seas

*The first experience can never be repeated. The first love, the first sunrise, the first South Sea island, are memories apart and touched a virginity of sense.*

Robert Louis Stevenson[1]

*Man's longed-for havens indeed are for the most part curiously simple in structure. But though the sweet, spoon-fed, simple dolce far niente of the South Seas may for a while allure his weary or indolent body, his true happiness must consort with desires of the mind.*

Walter de la Mare[2]

The earliest utopian myths describe a golden age of material abundance, long since past, a lost paradise to be found just beyond the perimeter of the known world. Often islands, and always out of reach, separated from *terra firma* by uncharted oceans and the burning heat of the sun, the locations of the Blessed Isles, of Elysium and Atlantis were impossibly remote, cut off from a present whose shortcomings they exposed. In the Hellenistic age, these myths of ideal societies were often accompanied by tales of imaginary voyages to strange new worlds, while Christianity was to supply a biblical myth which referred to both a paradise lost – the Garden of Eden – as well as that of an afterlife to come. Over time such myths were to become conflated, interchangeable in their descriptions of an otherworldly paradise lost in space and time. But another possibility remained which proved

71

equally persistent, an earthly paradise which existed still, located neither in the remote past nor the distant future but in the present, just over the horizon. The dimensions of the unknown portions of the globe were such, however, that the precise location of this terrestrial paradise was to remain tantalisingly out of reach. The Bible was to offer little help in finding the 'garden eastward in Eden', although the fact that God had deemed it necessary to place cherubim to guard it after the fall appeared to offer hope that it still existed.[3] In the *Mappa Mundi* of Hereford (c.1300) Jerusalem can be found in the centre and Paradise is marked as a circular island at the eastern end of the world, beyond India; while in Dante's *Inferno* (c. 1308–20) Paradise is to be found not in the east but in the southern hemisphere, also on an island, atop Mount Purgatory.[4]

The Renaissance voyages of discovery finally allowed such questions to be put to the test as the European powers despatched their ships across the globe. But the sailors who travelled in search of new worlds were seeking not merely the new, but were also looking for confirmation of the old – the existence of those mythical islands which formed the historical background to European thought. In this sense, the voyages of discovery can be viewed as a rediscovery of long-held beliefs, albeit transplanted to a new geographical location.[5] Travels to the Orient and the voyages of Columbus soon enlarged the extent of European geographical knowledge to the east and west, but while the contours of these areas were mapped, the hitherto uncharted expanses of the southern ocean remained out of reach. In fact it wasn't until 1513, three years before More's *Utopia* (1516) was to give its name to the new genre of speculative worlds, that a European was finally to set eyes on what was soon to become a repository of European hopes and desires, the South Sea:

On Tuesday the twenty-fifth of September of the year 1513, at ten o'clock in the morning, Captain Vasco Núñez

[de Balboa], having gone ahead of his company, climbed
a hill with a bare summit, and from the top of the hill saw
the South Sea. Of all the Christians in his company, he
was the first to see it. He turned back toward his people,
full of joy, lifting his hands and his eyes to Heaven,
praising Jesus Christ and his glorious Mother the Virgin,
Our Lady. Then he fell upon his knees on the ground and
gave great thanks to God for the mercy he had shown
him, in allowing him to discover that sea.[6]

'The South Seas', writes Neil Rennie, 'where voyagers
were to rediscover the lost Paradise, and also a Paradise lost,
have always depended on the observer's point of view.'[7]
Balboa, standing upon a peak in Darién (Darién Province in
eastern Panama), which runs from east to west, was looking
south at the ocean which Magellan would later name the
Pacific; and it was here that European dreams of paradise
would finally be realised.

## *Terra Australis* and the Utopian South

By the Middle Ages, with many geographers now holding
to a belief in a spherical earth, the *terra firma* of the known
world was contrasted increasingly with the unknown world
which was thought to be found at the Antipodes. The origin
of the myth of the Antipodes, that great unknown continent
thought to dominate the southern hemisphere, lies with the
second-century Greek geographer Ptolemy, who believed
that such a landmass must exist in the south simply to balance
the continents of the northern hemisphere, and to prevent the
planet from rolling over like a top heavy ball.[8] This great but
unknown southern land, the *terra australis nondum cognita*, was
to become a source of endless speculation for those seeking
the location of the terrestrial paradise.[9] But such dreams of
paradise were in fact interwoven with fears of their opposite,
and visions of utopian islands of ease and plenty on the one
hand, were shadowed by dystopian depictions of barren lands

inhabited by savages on the other. The prevailing depiction of *terra australis* was then, one which oscillated continually between these two opposing visions of heaven and hell.[10] But regardless of whether it was to be characterised as dream or nightmare, this was a realm which seemed to be constantly on the move, its location remaining stubbornly elusive and consistently beyond the boundaries of current geographical knowledge. As the limits of global exploration began to exclude both the east – formerly the favoured bearing for those seeking paradise – and the west, so did the *terra australis* become, in the minds of many Renaissance explorers and their paymasters, the best, and it would seem, final, hope for its discovery.

Throughout the Renaissance, utopian ideas were dominated by a triumvirate of dominant characteristics, to which all such speculative worlds were thought to conform, from Mandeville's *Travels* to More's *Utopia*, from Montaigne to Shakespeare: firstly, that of the island paradise; secondly, the conception of an ideal society, or rather a society perfectly governed; and finally, a belief in primitivism and the return to a simpler way of life free from the complexities and hypocrisies of contemporary European civilisation. These ideas were to form the basis of the utopian tradition which was to blossom in the wake of the Renaissance explorers, and which, following Balboa's sighting of the Pacific, came to be located, more frequently than in any other corner of the globe, in the 'empty' and uncharted expanse of the South Seas.

One of the earliest travel narratives, the Old Testament account of the expedition of Solomon's ships to Ophir (c.945 BC), is to be found in the Book of Kings: 'And they came to Ophir, and fet from thence gold foure hundred and twentie talents, and brought it to king Solomon.'[11] Rather disappointingly, however, this description of the source of Solomon's fabulous wealth fails to provide the details of its precise location. But the myth of Ophir proved persistent and, having failed to have been located elsewhere over the course of the next two millennia, by the time of the Renaissance it was thought, largely through a process of elimination, to be situated somewhere in the Pacific. In fact, the myth of Ophir took its place within a heady brew of biblical, classical, and even Indian myths, all of which were to be reworked into the creation of *terra australis*, and which were to inspire the Spanish exploration of the Pacific. Columbus was the first to claim he had discovered Ophir, thinking it to be in Hispaniola; but it was his successor, Mendaña, who was the first to locate Ophir in the South Seas, believing it was to be found in what are now known as the Solomon Islands. Mendaña's 'discovery' of the Solomon Islands in 1568 and the failure of the subsequent attempt to return and colonise them in 1595, offers a blueprint for much of the future European contact with the peoples of the South Pacific. Mendaña was unable to relocate the Solomon Islands but he did manage instead to find the island group which he was to name the Marquesas. Here, however, trouble was to begin almost immediately: 'They stayed for a fortnight, teaching the Marquesans "to make the sign of the cross" and shooting them. One Spaniard killed "lest he should lose his reputation as a good marksman."' By the end of this brief, but depressingly prescient episode, the tally of those killed exceeded two hundred. Such was the result of the first substantial contact between Europeans and Polynesians.[12]

There seems little to be found in this sorry account to inspire thoughts of a utopian paradise, and yet when news of Mendaña's discovery of the Solomon Islands reached England in 1572, it appears to have had precisely this effect, providing the impulse behind one of the most influential of all utopias. Francis Bacon presented his *New Atlantis* (1627) as a narrative of discovery in the South Seas; for like many others, he had identified America as the site of Plato's island of Atlantis, leaving him to create a newer alternative which he was to place, in familiar fashion, well beyond the limits of current maps, in 'that part of the South Seas [which] was utterly unknown; and might have islands or continents, that hitherto were not come to light.'[13] As Susan Bruce notes in her introduction to Bacon's tale, the isolation of such early modern utopias fulfils a necessary narrative function, lending them a plausibility that they would otherwise be denied.[14] Beginning with the line, 'We sailed from Peru [...] for China and Japan, by the South Sea', Bacon was careful to anchor his *New Atlantis* to a 'real' location, and his text reads much like a fictional travel guide in which the unnamed narrator offers the reader a detailed account of life on the utopian island of Bensalem, from his arrival and quarantine in the 'Stranger's House', to his meetings with Bensalem's inhabitants. The majority of the text is given over to his discussions during three such meetings, in which he is in turn informed of Bensalem's laws and history, its sexual and marital customs and, finally, the workings of its most important institution, Salomon's House. Named in honour of Bensalem's original 'lawgiver', Salomona, and in explicit confirmation of the influence of Mendaña, it is here that the narrator is informed of the scientific experiments and practices which dominate life on the island:

> We have engine-houses, where are prepared engines for all sorts of motions. There we imitate and practise to make swifter motions than any you have, either out of your muskets or any engine that you have [...] We represent also ordnance and instruments of war and engines of all kinds; and likewise new mixtures and compositions of gunpowder, wildfires burning in water, and unquenchable. Also fire-works of all variety both for pleasure and use. We imitate also flights of birds, we have some degrees of flying in the air; we have ships and boats for going under water, and brooking of seas [...] We imitate also motions of living creatures, by images of men, beasts, birds, fishes and serpents. We also have a great number of other various motions, strange for equality, fineness, and subtlety.[15]

The South Pacific was the last of the world's major oceans to be discovered by the Europeans and as a consequence it was also the first large region outside of Europe to be explored using the newfound methods of scientific enquiry. In this light, the voyages of discovery may be judged not merely as exercises in colonial expansion but as major scientific breakthroughs. For Bacon, as one of the founders of this new scientific methodology, which favoured experience and observation over the authority of the ancients, the Renaissance voyages had discovered a 'new continent' of truth, and these traveller's tales, which had formerly been regarded as little more than fiction, were now to provide the foundations for the scientific and philosophical revolutions which were to follow. Bacon's was only the first of many such fictional South Sea Islands which were to flourish during this period, helping to establish a tradition of such island paradises later to be discovered by an array of fictional voyagers. Uniquely, however, Bacon was to reject the emerging image of a natural paradise, in favour of an artificial one, and his futuristic fable on the benefits and dangers of science has since been described as the first science fiction novel.[16] His fantasy of scientific and geographical discovery is also explicit in its use of a pioneering voyage to the new world as a symbol of futuristic progress and it was this aspect of *New Atlantis* which was to prove so influential in subsequent accounts, both real and imagined, of southern exploration. Bacon's account was not the first to do so – it was preceded by Joseph Hall's *Mundus Alter et Idem*, or 'Discovery of a New World' in 1608 – but it was to set the tone and the direction (southerly) for much of what was to follow, from Henry Neville's fantasy of sexual wish-fulfilment, *Isle of Pines* (1668), to some of the most well-known works of western literature, amongst them Defoe's *Robinson Crusoe* (1719) and Swift's *Gulliver's Travels* (1726).

Throughout the seventeenth and early eighteenth centuries, the South Pacific was to become the site of a

seemingly endless series of imaginary islands of every
description, an industry of fictional discovery which was
matched only by the boom in travel narratives claiming
to offer factual accounts which were themselves no less
fantastic. In fact, by the early eighteenth century, such
accounts of voyages to foreign lands, which were, of
course, equally as fictional as their utopian counterparts,
had replaced the Romance as the principal source of
literary escapism.[17] The popularity enjoyed by travel
literature during this period was itself simply a reflection of
the increase in maritime activity, accounts of which were
notoriously unreliable. The sources of such material, the
voyagers themselves, were often equally well-known for
their literary endeavours, the most significant figure being
the writer and traveller William Dampier, whose accounts
of his own voyages were to be the catalyst for much of what
was to follow in his wake. His first book, *A New Voyage
Round the World* (1697), is often cited as the single work
with the greatest impact from this emerging genre, and it
was to revive interest not only in the voyages of discovery
generally, but more specifically in accounts of voyages to
the South Seas.[18] Dampier's *Voyage* describes not one but
several such journeys, which were to take him through
America, the Caribbean and the Pacific over a period of
more than 12 years before returning him to England.
Although he was to discover little of the South Seas during
this period, he was more than able to make up for such
deficiencies in his career as a sailor, through his career as
an author, and his accounts of a largely imagined south
were to prove enormously influential. In addition to being
a sailor and a writer, Dampier was also something of an
amateur scientist, which allowed him to add a further layer
of realism to his accounts through the use of botanical and
scientific language. In this way, the realistic imitation of
the travel narrative was born, in which the public demand
for exotic facts and colourful locations could be satisfied
while presenting an account written with the necessary

seriousness of scientific discourse. Dampier was to pave the way for numerous other such accounts, his particular blend of fact and fiction providing the template for works such as Edward Cooke's *A Voyage to the South Sea* (1712) as well as contributing to the utopian tradition outlined above. The cumulative effect of such works was to extend and reinforce an image of the South Seas in the public imagination which had its roots in the earliest myths of an earthly paradise. Yet when one returns to the accounts of that celebrated moment when the first Europeans were finally to make landfall on Tahiti, it becomes clear that the European imagination of the day was ill-prepared for what lay ahead.[19]

## Transit of Venus: De Bougainville, Cook and the Discovery of the South

Despite the vast array of myths and legends, alongside an ever growing series of fictional, and supposedly factual, accounts of the South Seas, throughout the early eighteenth century the idea of the *terra australis*, the stubbornly invisible southern continent, retained its position as a widely held geographical fact. Its existence was certainly given credence by the British Admiralty, which in 1766 officially took up the search, despatching Captain Samuel Wallis in the *Dolphin* to see if he might locate it. Wallis's secret instructions were 'to discover and obtain a complete knowledge of the Land or Islands supposed to be situated in the Southern Hemisphere.'[20] Wallis's endeavours have since been almost entirely overshadowed by those of his more celebrated compatriot, Captain James Cook, but contrary to legend it was Wallis and the sailors of the *Dolphin*, rather than Cook and the *Endeavour*, who, on 18 June 1767, spotted 'a great high mountain covered with clouds on the tope' and in the evening, 'at Sun Set, we now supposed we saw the long wishd for Southern Continent, which has been often talkd of, but neaver before seen by any Europeans.'²¹ This was not, of course, the Southern Continent, for Wallis, having completed a perfunctory tour of the southern latitudes, had been forced north by strong winds. What he had found, however, was to prove equally dramatic, both for the discoverers and for the newly discovered. The historian, JC Beaglehole, describes the consequences:

> So almost suddenly, so overwhelmingly, was the idea of the Pacific at last to enter into the consciousness, not of seamen alone but of literate Europe, in the form of this remarkable, this – as it were – symbolic island. It was not singular in its characteristics. Its primacy in natural beauty has been contested. One may exercise, in our later day, all due reserve. But it was the heart of Polynesia. Geographically, therefore, it was important. A few years more, and its importance would also be psychological. For Wallis had not merely come to a convenient port of call. He had stumbled on a foundation stone of the Romantic Movement. Not as continent, not as vast distances, was the ocean henceforth in common thought to be known. The unreal was to mingle with the real, the too dramatic with the undramatic, the shining light was to become a haze in which every island was the one island, and the one island the Tahitian dream.²²

On the following morning the *Dolphin* approached Tahiti and was soon surrounded by a flotilla of more than one hundred canoes. With signs of friendship having been exchanged, some of the men came aboard, where having immediately become entranced by the ship's iron fittings, they had to be persuaded to leave with the encouragement of a shot from the ship's nine-pound guns. In fact, over the following week the Tahitians were given several more examples of the power of the ship's guns, until they were finally subdued, allowing the British to land and Wallis to name the island, rather prosaically, 'King George the

Third's Island', by planting a pendant on the shore (which the Tahitians were to remove shortly afterwards). With the question of the island's ownership now settled, the terms of the Anglo-Tahitian relationship which was to follow were quickly established. The sailors, weakened from scurvy, wanted fresh food; the Tahitians, for whom the sight of iron in any shape or form proved irresistible, were more than willing to barter whatever they had to get it.[23] The result was that the Europeans had their desires satisfied in ways they might well have hoped for but never would have expected, with a trade in sexual favours quickly introduced in which the nail was to become the standard currency. Such was the popularity of this system that on leaving the island most of the men found themselves having to sleep on deck, the nails which had previously supported their hammocks now in Tahitian hands.[24]

The journals of Captain Wallis and George Robertson (the master of the *Dolphin*) were never published, but despite this, future visitors to Tahiti would prove the beneficiaries of this first meeting. For such was the impression made by the ship's guns on the unwary Tahitians, that in all subsequent encounters, the Europeans, still unaware of the effects of this initial encounter and the change of policy it had provoked, were not to know why the Tahitians had chosen 'to make love not war.'[25] Thus, within a few years of Wallis's arrival, the image of Tahiti as a prelapsarian paradise had developed rapidly. Wallis may not have discovered paradise, but the *Dolphin*'s guns had effectively ensured that his successors, de Bougainville, Cook, and Banks, were 'to be received with open arms by charming women, not savage men with spears and clubs, and to discover a new kind of noble savage, the nubile savage, erotic as well as exotic, inhabiting an Eden, it seemed, of prelapsarian innocence and bliss.'[26]

While Wallis was to describe his newly claimed island as 'romantic', his was the soul of a sailor not a poet, and it was the next European claimant to Tahiti who was to provide the poetic imagery with which the South Seas have been associated ever since. Louis-Antoine, Comte de Bougainville, the commander of the two ships to make the first French circumnavigation of the world, was a man of many parts: courtier, sailor and full-blown Romantic; he was to sight Tahiti first on 2 April 1768. De Bougainville was also a learned man and, although he was only to spend ten days on the island, this proved more than enough time for him to interpret his experience in terms of the utopian dreams of eighteenth-century Europe. In short, from the outset he was to find and to create the paradise of tropical sensuality that he, his shipmates and his audience back home had been searching for:

> The women are pretty [...] This people breathe only ease and sensual pleasure. Venus is the goddess who is worshiped here. The sweetness of the climate, the beauty of the landscape, the fertility of the ground which is everywhere fed by streams and waterfalls, the purety of the air, free from the legion of insects that are the scourge of hot countries – everything inspires voluptuous sensations. Accordingly, I have named it New Cythera.[27]

'La Nouvelle Cythère', the New Island of Love; de Bougainville's journal was to reveal the rediscovery of paradise that Europe had dreamt of, a land of beauty and sexual abundance, which seemingly offered proof of Rousseau's 'Noble Savage', where man lived still in a state of nature free from the corruption of the West. De Bougainville's first impressions record a return to the golden age of classical myth, yet while Tahiti appeared to conform to, if not surpass, all the necessary characteristics of a truly utopian society, it was not a place of dream and legend, the 'not place' of the imagined society, but the real thing, the 'beautiful place': 'la véritable Eutopie.'[28]

Spared by Wallis from the necessity of having to use force to achieve his ends, de Bougainville and his men were, on the contrary, met with a much warmer welcome, and his account of anchoring in Tahiti for the first time has become, as Richard Holmes notes, one of the most celebrated passages in French romantic travel writing:

> I have to admit that it was nigh impossible to keep 400 young Frenchmen at work, sailors who had not seen a woman for six months, in view of what followed. In spite of all our precautions, a young Tahitian girl slipped aboard and placed herself on the quarterdeck immediately above one of the big hatchways, which was fully open to allow air in to the sailors sweating at the capstan below. The young girl casually let slip the only piece of cloth which covered her, and appeared to the eyes of all the crew exactly as naked Venus appeared to the Phrygian shepherd. Truly, she had the celestial form of the goddess of Love. More and more sailors crowded to the foot of the hatchway, and no capstan was ever wound with such alacrity as on this occasion. Only naval discipline succeeded in keeping these bewitched young fellows from rioting; and indeed we officers had some difficulty in restraining ourselves.[29]

De Bougainville's account of his experiences, *Voyage autour du monde*, was published in May 1771, and unlike those of Wallis and later Cook, his was delivered not to the Admiralty but to the public. As a result, Tahiti quickly became the subject of the Parisian salons, presenting an image of utopia which both informed and scandalised in equal measure. For de Bougainville's *Voyage* was not only to confirm the view of Tahiti as a mythological paradise, but it was also to supply its readers with a more realistic account of the island, its inhabitants and their customs. These two Tahitis, however, sit rather uncomfortably together in the pages of de Bougainville's journal; the first, idyllic, more literary, impression based upon his own experiences; the other, more ethnographic and scientific, based upon the account of the native, Aotourou, who accompanied de Bougainville back to

Europe, where he was to be fêted as a living example of the noble savage. But a native Tahitian's account of his own less than paradisiacal existence could never hope to withstand the challenge of European Romanticism, and his contribution to the journal has since been entirely disregarded in favour of de Bougainville's initial impression of Tahiti as 'the land of Venus reborn', a paradise of free love amidst the palm trees.[30] 'I have often, in company with only one or two of our people, been out walking in the interior parts of the isle', writes de Bougainville, 'I thought I was transported into the Garden of Eden. [...] We found companies of men and women sitting under the shade of their fruit-trees. They all greeted us with signs of friendship. Those who met us upon the road stood aside to let us pass. Everywhere we found hospitality, ease, innocent joy, and every appearance of happiness among them.'[31] De Bougainville's journal has proved of greater merit as a literary endeavour than as a contribution to science. For despite his attempts to maintain a cool-headed factual perspective, de Bougainville is quite unable to downplay the welcome of the Tahitian women whose charms colour his entire perception of the island. And yet this Eden was not the paradise which it first appeared, and some weeks after leaving the island, de Bougainville was to discover that several members of his crew had been afflicted with venereal disease. Falling back upon traditional European enmities, he laid the blame for this outbreak upon Wallis and the British sailors who had visited the island previously, starting a long controversy.[32]

According to the predictions of Edmund Halley, the transit of the planet Venus across the sun was due in 1769, an event which would not recur for more than a century. By observing the transit of Venus from various specific locations on the earth's surface, one could then calculate the earth's precise distance from the sun. One such location was to be found in the middle of the Pacific, and it was ostensibly in order to take the necessary readings that Captain Cook was sent south by the Admiralty. Like Wallis before him, however, Cook's instructions also contained the stipulation that, following the observation of Venus, he was to search the Pacific south of Tahiti, where 'there is reason to imagine that a Continent or Land of great extent may be found.'[33] Driven partly by scientific curiosity, but mainly out of a sense of imperial competition, Cook's orders were to seek out the 'great Southern Continent', now thought to lie between a latitude of 30 and 40 degrees south, considerably further south than that part of Australia's eastern seaboard already discovered by Dutch navigators. Here, it was believed, was to be found a huge continent, rich in natural resources, whose northern tip was formed by New Zealand. If such a continent existed, it must be claimed and mapped before the French did so. Ultimately, however, Cook's voyage was to discover almost exactly the opposite of that which his superiors had hoped. For over the following decade, in his three voyages between 1769 and 1779, Cook effectively destroyed the myth of the southern continent; he charted New Zealand, the east coast of Australia, and the Marquesas; rediscovered the islands Mendaña had misplaced; as well as discovering New Caledonia and Hawaii. In short, he brought the era of European exploration to an end, leaving his successors, as a rival French Captain was to put it, with 'little to do but admire.'[34] Cook had established himself as the 'anti-Columbus' of the Pacific, responsible not so much for the discovery of the South as of its absence, and leaving in his wake a fragmented series of islands in a vast ocean.[35]

Cook and the *Endeavour* were to reach Tahiti, anchoring in Matavai Bay, on 13 April 1769. Due to adverse atmospheric conditions, however, their observation of Venus was only partially successful.[36] But during the three months that Cook and his crew were to spend upon the island, they were able to compile an extensive survey of Tahitian life, recorded both in Cook's journal and, in greater detail, in that of the ship's botanist, Joseph Banks. These accounts were in many ways to confirm the experiences of their predecessors, Wallis and de Bougainville, most notably in recording the

Tahitians' attitudes to private property and, in particular, their insatiable desire for anything made of metal; and also, of course, in their observations of the sexual bartering they were willing to employ in order to satisfy this desire. The theft of goods was a cause of constant disruption, and as Richard Holmes has indicated, there was perhaps no other activity which so exposed the divergent attitudes between these two civilisations:

> To the Europeans theft was a violation of legal ownership, an assault on private property and wealth. To the Tahitians it was a skilful affirmation of communal resources, an attempt to balance their self-evident poverty against overwhelming European superfluity. There was no source of metal anywhere on the island. The Tahitians' hunting knives were made out of wood, their fish hooks out of mother-of-pearl, their cooking pots out of clay. The Europeans clanked and glittered with metal.[37]

The system of sexual barter that had swiftly been established under Wallis and de Bougainville, soon flourished under Cook also, with any kind of usable metal object once again the preferred currency: 'Among the able seamen', writes Holmes, 'the initial going rate was one ship's nail for one ordinary fuck, but hyper-inflation soon set in. The Tahitians well understood a market economy. There was a run on anything metal that could be smuggled off the ship – cutlery, cleats, handles, cooking utensils, spare tools, but especially nails. It was said that the *Endeavour*'s carpenter soon operated an illegal monopoly on metal goods, and nails were leaving the ship by the sackful.'[38] This practice was also of concern to Cook, who disapproved of sexual bartering and attempted (unsuccessfully) to regulate the activity. It was a concern that was well-placed, however, considering the devastating medical effects this particular form of trade was to have on the Polynesian population in the years to come.

On returning to England, Cook and Banks were lionised

for their discoveries in the South Pacific. Unlike that of de Bougainville, however, the accounts of their adventures were passed directly to the Admiralty, and added to those of Wallis and Robertson. In order to support their claim to these newly discovered territories, the Admiralty was keen that an 'official' account of the voyages should also be published. The man chosen for this task was the poet, critic and editor, Dr John Hawkesworth (1715–1773). Predictably enough, the resulting *Voyages* was not a straightforward retelling of the journals it was based upon, but instead delivered a composite image of the discoverers and their achievements. For all of its exaggerations, omissions, and overblown style, Hawkesworth's account remained largely faithful to its subject and offered the public a vision of Tahiti much as it had been viewed by Wallis, Cook and Banks. Hawkesworth's *Account of the Voyages undertaken by the order of his present Majesty for making Discoveries in the Southern Hemisphere* was published in June 1773, and was soon followed by a second edition later the same year, in addition to American, French and German translations shortly afterwards. The public reaction, however, was one of shock at what was perceived to be Tahitian 'indecency', to the extent that (rather unfairly) it was Hawkesworth himself who was held responsible. It was generally agreed upon his untimely death only six months later that it was his *Voyages* which was responsible for his demise.[39] The Eden which had been proclaimed by de Bougainville and described by Cook and Banks, was soon found to have been rather less idyllic than had at first been believed. For Hawkesworth's account revealed not merely the utopian dream but the flawed reality, a society in which there was not only light but also darkness, in which alongside beauty and simplicity, sensuality and generosity, there were also darker elements, 'strong, even oppressive social hierarchies; endemic thieving; a strange religion haunted by ghosts and superstitions; infanticide; and warlike propensities just below the surface.'[40]

# The Arrival of the Missionaries

In February 1779, Captain Cook was killed by natives on a beach in Kealakekua Bay, Hawaii, during his third Pacific voyage, and the reputation which Tahiti and the South Seas had hitherto enjoyed in Europe, as an unalloyed paradise, was dealt a fatal blow. The legend that Tahiti had become was rapidly becoming tarnished, as it began to assume a new and less idealised identity. 'The Island', writes Richard Holmes, 'had started its long decline into a source of popular entertainment.'[41] This process was to reach its zenith a few years later, following the mutiny on the *Bounty* in 1789, perhaps the single event which, more than any other, has come to encapsulate the ambiguous relationship between Europe and the South Seas.[42] It was the accounts of navigators such as Bligh and other European explorers which had first helped to establish the idea of the noble savage, born in a state of nature, free from the taint of Western civilisation.[43] Such a view, which had taken a foothold in Europe through the writings of Rousseau and which was to receive further support from the Romantic Movement, was now facing the first signs of revolt, and where previously the public had seen (and been offered) only paradise, they now saw a paradise lost. The high point for the utopian vision of the South Seas had now been passed. Where once, and very briefly, Tahiti had appeared to offer Europeans a simpler and more appealing way of life, the island and its inhabitants were now in need of saving. Inspired by the pamphleteers who had disseminated Hawkesworth's vision, within twenty years Tahiti was to be rediscovered, this time by the missionaries. Already succumbing to the tragedy inflicted by disease, the Tahitians were now to become the victims of a moral onslaught from Europe. Leaving Tahiti at the end of his second mission, Cook wrote in his journal, 'I directed my course to the West and we took our final leave of these happy islands and the good people on them.' Some years later he was to add, 'It would have been far better for these poor people never to have known us.'[44]

The backlash by the religious orthodoxy of the day began in 1795 with the formation of the London Missionary Society. Immediately focusing its attention upon the Pacific, over the course of the next 50 years the missionaries were to challenge and eventually overturn the myth of the noble savage, replacing one myth with another, as they sought to establish the image of the depraved heathen awaiting redemption. In 1797, a convict ship bound for Australia was to put the first missionaries ashore on Tahiti, where, like de Bougainville and Cook before them, they were overwhelmed by the warmth of their welcome. Landing in Matavai Bay, they too were to experience the generosity of their hosts, who having little conception of private property were happy to grant them whatever they wished. The missionaries asked for Matavai Bay itself, and the local chief immediately fulfilled their request, only later to discover that he and his people were now to be debarred from the area.[45] Over the next seven years the Tahitians were to act as servants for the missionaries, building their homes and feeding them, but they remained stubbornly resistant to the Christian message their guests sought to convey to them and no converts were made. Finally the missionaries changed their approach, testing the new technique of supplying alcohol to the natives. This method gained immediate results and, having reduced the Tahitian Chief, Pomare, to an alcoholic, the missionaries then introduced the equally reliable colonising tool of divide and rule, backing him in a war against the other island chiefs, with the understanding that victory would be followed by enforced conversion, and supplying firearms to ensure the correct outcome. In his book *The Missionaries*, Norman Lewis describes the aftermath of Pomare's victory:

> There followed a reign of terror. Persistent unbelievers were put to death and a penal code was drawn up by the missionaries and enforced by missionary police in the uniforms of Bow Street Runners. It was declared illegal

to adorn oneself with flowers, to sing (other than hymns), to tattoo the body, to surf or to dance. Minor offenders were put in the stocks, but what were seen as major infringements (dancing included) were punished by hard labour on the roads. Within a quarter of a century the process by which the native culture of Tahiti had been extinguished was exported to every corner of the South Pacific, reducing the islanders to the level of the working class of Victorian England.[46]

Meanwhile a combination of syphilis, tuberculosis, smallpox and influenza was decimating the population of Tahiti, from the 200,000 estimated by Cook to 18,000 by the end of the eighteenth century. Following 30 years of missionary rule, only 6,000 remained. The missionaries soon widened their activities to the outlying islands, employing the same methods that had served them so successfully on Tahiti: a local chieftain would be baptised, crowned king, and presented with a portrait of Queen Victoria, then alcohol would be introduced and the process of conversion would continue. By 1850 their work was finished and the conquest of the Pacific was complete.[47]

Following the formal annexation of the islands of the South Pacific by the French and British, the work of what had been called the missionary protectorate was now over, but the islands had been utterly transformed and they were never to return to the society they had been at the time of their discovery less than a century before. 'Once the lives of the Polynesian and Melanesian people', writes Lewis, 'had been intertwined with the process of creation. They seemed under compulsion to decorate everything. But now the mysterious compulsion of art had left them. [...] The desire to produce beautiful things had gone – possibly through the long association, transmitted by the missionary teachings, of beauty with evil.'[48] With their objectives now largely achieved, by the end of the nineteenth century missionary work in the Pacific was much diminished. With little in the way of natural obstacles to prevent them, hundreds of islands across the Pacific had been reached and occupied, their inhabitants forcibly converted. Encountering little resistance, little more than a single native 'teacher' supported by a half dozen missionary police, was sufficient to take over almost any island in less than a week.[49] The missionaries were equally successful in changing perceptions of the South Seas at home in the West too, as the image of the noble savage was stripped of its nobility and left only with its savagery. What had previously been seen as fact was now understood as fiction, as one image of the South, imposed by the West, but now seen as misconceived, gave way to another, equally misguided, but for now regarded by many, including Coleridge, as the truth: 'The missionaries have done a great deal for us in clearing up our notions about savage nations [...] of course there never were such dear, good, kind, amiable people. We know now that they were more detestably licentious than we could have imagined.'[50]

## Paradise Lost: Melville and Stevenson in the South Seas

If the assault by the missionaries in the late eighteenth and early nineteenth centuries was to do much to destroy native Polynesian culture, the islands of the South Pacific were to retain their mythical status as outposts of Eden in the works of such writers as Herman Melville and Robert Louis Stevenson. These writers, and their successors, have since created a fictional south whose image has, at least in the minds of their readers, often proved more enduring than reality. In *Moby Dick* (1851), Herman Melville (1819–1891) compares Tahiti's isolation within the Pacific to the insularity of human existence:

> Consider all this; and then turn to this green gentle, and most docile earth; consider them both, the sea and the land; and do you not find a strange analogy to something

in yourself? For as this appalling ocean surrounds the verdant land, so in the soul of man there lies one insular Tahiti, full of peace and joy, but encompassed by all the horrors of the half-known life. God keep thee! Push not off from that isle, thou canst never return![51]

It was not *Moby Dick*, however, that was to establish Melville's position as the chief chronicler of the South Pacific, but rather his debut novel, *Typee* (1846). Melville's semi-autobiographical account of two sailors, Tommo (Melville) and Toby, who flee from a whaling ship to take refuge on Nuku Hiva in the Marquesas, has provoked a lengthy debate as to whether it is a work of fact or fiction, confusing his readers (as well as his publishers) who have been unable to untangle the adventures he recounts from his own experiences as a sailor. Documentary evidence has since been found to support Melville's claim to have deserted at Nuku Hiva in 1842, where he was to spend some 31 days, a period during which he would have been able to observe French colonial rule at first hand, as it set about dismantling and eventually destroying Marquesan culture.[52]

In Melville's novel the ship's arrival in the Marquesas is greeted in the customary fashion with young girls swimming out to meet it, and as evening falls, the girls, bedecked with flowers, put on a Marquesan version of the dances which so scandalised Cook and Banks. What follows is the by now obligatory description of the resulting chaos:

Our ship was now wholly given over to every species of riot and debauchery. Not the feeblest barrier was interposed between the unholy passions of the crew and their unlimited gratification. The grossest licentiousness and the most shameful inebriety prevailed, with occasional and but short-lived interruptions [...] Alas for the poor savages when exposed to the influence of these polluting examples! Unsophisticated and confiding, they are easily led into every vice, and humanity weeps over the ruin thus remorselessly inflicted upon them by their European civilizers. Thrice happy are they who, inhabiting some yet undiscovered island in the midst of the ocean, have never been brought into contaminating contact with the white man.[53]

Melville's 'savages' are depicted as children corrupted by contact with Europeans, a perception which sits uncomfortably alongside the dream of sexual gratification, for inevitably Melville's narrator is soon matched with a romantic heroine. Here, in the dreamlike valley of *Typee*, European notions of romance are satisfied in the form of Fayaway, one of many such fictional figures, in which the physical attributes of Polynesian beauty are allied to notions of tenderness and loyalty. Melville's vision of paradise is by no means an unblemished one, however, as the narrator soon discovers. But in its depiction of an unfallen world threatened by a corrupt European civilisation, Melville's idea of the South Seas owes as much to the utopian dreams of de Bougainville as it does to any notion of nineteenth-century reality.[54] In fact, literary critics have tended to read *Typee* in the light of a much earlier depiction of paradise, identifying its allusions to Milton's *Paradise Lost* and interpreting it accordingly, with the European colonists in this instance likened to the serpents entering the Garden of Eden.[55] Read in this light, Melville's novel is clearly an ambiguous one, in which the boundaries between fact and fiction are blurred, in which paradise is both found and lost, and in which the narrator displays an ambivalence about Marquesan life, which he begins the novel by running to but which he ends by running from. Incapacitated by a swollen leg, Tommo remains alone on the island after his companion leaves in search of help, never to return, but having regained his health he soon becomes unsure whether to stay or leave. Once again both he (and the reader) remain uncertain about life in paradise, an ambivalence which is highlighted by the fact that, while Tommo is constantly being fed, he is also often in fear of being eaten.[56] This ambiguity remains until he is confronted, firstly, with the prospect of having his face tattooed, thus barring a future return to civilisation, and secondly with the growing conviction that his hosts are cannibals, swaying the argument strongly in favour of leaving.[57] In the end, Tommo flees from the valley of *Typee*, but having already fled from civilisation it is unclear where there is left for him to go. This is, perhaps, the message of the novel, for one consequence of man's desire to escape from the confines of civilised life is the need to find or create a place free from such restrictions to escape to. In this instance, the wide expanses of the South Pacific at first appeared to offer such a possibility, and yet as Tommo discovers, civilised man's restlessness is such that there is unlikely to be a place anywhere on earth, even in paradise, which can overcome his desire to escape elsewhere.

More than 60 years later the spell cast by Melville's *Typee* was still luring people southward in search of the paradise he had described. But while Melville's was an ambiguous portrayal of a society under threat, by the time Jack London was to undertake a literary pilgrimage of his own to Nuku Hiva in 1907, there was little ambiguity in what he was to encounter. Sailing aboard the *Snark* in an attempt to outrun the demands of fame, it took Jack London and his wife Charmian two months to reach the Marquesas. At first he was delighted to be able to rent the same cottage as another idol of his, Robert Louis Stevenson, who had stayed there during his own six-week stay in 1888. Leaving the cottage, they followed the same trail through the valley that Melville had so memorably brought to life, as London's biographer, Alex Kershaw describes:

At the edge of the lake Jack stopped at a small thatched hut for a drink of water. An old-looking, yellowing woman offered him her gourd. In the background shuffled her husband, dragging one of his legs, bloated to twice its size with elephantiasis. Nearby, the couple's young children played in tall grass – they also showed signs of leprosy.

Jack and Charmian had not stumbled into paradise. Judging by the suffering they soon witnessed, they had arrived in killing fields fertilised by the devil. Colonisation had decimated the indigenous people; in two decades of French rule, because of imported illnesses such as tuberculosis and asthma, the population had plummeted from fifty thousand to just five thousand. 'All this strength and beauty has departed', Jack mourned. 'Life has rotted away in this wonderful garden spot.'[58]

Deeply disillusioned by what he was to find on Nuku Hiva, London, a believer in many of the more unpalatable racial theories of the day, became attracted to the idea that white people flourished in such conditions. For just as immunity to disease was built up through natural selection, so too, he concluded, must the Polynesians 'undergo the same bath of organic poison before they could lay the foundations of a new people'.[59] London's bitter assessment of man's struggle for survival in a hostile environment seems a world apart from the prevailing myths of the noble savage which had informed earlier depictions of Polynesian life. Yet Melville's portrait of a society on the cusp of decline, an image of a paradise soon to be lost, was to point the way towards the more realistic fictional portrayals of life in the South Seas which were to follow.

At 5 am on 28 June 1888 the chartered yacht *Casco* passed from San Francisco through the Golden Gate into the Pacific, and so began Robert Louis Stevenson's journey to the South Seas and to his eventual resting place on Samoa. Stevenson had dreamt of the South Seas since he was a boy, and at the age of 12 he had written 'Creek Island, or Adventures in the South Seas'; while at 15 he was to introduce himself to another Edinburgh writer, R M Ballantyne, author of *The Coral Island: A Tale of the Pacific Ocean* (1858).[60] Having arranged for his cruise to be paid for through a series of South Sea letters to be syndicated in the papers (they were

to be published posthumously in 1896 as *In the South Seas*),
Stevenson was accompanied on his voyage by his wife Fanny,
his widowed mother and his stepson Lloyd. Having read both
Melville's *Typee* and its sequel *Omoo*, Stevenson's first stop
was Nuku Hiva. Eager to catch a glimpse of his first Pacific
island, Stevenson was up on deck at four, waiting for the
island to emerge out of the darkness. 'I have a fine book of
travels, I feel sure', he wrote to his friend Charles Baxter, 'and
I will tell you more of the South Seas after very few months
than any other writer has done – except Herman Melville
perhaps'.[61] Like Melville, however, Stevenson was alert to
the destructive impact of European colonialism, making
the surprising but acute comparison between the plight of
the Marquesans under French rule and that of the Scottish
Highlanders in the seventeenth and eighteenth centuries.
For, like the Highlanders, not only were the Polynesians
persecuted and driven off their land, but they were prevented
from practising precisely those customs which maintained
their identity: tattooing in the case of the Marquesans, the
wearing of tartan and herding of cattle for the Highlanders. In
much the same fashion, the islander's chiefs were deposed and
their men disarmed, resulting in what Stevenson recognised
as a state of demoralisation similar to that experienced by the
Highlanders, forced into a 'convulsive and transitory state'
through the interference of the colonising powers.[62] The
Marquesas were the Stevensons' first port of call on what was
to prove an extensive series of journeys across the Pacific:
Tahiti was to follow, before a journey to Hawaii, and on to
the Gilbert Islands, before finally arriving in Apia on Samoa,
where he bought the site of his future home at Vailima.
Further travels were to follow to Australia, New Caledonia
and other islands before he returned to settle in Vailima late
in 1890. Describing his ongoing work in a letter written in
1889 to his friend Sidney Colvin, Stevenson writes: 'At least,
nobody has had such stuff; such wild stories, such beautiful
scenes, such singular intimacies, such manners and traditions,
so incredible a mixture of the beautiful and the horrible, the

savage and the civilised [...] I propose to call the book *The South Seas*: it is rather a large title, but not many people have seen more of them than I, perhaps no one – certainly no one capable of using the material.'[63]

Stevenson was fond of what he believed to be a Polynesian saying – 'The coral waxes, the palm grows, but man departs' – citing it twice in his work, seemingly unaware that it was actually coined by Melville.[64] But the theme it encapsulates, the inevitability of death and the transience of all things, perfectly captures the melancholic mood with which so much of Stevenson's Pacific writings are infused. The Edinburgh edition of *In the South Seas*, his account of his own experiences in the Pacific, was published posthumously in 1896. What Stevenson's readers were expecting from the author of *Treasure Island*, however, was not melancholy reflection but rip-roaring adventure and, as a result, his work was both a commercial and critical failure. For, as Neil Rennie has noted, the problem was that, while the public wanted to read about Stevenson in the South Seas, Stevenson himself had more ambitious, but unachievable, plans, attempting to transcend the personal travel narrative altogether, in favour of an anthropological and historical work that would take in the South Seas in their entirety. In short, Stevenson wanted, 'not the story of his travels *In the South Seas*, but *The South Seas* themselves.'[65]

Since his death, Stevenson's South Seas writings have been largely overlooked.[66] Yet alongside his account of his own experiences, there remains his fictional portrayal of the Pacific in which he introduces a bracing dose of realism into the depiction of Polynesian life, revealing the devastating impact of European colonialism. The best of these works, which were to anticipate the broader move towards modernism in European fiction, is 'The Beach of Falesá' (1892). In a startling evocation of the cynicism, greed and questionable morality of European involvement in the Pacific, 'The Beach of Falesá' is narrated by John Wiltshire, a British copra trader on the island of Falesà who colludes with a rival trader, Case, in tricking a local girl, Uma, into a sham marriage. But the marriage is taboo in the eyes of the native community who then refuse to do business with him. Finding that Case has engineered the situation to deprive him of trade, Wiltshire, who has by now fallen in love with Uma, also discovers that Case has come to dominate the villagers by fooling them into believing he possesses demonic powers. Wiltshire confronts Case, the two men fight, and Case is killed. The story closes with Wiltshire now living upon another island, still married to Uma and by now the father of her children. With its themes of greed and duplicity, of sexual exploitation and inter-racial marriage, and, most controversially, its contrast between the clearly inferior morality of the European characters to that of their native counterparts, 'The Beach of Falesá' was censored by Stevenson's publishers. Needless to say, Stevenson's story was poorly received, although over time it has finally gained critical recognition. With its use of native slang, alongside its references to real people and places, Stevenson was forging a newly realistic representation of the South Seas, free from the romance behind which the true nature of European intervention had for so long been concealed. In a letter to his friend Sidney Colvin he was to describe his story in the following terms:

It is the first realistic South Seas story; I mean with real South Sea character and details of life. Everybody else that has tried, that I have seen, got carried away by the romance, and ended in a kind of sugar candy sham epic, and the whole effect was lost – there was no etching, no human grin, consequently no conviction. Now I have got the smell and look of the thing a good deal. You will know more about the South Seas after you have read my little tale than if you had read a library.[67]

Stevenson's depictions of the melancholy end of paradise in the South Seas, as native culture was finally subdued and depleted by commercial greed might be thought to mark the end of utopian visions of the South Seas in Europe, a dream or delusion which had endured for several centuries. Yet one should not underestimate either the need for such a dream, nor the force of its imagery. For despite the lament for the loss of paradise to be found in the work of Melville, Stevenson and others, the vision of a Tahitian Eden was to remain very much alive, and as the twentieth century approached, so continued the influx of writers, artists and dreamers still searching for an escape from civilisation.

## *Noa Noa*: Gauguin and the Tahitian Dream

'It is notable', writes Ian Littlewood, 'that France, which had the most extensive colonial possessions among the Pacific islands, should also have produced the most powerful response to the intertwined appeal of the exotic and the erotic.'[68] One need not look far through the history of French literature to find confirmation of Littlewood's observation, but nowhere has this blend of exotic and erotic, or travel and sex, been combined to greater effect, and to greater popular acclaim, than in the work of Pierre Loti. Born Louis Marie Julien Viaud, Loti was given his pseudonym by the Tahitian women he met during his first visit to the island in January 1872. Arriving as a sailor aboard the frigate *La Flore*, his affair with a young Tahitian girl was to form the basis of his most successful work, *Le Mariage de Loti* (1880). It barely seems necessary here to supply a summary of the plot, for needless to say, the heroine of the piece, the 14-year-old, Rarahu, combines the necessary attributes of primitive sensuality on the one hand, and infatuation for the narrator on the other. Loti's novel is characteristic of a body of work which incorporates the twin motifs of love and loss in a foreign clime, and while he is little read today, his peculiar blend of sentimental fantasy and colonial wish-fulfilment proved hugely successful, having a major impact on popular perceptions of travel across Europe, Asia and the South Pacific. The success Loti was to enjoy with this novel results from the way in which he was able to tailor his own experiences to fit the expectations of a European audience eager to immerse themselves in the romantic mythology of the South Seas. For, as the notes from Loti's journal from Tahiti indicate, far from being an accurate reflection of his own experience, Le Mariage de Loti deliberately enhances the relationship between himself and Rarahu to encapsulate 'all the traveller's subversive dreams – sexual freedom, romantic love, escape from civilisation, magical access to a new world and a new identity.'[69]

Visitors to Tahiti today will find a commemorative monument to Loti, unveiled in 1934, yet while Loti's reputation may since have waned, the impact of Le Mariage de Loti endures, not least through the effect it was to have on the French painter, Émile Bernard, who was at the time of the novel's publication hoping to embark on a new life in Madagascar with his friend Paul Gauguin. Having finished Le Mariage, Bernard wrote to Gauguin suggesting a change of destination, and having overcome his initial doubts, Gauguin agreed to swap Madagascar for Tahiti.[70] So closely has Gauguin's life and work since become entwined with the myth of the South Seas, that it is now difficult to separate the one from the other, and in this respect his change of heart, thanks to Loti, marks a turning point in the history not only of his own life, but in that of European perceptions of the South Seas. For just as in the nineteenth century, Byron came to symbolise the figure of the poet who turns his back on civilisation, so does the life of Gauguin provide a twentieth-century equivalent, banishing the idea of Tahiti as a lost paradise and restoring, once again, its position as an alternative to, and an escape from, a Europe 'gone rotten.'[71]

If Gauguin was to restore the myth of the South Seas, his painting celebrating the primitivism and sensuality of an earlier age, he was to do so by mythologising his own life, establishing the legend of the man who impulsively turned his back on civilisation in search of freedom, a legend divorced from a much less appealing reality. Arriving in Papeete in 1891, three years after Robert Louis Stevenson, Gauguin's romantic vision of Tahiti, and of himself, are displayed in his journal *Noa Noa* ('Fragrance').[72] As the title suggests, Gauguin's account is one in which sensuality is at the forefront, his experience, from the outset, one markedly at odds with the melancholy that infuses Stevenson's work. 'On the eighth of June', he writes, 'during the night, after a sixty-three days' voyage, sixty-three days of feverish expectancy, we perceived strange fires, moving in zigzags on the sea. From the somber sky a black cone with jagged indentations became disengaged. We turned Morea and had Tahiti before us.'[73] But Gauguin was quickly disappointed by what he was to discover in Papeete, finding all the hallmarks of the European society he had sought to leave behind:

It was Europe – the Europe which I had thought to shake off – and that under the aggravating circumstances of colonial snobbism, and the imitation, grotesque even to the point of caricature, of our customs, fashions, vices, and absurdities of civilisation. Was I to have made this journey, only to find the very thing which I had fled? [...] Both the human beings and the objects were so different from those I had desired, that I was disappointed. I was disgusted by all this European triviality. I had disembarked too recently yet to distinguish how much of nationality, fundamental realness, and primitive beauty still remained in this conquered race beneath the artificial and meretricious veneer of our importations. I was still in a manner blind.[74]

Gauguin felt that he had been cheated of the dream which had brought him south, only to discover a reality that in attempting to imitate the West merely magnified its faults. 'It was the Tahiti of former times which I loved', he wrote, 'That of the present filled me with horror.'[75] The European 'dream' which Gauguin sought was one which no longer existed, or rather one which had never existed, a Tahiti free from European contamination, yet born of European desires and frustrations. Gauguin resolved to leave Papeete in search of a more 'authentic' locale and settled some 45 kilometres south along the coast, in Mataïea. Here, he hoped to live out his fantasy of the noble savage, free from the constraints of work and money, and in harmony with nature. Finding himself wholly ill-equipped to do so, however, he quickly acquired a 'wife', Tehura, with whom he could share this dream of simple abundance in accordance with even earlier myths: 'We lived, both of us, in perfect simplicity. How good it was in the morning to seek refreshment in the nearest brook, as did, I imagine, the first man and the first woman in Paradise. Tahitian paradise, navé navé fénua, – land of delights! And the Eve of this paradise became more and more docile, more loving. I was permeated with her fragrance – noa noa.'[76]

Gauguin's return to Eden proved unsuccessful. He had found paradise, an Eve to share it with and all his needs were catered for. But he had arrived too late, for he felt that Tahiti had by now been unmistakably tainted by its contact with European civilisation, whose alien customs and religion had destroyed something which could not be restored:

They had been richly endowed with an instinctive feeling for the harmony necessary between human creations and the animal and plant life which formed the setting and decoration of their existence, but this has now been lost. In contact with us, with our school, they have truly become "savages," in the sense which the Latin occident has given this word. They themselves have remained beautiful as masterpieces, but morally and physically (owing to us) they have become unfruitful.[77]

Gauguin's journal is a curious blend of joy and despair, at one moment recording his certainty that he has found paradise, only to reveal shortly afterwards his conviction that paradise has in fact been lost forever. In this respect, his outlook seems to capture perfectly the contradictory reaction the South Seas have provoked in the European mind ever since their discovery, oscillating between these two extremes. In 1893 Gauguin was to leave for Europe, only to return two years later in 1895. He remained on Tahiti until 1901, when he moved to the Marquesas where he was to die in 1903. *Noa Noa* ends with his departure, a parting he describes with an almost biblical flourish:

> I am leaving, older by two years, but twenty years younger; more barbarian than when I arrived, and yet much wiser. Yes, indeed, the savages have taught many things to the man of an old civilisation; these ignorant men have taught him much in the art of living and happiness.
>
> Above all, they have taught me to know myself better; they have told me the deepest truth. Was this thy secret, thou mysterious world? Oh mysterious world of all light, thou hast made a light shine within me, and I have grown in admiration of thy antique beauty, which is the immemorial youth of nature. I have become better for having understood and having loved thy human soul – a flower which has ceased to bloom and whose fragrance no one henceforth will breathe.[78]

Gauguin's overblown rhetoric with its tone of moral improvement is rather at odds with the expressions of peevish irritation with which he begins his journal. But in fact very little of Gauguin's account should be taken at face value, for while he presents within its pages a celebration of his spiritual renewal, it appears that the reality of his time in Tahiti was rather less wholesome and uplifting. Those viewing Gauguin's paintings will find a primitive landscape in which the realities of late nineteenth-century colonial life, with its ugly architecture of plank houses and corrugated iron, not to mention the Europeans themselves, are nowhere to be found. But just as these European encumbrances have been removed from Gauguin's work, so too in his own story has the backdrop of financial worries, entanglements with the colonial authorities, and the unpleasant side-effects of his sexual liaisons been similarly airbrushed from the record.[79]

*Noa Noa* was written after Gauguin's return to France, as he attempted to establish a market for his pictures, and should be read both as a product of nostalgia and as a means to self-publicise himself and his work, an attempt – a successful one – to transform his life into myth. And like so many of the myths that Europe was to propagate about the South Seas, at its heart were the sexual fantasies which had in large part prompted Gauguin's initial journey. *Noa Noa* records Gauguin's brief encounter with the mulatto girl, Titi, in Papeete, as well as his 'marriage' to Tehura, and it was these relationships which were to cement Gauguin's vision of Tahiti as the home to a sensuous, primitive existence at odds with a 'civilised' but repressed Europe.[80]

Of course, the reality of Gauguin's South Sea experiences could never hope to match the idealised portrait he was to create for himself, and having returned to Tahiti in 1895, Gauguin's attempts to recapture the life he had left behind were doomed to failure. The syphilis which he had most likely brought with him from Europe prior to his first visit was now more evident and his approaches to his former wife, Tehura, were rebuffed. Despite an ankle injury he had picked up during a fight in France, in addition to his unsightly sores, Gauguin did manage to persuade another young girl, the 14-year-old Pau'ura, to take Tehura's place. But as his health declined and his attractiveness to young Polynesian girls began to wane, Gauguin decided upon the alternative of the Marquesas, home to a poorer, and cheaper, population of complaisant women ready to be bartered, or so he hoped, with a sackful of sweets.[81] By now Gauguin's frankly repellent existence had very little in common with the noble sentiments he had espoused in *Noa Noa*, approaching instead the more tawdry reality of Stevenson's 'The Beach of Falesá' with its collection of depraved and diminished Europeans. It was in the Marquesas, however, that Gauguin's mythical existence reached its apotheosis, as he set up home with another young bride, Vaeoho, in his house in Atuona, the lintel inscribed with the words 'Maison du Jouir' (roughly speaking, 'House of Pleasure').[82] By now reduced to a syphilitic wreck, he was to spend the final twenty months of his life on Atuona, continuing to paint and fathering a child, before his death, aged 54, in 1903.

Gauguin's life, more than any other, perfectly encapsulates the gulf between myth and reality in European perceptions of the South Pacific, the myth of freedom and escape from civilisation masking an unsavoury reality of disease and sexual exploitation. At the heart of this contradiction lies the idea of romantic primitivism, and the assumption that the gap between savagery and civilisation mirrors a corresponding contrast between sexual restraint and abandon.[83] This is the contradiction concealed within so many European representations of the south, from Banks and de Bougainville, to Melville and Gauguin, in which the archetypes of freedom and escape always outweigh the violation and exploitation they obscure. From Loti to Melville and on to Gauguin, this colonial fantasy is achieved by characterising the Tahitians as children (and child-brides), as innocents free from the taint of civilisation and its burdens. But what such an idealised image fails most significantly to consider, and of which the life and death of Gauguin provide an uncomfortable reminder, is the horrifying impact of the spread of disease, from syphilis and smallpox, to dysentery, tuberculosis, measles and flu. For the appalling effects of such diseases offer a clear and compelling corrective to European notions of paradise, establishing an alternative history in which the freedom and love celebrated in the West are experienced against the backdrop of a sickly and decimated population. 'Paradise is regained', concludes Littlewood, 'but only at the cost of laying it waste. [...] The history of tourism is the story of desire consuming its object.'[84]

## The Nuclear South

The vision of Tahiti depicted by Gauguin and Loti, of a Polynesian paradise devoted to the pleasure and self-fulfilment of its Western visitors, was to reach its zenith in 1955 with the opening of the first Club Med village on the island. Advertised as a 'pilgrimage to the source', the village was presented via the deliberate evocation of a pre-industrial way of life no longer to be found beyond the perimeter of the compound. With its traditional architecture of thatched huts and the sarong as the preferred form of dress (available from the Club's mail-order catalogue), this vision of an 'authentic' Polynesian experience was summarised in the Club magazine, Le Trident: 'the arch of the beach, the Polynesian huts under the palms, men pushing their dug-out canoes into the surf, chasing young girls wearing flowers, and fishing all day.'[85] Club Med had successfully created a version of Tahiti perfectly aligned to the expectations of its European clients, in which 'the return to Eden is available at an all-inclusive price.'[86]

The colonial impulse which had propelled the first European voyagers in search of terra australis, which had dispatched the missionaries from London to spread an alien gospel, and which had provoked a literary response in a plethora of excited portrayals of erotic freedom, had now, by the latter half of the twentieth century, given way to its latest incarnation, the tourist. And just like their predecessors, these middle-class western tourists found themselves in an environment where they could live like kings, with native servants on hand to cater for their every need. The stark imbalance between the advanced economies of the West, and those of the Pacific islands, makes it difficult to avoid the conclusion that the role of the tourist in this context is not without a colonial component. But if tourism was to disguise such motivations, both from the native population, as well as from the tourists themselves, then the islands of the South Pacific were soon to be exposed to a form of colonial exploitation much more difficult to conceal.

In February 1946, the US Navy evacuated the inhabitants of Bikini Atoll in the Marshall Islands: 'For the good of mankind' the navy officers told the islanders, 'and to end all world wars.' Shortly afterwards they were to conduct the first of 23 atmospheric nuclear tests that were to take place there between 1946 and 1958.[87] The Japanese-held Marshall Islands were a 'gift' to America after the Second World War, and over the next 50 years the West (the USA, Britain and France) were to conduct more than 250 nuclear tests across the 'empty' expanses of the Pacific.[88]

In February 1960, the French carried out their first successful nuclear test at Reggane in the Algerian Sahara, joining an exclusive club that at that time consisted of only the USA, the Soviet Union and Britain. It is interesting to note how these northern powers came to favour the southernmost available locations for the testing of these devices, either in their own countries, or more commonly, within their wider colonial possessions: the USA in New Mexico and the Pacific; the Soviet Union in Kazakhstan; and most successfully, in terms of the distance generated between the country of origin and the site of the testing, the British, in the Pacific and later Australia. In an ironic reversal of their failure to find the elusive *terra australis*, the British claimed as their test site the *terra nullius*, or empty space, of Southern Australia; empty, that is, apart from the ancestral homes of the aboriginal tribes that lived there and whose permission was never sought. There is, perhaps, no better example of the lasting inequality between north and south, than the twentieth-century process by which the 'empty' spaces of the south became a convenient depository for the unwanted refuse of the north, in this case the lingering irradiation of nuclear contamination.

By the 1950s the French had identified two general locations which they saw as suitable for the testing of nuclear weapons, regions which were thought sufficiently distant from large centres of population, were easily defensible and which were currently under complete French sovereignty. In 1962, however, the French granted independence to Algeria, and in the process they lost the use of their North African test ground. Thus the unoccupied regions

MERLIN COVERLEY

of the Algerian Sahara gave way to what was assumed to
be a similarly unoccupied region of the Pacific in French
Polynesia. In choosing to establish a test site at the remote
atoll of Mururoa, De Gaulle saw the opportunity to inject
capital and provide employment for French Polynesia's
moribund economy. In fact, and as extraordinary as it
may now seem, in conversations with Polynesian leaders
he implied that the facility should be considered as
something of a 'reward' for the support Polynesians had
given to the Free French during the Second World War and
their loyalty during the 1950s.[89] Of course, once the tests
were underway on Mururoa, tensions in the surrounding
islands and across the Pacific rose quickly and, in 1974,
the French abandoned atmospheric tests and moved
testing underground. Arguments and counter-arguments
continued but failed to prove that the nuclear tests were
either entirely safe or as harmful as was suggested. But
while the majority of the world remained largely oblivious
to French testing, in Australasia and the South Pacific a
consensus soon grew that the tests were at the very least
potentially dangerous to human life and the environment,
and that they should be stopped. In 1985, the South Pacific
forum adopted a proposal for a South Pacific Nuclear-Free
Zone, and in May of that year relations between France
and French Polynesia reached a new low with the sinking
of the Greenpeace ship *Rainbow Warrior* in New Zealand
by French intelligence agents.[90] In 1992, the leaders of the
Polynesian Liberation Front (formed in 1977) gathered in
Salzburg to voice their opposition to the testing. 'Now this
island of Mururoa – you know what Mururoa means?'
asked Myron Mataoa, 'Mururoa means "the land of the
secret". The land of secret. And today that land is really
a land of secret where we don't get any information from
the French administration on how bad was their testings
since 1966.'[91] The last French nuclear test was in 1996,
after which the test site at Mururoa was dismantled, but
since then information about the tests and their aftermath

has remained hard to come by. In recent years, however, evidence has begun to appear which suggests that the Pacific tests of the 1960s and 1970s were far more toxic than had previously been acknowledged, subjecting a vast swathe of Polynesia to radioactive fallout, including both Tahiti itself and the tourist island of Bora Bora. From 1960 to 1996, France carried out some 210 nuclear tests, 193 of which took place in French Polynesia, and for decades afterwards France argued that these controlled explosions were clean. Recently declassified papers, however, show that on 17 July 1974, one such test exposed Tahiti to 500 times the maximum allowed level of plutonium fallout, while in 2006 a French medical research body found that nuclear testing had caused an increase in cancer on the nearest inhabited islands.[92]

In 2012, Julian Evans, author of *Transit of Venus* (1993), an account of his travels across the Pacific, described his return to the region to see what, if anything, had changed in the intervening period. What he found was 'a post-nuclear Paradise Lost of bad politics, bad foreign aid, crackpot colonialism, wacky Christianity, beachcombers, booze and military bases.' 'Geostrategically', he adds, 'it was a mess (and still is). It was an American lake: the US Pacific fleet was spending more time at sea than in the Second World War, trying to outdo the Russians and Chinese (it still is).'[93] The Pacific that Evans re-discovers has little in common with that of Melville or Stevenson, Gauguin and Loti. Far from providing an escape from the West, it seems to have become mired within western geopolitics, its romanticism now somewhat debased by the military, economic and political anxieties of the northern hemisphere. For in the latter part of the twentieth century, as various northern powers continued their familiar jockeying for global influence, the Pacific returned to fashion. And, in a curious echo of the colonial expeditions of the eighteenth century, the Pacific and its islands once again came to represent, in the minds of the western powers at least, one of the last frontiers where they could acquire influence, and these emerging rivalries resulted in a new 'scramble for the Pacific.'[94] Amidst new (but all too familiar) concerns of an economically strong Asia seeking to expand southwards, fear of overpopulation in the West, allied to the ever-present threat of nuclear catastrophe, the 1980s saw a resurgence of the idea of the South Pacific as a last refuge for a threatened (western) humanity. Once again the South Seas came to be viewed with utopian longing as part of the 'empty' south, the 'New World' towards which the escapees of any future western calamity might flee.[95]

The fall of the Berlin Wall and the end of the Cold War put paid to such fears, for the time being at least, although the islands of the Pacific basin have retained their strategic importance to the military and economic powers of the north. Whether the Pacific can challenge the Atlantic and the Mediterranean, however, for supremacy within the new world order of the twenty-first century is unclear. It was in response to precisely such a scenario, however, and in the face of the disconcerting possibility that the 'centre' of the world might be about to shift southward from its western axis, that Régis Debray (an adviser to the then French President François Mitterrand) proclaimed: 'In a world which fortunately has several centres, the Pacific must not become a myth. [...] The South Pacific is a different place, where the schemas of East and West and of North and South do not fit. As for strategic issues, the centres of the world will long remain the Atlantic and the Mediterranean.'[96] No longer beyond western conceptions of time, perhaps, the South Pacific appears to have retained its ambiguous position within western conceptions of space, free-floating at the bottom of the world, and seemingly farther than ever from the more geographically anchored world to be found in the north. In this respect, the myth of the Pacific that Debray warns against, appears still to be alive and well some 250 years after the first European contact. This puzzling region and its islands remain as disorientating as ever to those most distant from them, 'a different place' in which the rules governing the remainder of the globe seem not to apply.

## Notes

1. Stevenson, *In the South Seas*, p. 6.
2. de la Mare, p. 17.
3. Rennie, p. 11.
4. Rennie, p. 11.
5. Rennie writes (p. 1): 'So travel from civilization tended to be regressive, the traveller discovering not a new land so much as a new location for old, nostalgic fictions about places lost in the distant past, now found in the distant present, found and confirmed, it seemed, in the form of exotic facts.'
6. Gonzalo Fernándes de Oviedo, *Historia general y natural de las Indias*, ed. Juan Pérez de Tudela Buesca (Madrid, 1959), trans. by John H Parry, in *The European Reconnaissance: Selected Documents* (London, 1968), quoted in Rennie, p. 28. For the perfect encapsulation of Balboa's story see Stefan Zweig, 'Flight into Immortality: The Discovery of the Pacific Ocean', in *Shooting Stars: Ten Historical Miniatures*, pp. 11–38.
7. Rennie, p. 28.
8. Lansdown, p. 15. This idea of 'balancing' the hemispheres was to prove surprisingly durable, with the mathematician, astrologer and adviser to Elizabeth I, Dr John Dee, also arguing (some 1400 years after Ptolemy) that in order to offset the combined mass of Europe, Asia and Africa, a southern continent must exist 'stretched in all directions from the South Pole, uniting with Tierra del Fuego and reaching north almost to Java in the western Pacific.' See Evans (1993), p. 31.
9. Rennie, p. 11.
10. Lansdown writes (p. 16): 'This bipolar vision is much the most influential intellectual inheritance Westerners brought to the Pacific.'
11. Kings, 9:28, quoted in Rennie, p. 1.
12. Rennie, p. 41.
13. Rennie, p. 43.
14. Bruce writes (Introduction, pp. ix-xii):

The opportunities for narrative plausibility here were vastly increased by the explosion of knowledge about the globe which took place over these years: underlying the construction of the early modern utopia was the sense of discovery and possibility afforded by the Renaissance voyages of exploration. [...] Early modern utopias, then, even as they embraced fiction as their mode of representation, insisted on the location in real space of the communities that they described.

15. Bacon, 'New Atlantis' in Bruce, 149–187, pp. 182–3.
16. 'It is remarkable', writes Rennie (p. 47), 'that on this first South Sea island of fiction, the voyagers should discover, of all things, a 'happy land' of art, not nature, of synthesizers, telephones, aeroplanes, submarines, and the like. [...] If the voyagers of the Renaissance could discover a state of nature, they could also discover, by contrast, the state of art in Europe and the possibility of progress.'
17. Rennie, p. 59.
18. Rennie, p. 64.
19. As Julian Evans notes, such a failure of imagination is one which still afflicts European visitors to the South Pacific: 'Even today the Pacific islands have not lost that sense of acute otherness. They are hard to imagine. Or they're easy to imagine, but only as idealised versions of themselves, as those paradises mythologised from the accounts Cook brought back. This isn't a failure of imagination on our part, so much as a sense that for northern earthlings the conditions of Pacific life are more ethereal than material.' See Evans (2012).
20. Rennie, p. 84.
21. Rennie, p. 84. In fact, it now seems likely that Wallis was not the first European to have reached Tahiti, the Spanish expeditions under Quiroz or Torres having probably reached Tahiti in the late sixteenth century, claiming it for Spain. See Holmes, p. 3.
22. JC Beaglehole, ed., *The Journals of Captain Cook: The Voyage of the 'Endeavour' 1768–1771*, Cambridge, 1968, pp. xciv-xcv, quoted in Rennie, p. 84.
23. Rennie, p. 85.
24. Littlewood, p. 146.
25. Rennie, p. 87.
26. Rennie, p. 107.
27. Bougainville, *Journal*, 7 April 1768, quoted in Littlewood, p. 147.

28. Rennie, p. 89.
29. Bougainville, *Voyage autour du Monde* (1771), Chapter 8, 'Mouillage à Tahiti', quoted in Holmes, p. 4.
30. Rennie, p. 118.
31. Bougainville, 'A Voyage Round the Whole World. Performed by Order of his Most Christian Majesty, in the Years 1766, 1767, 1768 and 1769' (1772), trans. by John Reinhold Forster, quoted in Carey, p. 155.
32. Rennie, p. 89.
33. Rennie, p. 90.
34. Evans (1993), pp. 9–10.
35. Rennie, p. 90.
36. Julian Evans writes (1993; pp. 183–4):

The Captain's reason for being there, to observe on 3 June 1769 the transit of the planet Venus across the sun, paled into insignificance next to the descriptions of the Polynesians on Tahiti. [...] When the *Endeavour*'s quadrant and telescopes proved inadequate to record the exact passage of the planet after seven weeks of preparation, all Cook could manage about the experiment was a couple of lines. [...] The real Venus that Cook observed, in the reports that he brought back from his first confrontation with the Pacific, had nothing to do with the shade of another planet tricking across the face of the sun. The real Venus observed was in those mythical anecdotes, of freedom and desire that men are always astonished to relate about women.

37. Holmes, p. 16.
38. Holmes, p. 17.
39. Rennie, p. 102.
40. Holmes, p. 36.
41. Holmes, p. 54.
42. Littlewood writes (pp. 149–150):

The mutiny of 1789 defined the South Seas for the next two centuries as a paradisal alternative to all that was constrained, sunless and oppressive about life in the civilised west. The opposition could not have been more starkly drawn. On one side was the institutional brutality of life in His Majesty's Service: backbreaking work, rigid discipline, ferocious punishments; on the other, a carefree life of childlike leisure and untroubled sensuality. It was the fallen world we know against the unfallen world we dream of.

43. Lansdown writes (p. 18):

The myth of the Noble Savage is older than the discovery of Tahiti. But Tahiti seemed to prove that this was no myth or that the myth had been proved true. Nothing Europeans had seen in Asia, Africa, and America had a remotely similar intellectual effect. The noble savage soon found its opposite incarnation: the ignoble savage. What unites these ideas, and is a core principle of primitivism in any guise, is the Western belief [...] that for certain peoples of the earth progress had come to a stop or never started.

44. Cook, quoted in Lewis, *The Missionaries*, p. 9.
45. Lewis, *The Missionaries*, p. 10.
46. Lewis, *The Missionaries*, p. 11.
47. Lewis, *The Missionaries*, pp. 12–14.
48. Lewis, *The Missionaries*, pp. 14–15.
49. Lewis, *The Missionaries*, p. 15.
50. Coleridge in conversation, recorded in John Sterling, *Essays and Tales*, ed. by JC Hare, London, 1948, pp. xx-xxi, quoted in Rennie, p. 181.
51. Melville, *Moby Dick*, p. 248.
52. At the time of Melville's visit the Marquesan population was 6,000. This had been reduced to 682 by the beginning of the twentieth century. See Rennie, p. 186.
53. Melville, *Typee*, p. 15.
54. Littlewood, p. 152.
55. Rennie, p. 189.
56. Rennie, p. 191.
57. Despite Tommo's reservations, the tattoo has since proven a successful import to the West:

In a society without capital, the tattoo was a principal means by which power and status could be acquired. All it needed was the capacity of the individual to endure great pain. After recovering from the ordeal, proof of their strength was available for all to see. The European sailors who acquired tattoos for themselves then introduced this skin economy into the West, where it still flourishes today, particularly among those who do not have access to other forms of capital. The tattoo is one of the most visible ways in which the South has imprinted itself on the rest of the world.

See 'Tahiti – Time to Eat Time!' (2008) at http://ideaofsouth.
net/journey/tahiti-time-to-eat-time
58. Kershaw, pp. 192–3.
59. London, pp. 7–8.
60. Ballantyne's novel was hugely successful, and yet its author never actually visited the Pacific, the story coming to him while looking out across the Firth of Forth to the island of Inchkeith. See Rennie, p. 210.
61. Letter to Charles Baxter, 6 September 1888, quoted in Stevenson, *In the South Seas*, Introduction, pp. vii-xi.
62. Harman, pp. 366–7.
63. Stevenson to Sidney Colvin, 2 December 1889, *Letters*, iii. 139, quoted in Rennie, p. 214.
64. Rennie, Introduction, Stevenson, *In the South Seas*, p. xxix.
65. Rennie, Introduction, Stevenson, *In the South Seas*, p. xxv.
66. Roslyn Jolly writes (Introduction, Stevenson, *South Sea Tales*, p. xxx):

It was as if this body of work simply did not exist. [...] the most important reason for the critical neglect into which these works almost immediately fell was the unfamiliarity of the world they presented; unlike the India depicted by Kipling, to which British culture and society were closely bound by an immense apparatus of colonizing institutions, the Pacific world seemed to readers too marginal, too eccentric, to be the setting for important literature.

67. Letter to Sidney Colvin, quoted in Stevenson, *South Sea Tales*, Introduction, p. xxvii.
68. Littlewood, pp. 155–156.
69. Littlewood, p. 161.
70. Littlewood, p. 161.
71. Littlewood writes (p. 161):

This was the start of a story that would cast as long a shadow over tourism in the twentieth century as Byron's had in the nineteenth, providing a template for our fantasies that is if anything more potent today than it was a hundred years ago. An icon of defiant escapism, Gauguin has left us with an array of brilliantly coloured images that are central to the tourist ideal; but like respectable heirs to a dubious fortune, we tend not to enquire too closely into their origins.

72. During Gauguin's first visit to Tahiti, Stevenson was living on Samoa, where he was to die in 1894. While it is Stevenson who is still commonly thought of as the Romantic, his early adventures establishing a reputation he was unable to overturn, his *South Sea Tales* may be regarded as the first realist account of the region. Conversely, while Gauguin is now regarded as a modernist and stylistically as an innovator, his journal reveals a Romantic's vision of the South Seas as a fallen paradise. See Harman, pp. 367–8.
73. Gauguin, p. 1.
74. Gauguin, pp. 2–3.
75. Gauguin, p. 7.
76. Gauguin, p. 32.
77. Gauguin, p. 47.
78. Gauguin, p. 65.
79. Littlewood, p. 162.
80. Littlewood, p. 163.
81. Littlewood, p. 165.
82. Littlewood, p. 165.
83. Littlewood, p. 166.
84. Littlewood, p. 170.
85. Littlewood, p. 209.
86. Littlewood, p. 209.
87. Evans (1993), p. 5.
88. The United States conducted 213 atmospheric explosions in the Pacific from 1946 to 1963; Britain carried out 21 between 1952 and 1957; while France made 45 tests over the same period. In the face of mounting protests the French were later to point out that out of a total of 167 megatons exploded in Oceania, their share amounted to only 11.8 megatons. See Aldrich, p. 309.
89. Aldrich, p. 304.
90. Aldrich, p. 314.
91. 'Tahiti – Time to Eat Time!' (2008) at http://ideaofsouth.net/journey/tahiti-time-to-eat-time
92. 'French nuclear tests "showered vast area of Polynesia with

radioactivity", *The Guardian*, 3 July 2013, at http://www.
theguardian.com/world/2013/jul/03/french-nuclear-tests-
polynesia-declassified
93. Evans (2012).
94. Aldrich, p. 317.
95. Aldrich, p. 323.
96. Interview in *Libération*, 14 February 1986, quoted in Aldrich, p.
327.

*John Muir* by Francis M. Fritz (1907)

# 3

## Magic South

*Tell about the South. What's it like there. What do they do there. Why do they live there. Why do they live at all.*

William Faulkner[1]

*I looked over the map: a total of over a thousand miles, mostly Texas, to the border at Laredo, and then another 767 miles through all Mexico to the great city near the cracked Isthmus and Oaxacan heights. I couldn't imagine this trip. It was the most fabulous of all. It was no longer east-west, but magic south. We saw a vision of the entire Western Hemisphere rockribbing clear down to Tierra del Fuego and us flying down the curve of the world into other tropics and other worlds. 'Man, this will finally take us to IT!' said Dean with definite faith. He tapped my arm. 'Just wait and see. Hoo! Whee!'*

Jack Kerouac[2]

'The idea of the South – or more appropriately, the ideas of the South', as one commentator writes, 'belong in large part to the order of social myth. There are few areas of the modern world that have bred a regional mythology so potent, so profuse and diverse, even so paradoxical, as the American South.'[3] The truth of this statement may be confirmed by any cursory internet search using the word 'South' as a keyword – one will have to trawl through endless references to the American

South before any other southern region of the world is even acknowledged. The Deep South; the Romantic South; the Antebellum South; the Old South (and the New); the Southern Renaissance; Southern politics; Southern manners; the Southern accent: it seems quite superfluous to mention the United States as we all know instinctively to which region these labels apply. And as a consequence of the unquestioned pre-eminence the American South maintains within the global usage of this particular cardinal point, there have been a vast assortment of novelists, poets, academics and theorists eager to explore the region and to explain the unwavering hold it continues to exert over the public imagination both in the United States and elsewhere.[4] In his book *The Idea of North*, Peter Davidson chooses several northern locations as topographical case-studies, but forgoes the choice of the United States, arguing that it is hard to discern a particular 'idea of north' in that country.[5] He suggests that this is because of Canada's dominant position on the northern horizon on the one hand, whilst Alaska's frontier status is subsumed by the more powerful metaphor that is the American West. But perhaps the real reason that the North in the United States is less clearly identifiable as a discrete region, is precisely because of the fact that the South is so powerfully defined, the mythological attraction of the southern states somehow diminishing that of their northern counterparts.

I do not aim, nor am I qualified, to add to what is already a seemingly endless body of work that has examined the American South from every conceivable standpoint, but I would like instead to look at the South here less as a region than as a direction, a trajectory that not only encompasses the North American continent but which continues south across the border, and which in Kerouac's expression above, no longer moves from east to west, but downward towards the 'magic south'. Of course, just as the South is the most easily recognisable, and perhaps the most mythologised, region of the United States, it is the West which exerts the greatest force as the prevailing current of American history, the expansion of the United States westward in the nineteenth century underpinned by the doctrine of Manifest Destiny through which the continental United States would grow from coast to coast, refashioning the West in its own image. The dominance of this westward orientation is best encapsulated in the phrase often attributed to the American newspaper editor, Horace Greeley, whose exhortation to 'Go West, young man', in 1865, came to symbolise the idea that by expanding to settle and cultivate the 'empty' spaces of the West, America could truly fulfil its promise as the land of opportunity. In this light, the journey that John Muir was to embark upon in 1867, only two years after Greeley's proclamation, travelling on foot on his 1,000-mile journey southwards from Indianapolis to Florida, was very much against the grain of his era, and as we shall see, it was a journey whose ultimate destination was not the American South but South America. Similarly, the movement initiated by Kerouac and the Beats in post-war America was not simply one whose ultimate destination would be the celebrated countercultural centres of the West Coast, but rather it was a journey whose end lay southwards across the border into Mexico and beyond in search of an alternative way of life. These two journeys were both initiated within the United States but they reflect an urge to move southwards beyond its borders, an urge to head southwards and to keep going. The final destination in this chapter then, is not Mississippi or Mexico but rather the 'magic south' of Borges' Buenos Aires and the southernmost reaches of the South American continent. From the Deep South to the Far South; two regions separated by more than 5000 miles, which share a distinctive southern character that has done much to shape their respective continents.

## Deep South

The idea that character is to some degree determined by geography goes back at least as far as the American

Enlightenment. In a letter of 1785 from Thomas Jefferson to the Marquis de Chastellux, Jefferson describes the differences in temperament to be found between northerners and southerners: 'In the North they are: cool, sober, laborious, independent, jealous of their own liberties, and just to those of others, interested, chicaning, superstitious and hypocritical in their religion. In the South they are: fiery, voluptuary, indolent, unsteady, zealous for their own liberties, but trampling on those of others, generous, candid, without attachment or pretensions to any religion but that of the heart.' According to Jefferson, however, such regional differences are not rigidly inscribed, but rather they increase or decrease in proportion to one's movement along a north-south axis, with Pennsylvania providing a happy medium.[6]

Quite apart from those characteristics which constitute the southern character, the exact geographical dimensions of the South are themselves also open to debate. The Mason-Dixon Line has generally been regarded as marking the border between North and South, originally separating the 'free' states of the North from their slave-owning southern counterparts. And yet Missouri, Kentucky, West Virginia, and Maryland, all states which never joined the Confederacy, are found to the south of this dividing line. Furthermore, of the eleven states that made up the Confederacy, both Arkansas and Texas have become more western than southern in their cultural outlook in the years since the American Civil War – or rather the War between the States, as southerners tend to refer to it. This leaves the remaining nine states which may be regarded as comprising the 'Deep South': Louisiana, Mississippi, Alabama, Georgia, Florida, the Carolinas, Virginia, and Tennessee. Here then, is the South as it is commonly understood, an area both geographically and culturally diverse, yet one bearing the unmistakable essence of *South*. 'The "southern accent" is harder to detect on the printed page than in the spoken language', writes Sara Marshall, 'but there does seem to be some essence of *South* which knits together – however loosely – such diverse subcultures as Faulkner's Yoknapatawpha County, the Creole mystique of New Orleans, the foxfires of North Carolina, the subtropics of Florida.'[7]

In the popular imagination, or rather in my own, the true nature of the American South lies somewhere between that which is depicted in the films *Gone With the Wind* (1939) on the one hand, and *Deliverance* (1972) on the other, the romance and privilege of the former more than offset by the savagery and backwardness of the latter. In *The Oxford Book of the American South*, however, the history of the South is dealt with in a rather more precise and objective fashion, and is divided into four distinct periods: 'The Old South' (late eighteenth century to 1861); the American Civil War (1861–5) and its aftermath; 'Hard Times', the period between 1915–1940 encompassing WWI, the Great Depression, and the literature of the Southern Renaissance; and finally, 'The Turning' of WWII and the Civil Rights Movement of the 1950s. Of these four periods, it is undoubtedly the first, the 'Old' (or 'Romantic', or 'Antebellum') South, which resonates most strongly today. This period is summarised, or rather, caricatured, by WJ Cash in his *The Mind of the South* (1941), an indisputable classic within the mass industry of writings on this subject:

It was a sort of stage piece out of the eighteenth century, wherein gesturing gentlemen move soft-spokenly against a background of rose gardens and duelling grounds, through always gallant deeds, and lovely ladies, in farthingales, never for a moment lost that exquisite remoteness which has been the dream of all men and the possession of none. [...] They dwelt in large and stately mansions, preferably white and with columns and Grecian entablature. Their estates were feudal baronies, their slaves quite too numerous ever to be counted, and their social life a thing of Old World splendour and delicacy. What had really happened here, indeed, was that the gentlemanly idea, driven from England by Cromwell, had taken refuge in

the South and fashioned for itself a world to its heart's
desire: a world singularly polished and mellow and poised,
wholly dominated by ideals of honor and chivalry and
noblesse. [...] Beneath these was a vague race lumped
together indiscriminately as the poor whites – very often,
in fact, as the "white-trash." These people belonged in the
main to a physically inferior type, having sprung for the
most part from the convict servants, redemptioners, and
debtors of Old Virginia and Georgia, with a sprinkling of
the most unsuccessful sort of European peasants and farm
labourers and the dregs of the European town slums. And
so, of course, the gulf between them and the master classes
was impassable, and their ideas and feelings did not enter
into the make-up of the prevailing Southern civilisation.[8]

Cash's depiction of the attractive veneer of an imported
European civilisation concealing the less appealing reality
of an unacknowledged underclass reveals a society in which
three distinct populations may be identified: a white/
European ruling class; a 'white-trash' underclass; and a
black population, present, populous but largely invisible. A
strictly rural society dominated by its plantations, the Old
South was effectively abolished by the Civil War, although
the rigid social system which sustained it, and which Cash
describes above, was to remain largely intact. Hence, the
new South which grew up in its place, whilst shorn of its
political expression, was in many respects a continuation of
the old. Indeed, in maintaining the contradictory position
of both embracing the new whilst upholding the traditions
of the old, the South that was to emerge from the Civil War
was to preserve and promote an idea of this region which in
reality no longer existed (if it ever had). It is this idea of the
South which has subsequently been mythologised and which
has long since outlived the destruction of the society which
gave birth to it.[9]

Recalling his first visit to the US as a young student in
1968, Michael O'Brien, author of *The Idea of the American*

*South: 1920–1941*, describes how even then, with the South now at the forefront of American political life through the furore generated by the Civil Rights Movement, he was unable to find any agreement on the meaning of the term 'the South':

> The South, I was told, is a splendid old European civilisation, gentle, leisurely, polite, now somewhat ravaged by time and the contagious acquisitiveness of frantic Northerners. The South, I was told by anxious liberals, is a land of peculiar hypocrisy and oppression to poor whites and blacks alike, its pretensions a sham. [...] The South, I was told, is a quite separate culture. The South, I was further informed, was just like the rest of the United States. The South, it seemed to me by the end of that summer, was anything anyone wanted it to be. But one thing was apparent; it seemed desperately important to Southerners to work out a definition of Southern culture and fix their place in it.[10]

O'Brien was to conclude that in the absence of any consensus on the subject it was clear that what had hitherto been regarded as a single, identifiable entity with shared characteristics common to all, was in reality defined solely by the absence of any such features. In other words, while the idea was intact, the reality was 'broken', and 'No man's South was the same as another's.' While the South had for so long appeared as a shorthand for a community judged to be so well-known that no further comment were necessary, in fact the only real community to be found was, ironically, that created 'so men could talk about different things while imagining that they discussed the same entity.'[11] Is this then the reality of how the American South should be understood, as that community of people who are able, willing, or compelled to discuss their vision of the South, regardless of the nature of that vision?

# Walking South: John Muir's *A Thousand-Mile Walk to the Gulf*

A celebrated naturalist and the author of a dozen books; a founder member of the Sierra Club and a renowned conservationist whose efforts led to the formation of Yosemite and Sequoia National Parks; the life of John Muir (1838–1914) is today most closely associated with California and the American West. He was also to find fame as an explorer of America's most northerly frontier; he was to make seven expeditions to Alaska, many undertaken alone or with just a few native guides. Yet despite these achievements, on which his reputation now rests, it was not to the north or the west to which he was unerringly drawn, but to the south, which was to remain his abiding impulse and which was to haunt his imagination over the course of his lifetime: 'For many a year I have been impelled toward the Lord's tropic gardens of the South. Many influences have tended to blunt or bury this constant longing, but it has outlived or overpowered them all.'[12]

Born in Scotland in 1838, John Muir and his family immigrated to the United States in 1849 where they started a farm near Portage, Wisconsin. A deeply religious man, Muir was also a keen botanist and it is these twin passions for God and nature which inform his writing. Like Emerson and Thoreau before him, Muir was inspired by the pedestrian ordeals and botanical zeal of the great German explorer and scientist, Alexander von Humboldt, who during a five-year (1799–1804) expedition through Central and South America had covered more than 6,000 miles, largely on foot, in search of new specimens. It was from reading von Humboldt that Muir was to discover the thrill of wilderness adventure and from whom he was to acquire his greatest yearning, to follow in his footsteps by exploring the tropical rainforests of the Amazon basin. By 1867, however, Muir was no closer to achieving this ambition; in fact, he was employed as a machinist in a factory in Indianapolis. But on the evening

of 6 March 1867, while working late in the factory, Muir
seriously damaged his right eye, and it was this event which
was to mark the turning point in his life. For during his
four-week convalescence he resolved to fulfil his long-held
ambition and to embark on 'a long botanical ramble through
the American South and then on to South America.'[13] As
soon as he had recovered, he quit his job and by September
of that year he was ready: 'I propose to go South and see
something of the vegetation of the warm end of the country,
and if possible to wander far enough into South America
to see tropical vegetation in all its palmy glory.'[14] But
despite long deliberations over his choice of route, Muir,
then aged 29, was wholly unprepared for what lay ahead.
In 1867, with the Civil War having ended only two years
before, the scars were still unhealed and the American South
remained a largely lawless territory, blighted by poverty,
violence and disease. 'With its swamps, prickly vines, briars,
heat, humidity, predatory animals, poisonous snakes, and
dangerous diseases,' notes one commentator, 'his Southern
route promised a significant challenge, which was intensified
by the South's postwar destruction, dislocation, and turmoil.
Armed, unemployed, desperate men lurked through the
countryside. Disease was pervasive, and no one knew how
malaria was transmitted.'[15] Faced with such a plentiful array
of potential hazards, it was surely only his ignorance of the
South and what awaited him there that prevented Muir from
abandoning his plans altogether.

The journal that he was to write during his epic journey
south was not published until 1914, the year of his death,
and was given the title *A Thousand-Mile Walk to the Gulf*.[16] It
begins with Muir in an exultant mood, as guided only by his
compass, he walks literally out of his front door and heads
southwards:

I had long been looking from the wild woods and gardens
of the Northern States to those of the warm South,
and at last, all drawbacks overcome, I set forth [from

Indianapolis] on the first day of September, 1867, joyful and free, on a thousand-mile walk to the Gulf of Mexico [...] My plan was simply to push on in a general southward direction by the wildest, leafiest, and least trodden way I could find, promising the greatest extent of virgin forest. Folding my map, I shouldered my little bag and plant press and strode away among the old Kentucky oaks, rejoicing in splendid visions of pines and palms and tropic flowers in glorious array, not, however, without a few cold shadows of loneliness, although the great oaks seemed to spread their arms in welcome.[17]

The following morning Muir crossed the Ohio River and began walking through Louisville. Dressed in tough woollen clothing, he carried with him only a plant press and a small bag containing underclothing, a brush, a towel and books: Robert Burns's poems, John Milton's *Paradise Lost*, a New Testament, and Woods's 1862 edition of *Class-Book on Botany*.[18] Despite having walked this journey in his head for so many years, as soon as he was actually underway he appears to have taken a more relaxed approach to planning, writing a week after his departure, on September 9: 'I was a few miles south of Louisville when I planned my journey. I put my map under a tree and made up my mind to go through Kentucky, Tennessee, and Georgia to Florida, thence to Cuba, thence to some part of South America, but it will be only a hasty walk.'[19] Averaging an astonishing 25 miles a day, Muir passed swiftly through Indiana and Kentucky and soon approached the southern states, 'an open wound still festering from the Civil War.' Evangelical in tone and lushly descriptive in style, Muir has surprisingly little to say about the aftermath of those events. Indeed he often appears to have little to say about anything he encounters except the plants and wildlife. Avoiding towns and cities in favour of the mountains, forests and swampland of the South, Muir's journal is in fact a strangely uneventful document, in which short episodic entries dwell on distances covered and wildlife observed: 'September 4 – Walked ten miles of forest. Met a strange oak with willow looking leaves [...] September 30 – Traveled to-day more than forty miles without dinner or supper [...] October 4 – New plants constantly appearing. All day in dense, wet, dark, mysterious forest of flat-topped taxodiums.'[20] Yet while Muir's journal often overlooks the historical background to the regions he passes through, he is always alive to the natural world, and his prose frequently becomes more excitable as he struggles to relate, with biblical phraseology, the sheer exoticism of the landscapes he encounters:

> I am now in the hot gardens of the sun, where the palm meets the vine, longed and prayed for and often visited in dreams, and, though lonely to-night amidst this multitude of strangers, strange plants, strange winds blowing gently, whispering, cooing, in a language I have never learned, and strange birds also, everything solid or spiritual full of influences that I never before felt, yet I thank the Lord with all my heart for his goodness in granting me admission to this magnificent realm.[21]

For Muir, one senses that writing is always subordinate to walking, which is itself simply a means to the botanical end he has set himself. But while he lacks the style of Emerson and Thoreau, Muir achieves a degree of absolute identification with the natural world that surrounds him; for this is total immersion in the landscape to the point at which all extraneous material – society, politics, history – is stripped away to reveal the ecology that lies beneath. Yet if Muir is clearly at home within a botanical setting, *A Thousand-Mile Walk to the Gulf* is also the record of a young man attempting to find his way; a sense of uncertainty is palpable in Muir's account, and it has been described as 'a narrative of a man who had not yet made up his mind.'[22] For apart from his steadfast determination to keep heading south – although events conspired to change his direction – his purpose remains unclear, although what he finds in the South does not always live up to his expectations. Florida, most notably, was to prove something of a disappointment. He had dreamt of what he would find there, but 'his first view was of a vast salt marsh, gloomy and nearly impenetrable.'[23] Yet despite his adherence to his botanical obsessions, Muir was not wholly blind to the more human aspects of his journey and his journal reveals him to be, on occasion, an acute observer of the situation in the South after the Civil War.[24] In one of his infrequent portraits of the people he encounters along the way, Muir offers a discussion of southern customs, all of which would have been entirely alien to a northerner such as himself, as well as offering a vivid description (using his customary botanical metaphor) of the ongoing hardships borne by the population of the post-bellum South:

> The traces of war are apparent not only in the broken fields, burnt fences, mills, and woods ruthlessly slaughtered, but also on the countenances of the people. A few years after the forest has been burned another generation of bright and happy trees arises, in purest, freshest vigor; only the old trees, wholly or half dead, bear marks of the calamity. So with the people of the war-field. Happy, unscarred, and unclouded youth is growing up around the aged, half-consumed, and fallen parents, who bear in sad measure the ineffaceable marks of the farthest-reaching and most infernal of all civilized calamities.[25]

Despite observations such as these, in which Muir momentarily turns his attention to the human specimens he encounters, the unavoidable conclusion of reading Muir's journal is the idea that man is not only less important than he thinks, but that he is also of considerably less interest than the botanical world which surrounds him: 'It is very doubtful that a thoroughgoing Humanist would enjoy Muir's writings very much', one critic concludes.[26]

Having reached Cedar Key in Florida, Muir succumbed

to a serious bout of malaria. He recovered slowly, and it was the hope of reaching his final destination of South America which gave him the impetus to overcome his illness: 'Hope of enjoying the glorious mountains and the flower fields of S. America does much to sustain me.'[27] However, as the title of Muir's book indicates, he was unable to complete his journey. Having recovered from his illness and, like von Humboldt before him, having travelled as far as Cuba, he was unable to find passage further south, and still in a weakened condition, he turned back to New York before making his way west to California. But the fact remains that the Gulf was neither the ultimate goal of his walk nor his final destination. Indeed, the Gulf was no more than an unplanned stopover, forced upon him through illness and ill-fortune, his journey thus far merely a part of what he himself viewed as a much longer expedition onwards into the Amazon and beyond:

> I made up my mind to push on to South America while my stock of strength, such as it was, lasted. But fortunately I could not find passage for any South American port. I had long wished to visit the Orinoco basin and in particular the basin of the Amazon. My plan was to get ashore anywhere on the north end of the continent, push on southward through the wilderness around the headwaters of the Orinoco, until I reached a tributary of the Amazon, and float down on a raft or skiff the whole length of the great river to its mouth. It seems strange that such a trip should ever have entered the dreams of any person, however enthusiastic and full of youthful daring, particularly under the disadvantages of poor health, of funds less than a hundred dollars, and of the insalubrity of the Amazon Valley.[28]

Muir's decision in that moment of misfortune was to turn his trajectory from south to west, a choice which was to change his life. It was also, no doubt, a blessing in disguise, for as his plans above reveal, an attempt to penetrate the jungles

of South America, to locate a tributary of the Amazon and
then to float down it on a raft as far as the Atlantic, may have
proved too much even for a man of Muir's determination,
as he himself was to acknowledge in later life.[29] One would
be mistaken, however, in believing that having come so far
Muir would be willing to abandon his plans, and long after
he moved to California his letters reveal that he continued
to be fascinated by the forests of South America and that
he never gave up hope of reaching his ultimate destination.
Fate may have forced him to curtail his journey, but as it
turned out, the next four decades were merely to prove a
postponement, albeit a lengthy one, frustrating his southerly
trajectory for a considerable time, but unable to prevent him
from completing his life's dream. Muir spent the next 30
years residing in California, and he was to make a return
visit to the South in 1889. He continued to travel to remote
wilderness areas, right up until his death in 1914. And that,
at least in the commonly held account of his life, appears
to bring Muir's biography to its close. Yet that isn't quite
the full picture, for Muir still had one major journey left to
undertake.

Shortly before his seventy-third birthday, Muir was asked
if he still harboured hopes of ever voyaging to South America:
'Have I forgotten the Amazon, Earth's greatest river?' he
replied, 'Never, never, never. It has been burning in me half a
century, and will burn forever.'[30] That same year, against the
wishes of his friends and family who thought it unlikely he
would return, Muir embarked on his final journey, departing
alone from Brooklyn, New York on 12 August 1911 on what
would prove an eight-month, 40,000-mile voyage to South
America and Africa. First he sailed south through the Atlantic
and Caribbean to Belém (then Pará), in Brazil, before sailing
1,000 miles up the Amazon, then down the Atlantic Coast
and across the continent into the Chilean Andes before re-
crossing the pampas to Buenos Aires.[31] Believing it to be the
conclusion of the journey that he had begun, on foot, more
than four decades earlier, Muir regarded this adventure as

amongst the most important that he had ever undertaken and the culmination of his life's work. Ever since 1867 he had longed to follow in von Humboldt's footsteps and when the long-deferred journey south was finally completed, 44 years after his first attempt, Muir spoke of it as the fulfilment of those youthful dreams which had first inspired his 1,000–mile walk to the Gulf.[32]

Yet oddly enough, amongst the many commentators on Muir's life and work, this final journey has passed almost entirely unheralded, seen merely as an unimportant footnote to a life whose major achievements were conducted elsewhere. Taking this journey into account, however, Muir's life can then be seen in its entirety, a life book-ended by his two excursions southward with a 44-year hiatus separating these two attempts to reach the Amazon. It is only when Muir's life is viewed in this fashion that one can see that his compass was always set to the south, and not to the west or north as is more commonly supposed. For though Muir 'deeply admired the Sierra', as one of his more observant critics has indicated, 'even his much-celebrated early experiences in the mountains of California never fully eclipsed his Amazonian ambitions.'[33] And why is it, this same critic asks, that so little attention has since been paid to this last journey of his, a journey which Muir himself was to regard as the most rewarding of his life? The answer, he suggests, is twofold: firstly, because much analysis of Muir's work is 'Americo-centric' and simply chooses to ignore those parts of his life which deal with his travels beyond the borders of the United States; and secondly, because by the time Muir had finally accomplished his southward ambitions he was an old man, and once again critics are pre-disposed to ignore this phase of his life, in favour of his younger, more vigorous self, disregarding anything that might distract from this more 'heroic' phase of his long life.[34] But the fact remains that if Muir had not succumbed to illness in Cedar Keys in 1867, if he had been able to find passage southward from Cuba, then the desire that he was to harbour for the rest of his life might well have been satisfied as a young man and his future would have been quite different. Fate intervened to turn him westward, but this was neither inevitable nor preordained, and while it may have altered the course of his life, ultimately it could not suppress his unwavering instinct to turn southward once again.

## Southland

Throughout the nineteenth century, North Americans, like their European counterparts, steadfastly viewed the tropical zone to their south with a mixture of fear and attraction: fear, because as everyone knew, this was the 'white man's grave', a region impregnated with infectious disease fatal to the unprepared and defenceless northern constitution; attraction, because it was also believed to be home to a sensuous and seductive way of life with little of the industriousness and formality to be found at home. Implicit within this outlook was the widespread belief that geography was one of the chief influences upon character, as was the notion that climate determined behaviour and morality. In this respect, the choice of clothing one chose to wear was determined by much more than mere convention, as Catherine Cocks explains in her book *Tropical Whites: The Rise of the Tourist South in the Americas*:

> Donning sheer, snowy garments, northerners opened themselves to summer, the season when – and in the case of travel southward, the place where – nature's powers reached their zenith and the virtuous necessity for human labor its nadir. A realm of steamy fertility, scantily-clad dark-skinned primitives, leisure, and self-indulgence, the tropics were the opposite – and in the nineteenth century the enemy – of the winter-hardened civilization established in the earth's temperate zones by hard-working, self-disciplined, modestly attired whites.[35]

*Tropical Whites* explores the development from the late nineteenth century to the mid-twentieth century of what Cocks calls 'the Southland', the global tourist south which was to grow up through Florida and California before spreading beyond America's borders as far as Mexico and the Caribbean. Between 1880 and the 1940s, American perceptions of this region to their south underwent a complete transformation, from pestilent no-man's-land to the ideal winter holiday destination. This process was, of course, part of the wider emergence of modern, industrialised society in the North, along with the moral and economic liberalisation that was to follow, but the development of tourism was an integral part of this transformation, through the creation of 'tropical whites', a new social class more than willing to exchange their familiar lives in the North for a less oppressive southern alternative, to become, albeit only for a week or two, 'civilised, pale-skinned people with the youthful, sensuous joy of dark-skinned primitives.'[36]

As Cocks readily acknowledges, however, the majority of this new tourist nation, Southland, was, despite its 'tropical' designation, actually outside the tropical zone, as neither Southern California, Florida nor northern Mexico are to be found between the tropics of Cancer and Capricorn. But as every travel agent knows, it is the idea of the destination that sells rather than the reality. In light of which the resorts of Southern California were soon to be labelled 'Mediterranean', a stretch of the geographical imagination, admittedly, and yet no more than an attempt to equate the lifestyle that these burgeoning resorts offered with their equivalents on the French Riviera.[37] And just as the resorts of the Riviera were to flourish following the opening of the first rail services from London in the mid-nineteenth century, so too were the resorts of the Southland to experience a similar boom in the 1880s, as a network of steamships and railroads first linked Southern California and Florida to the rest of the continental United States, before gradually extending their reach to Mexico and the Caribbean. But if advances in transportation and infrastructure were to make Southland a viable proposition, what was really to ensure its future prosperity was the advance of medical science, and in particular the development of germ theory which was first to regulate the management of infectious disease in the tropical belt. These two advances in medicine and transportation, alongside the development of commercial horticulture and the growth of fruit plantations in the southern United States, were to play a decisive role in reducing 'the awesome seductive powers of the tropics to resources selectively available for the rejuvenation of weary northerners.'[38] Or, at least, for those weary northerners wealthy enough to afford it – it would require another half-century or so before the gates of Southland were opened to the masses. In fact, just as had been the case in the south of France a generation earlier, many of the northerners attracted to the Southland were not merely weary but positively unwell. In a remarkable turnaround, these tropical (or almost tropical) destinations that had so recently been regarded as fatal to the health of the northerner now came to be seen as a source of health and vitality; and a climate which had previously been judged as both morally and physically corrupting was increasingly diagnosed as beneficial. Soon the heliotherapy which was in fashion in southern Europe was equally in demand in the Southland, as these wealthy but unhealthy northerners once again proved the vanguard for the explosion of mass tourism that was to come.[39]

By the 1930s the transformation was complete and large swathes of the southern United States, Mexico and the Caribbean were now home to a transitory population of wealthy, often elderly, frequently unwell, northerners very much at home in the benign, health-improving, international playground that the tropics had become. Just as in southern Europe and the South Pacific, a sense of cultural authenticity was in demand that was satisfied through an interchangeable stage-set of Latin or African costumes, dances, and cuisines in which the lifestyles (and the lives) of the indigenous populations were often reduced to little more than a walk-on part in the tropical fantasy of youthful sensuality which they were required to display. Needless to say, the exchange between the north and south was, and remains, an unequal one, in which the celebration of 'tropical' cultures rarely translated into greater rights, political representation, or even a great deal of improvement in the economic situation for the populations involved.[40] The popularisation of tropical life was, however, to prove enormously influential, as today's global tourist south demonstrates as strongly as ever. And while it remains easy, and tempting, to characterise the growth of the Southland and its global satellites within a narrative of capitalist and neo-imperialist exploitation, it is also undeniable that, in cultural and racial terms, the once commonly held, and almost wholly negative, assumptions of North Americans, and Europeans, towards the tropical south has undergone a conversion from suspicion and disdain to something approaching a romantic attachment: 'As white North Americans learned to love the tropics, they also learned to question one of the founding assumptions of white supremacy: that it represented the best and most moral way of life. They learned that in the tropics they might not be in danger of losing their souls but recovering them.'[41]

## South of the Border: Kerouac in Mexico

In *The Lawless Roads* (1939), an account of his travels through southern Mexico in 1938, Graham Greene records his experience of crossing over the border from the United States, capturing that moment, which he equates to a kind of rebirth, as one leaves the familiar behind in search of something new and unexpected:

> The border means more than a customs house, a passport officer, a man with a gun. Over there everything is going to be different; life is never going to be quite the same again after your passport has been stamped and you find

yourself speechless among the moneychangers. The man seeking scenery imagines strange woods and unheard-of mountains; the romantic believes that the women over the border will be more beautiful and complaisant than those at home; the unhappy man imagines at least a different hell; the suicidal traveller expects the death he never finds. The atmosphere of the border – it is like starting over again.[42]

Despite these comments, Greene himself was to experience no such epiphany; in fact, he was largely unimpressed by what he perceived to be the cruelty and ugliness he encountered in Mexico. The expropriation of the oil industry by the Mexican government in 1938 had resulted in the breaking of diplomatic relations with the UK for three years and Greene was to face some hostility as a result. Recording in detail his disgust with almost every aspect of Mexican society, its government and its people (an exception being made for the priests), Greene's account has since been described as 'one of the most ill-tempered books ever written about Mexico.'[43] The Mexico that Greene was to describe in the 1930s, however, was far from virgin territory for visitors from Europe and America, as the development of the 'Southland' indicates. But alongside the emergence of official tourism, there was also the gradual growth of a secondary 'unofficial' or countercultural movement. Many of Greene's fellow travellers would have shared a liberal, if not bohemian, outlook, and the majority of these were attracted by images of a culturally authentic, indigenous Mexico, which in their eyes would have reflected an alternative America, 'a premodern, Indian-centered world free from the hassles of modern, "straight" America.'[44] Although such visitors were at first few in numbers, by the 1950s Mexico was becoming the destination of choice for America's emerging countercultural movement. In search of the exotic, the primitive, the criminal, in fact anything that was at odds with the values of the American middle class, Mexico was the nearest 'alien culture' to America, the gateway to the 'magic south.'[45] Soon their presence was to draw the attention of the Mexican authorities and the press and it was through their highly visible display of disdain for the way of life of the majority of their countrymen back home, that they were to influence the emergence of Mexico's own home-grown countercultural movement, *La Onda*. The Beat Movement, as it came to be known, was thus, from the outset, to have a significance far beyond the borders of the US, moving southwards to offer a corrective to the prevailing image of North American tourism, a counter-narrative which was to be immortalised in the sacred text of the Beats, Jack Kerouac's *On the Road* (1957). More than any other book, Kerouac's novel has since come to symbolise the freedom of the American road, a journey that is fixed firmly within the popular imagination as one which moves, repeatedly, along an east-west axis, as Dean Moriarty and Sal Paradise criss-cross the United States in search of the next experience. Yet the journeys and the characters that *On the Road* describe are much less predictable than this suggests, their movements impulsive and digressive, as they veer repeatedly from their course. For the continent that they explore is one that extends well beyond the boundaries of the United States, both to the south and to the north, *On the Road* providing a constant reminder to the reader of the wider North American continent and those lands that lie to its south.

In March 1950, shortly after the publication of his first major work, *The Town and the City*, Kerouac (1922–1969) had returned to Denver in search of a change of scene and a cure for the writer's block which was jeopardising his attempts to write his 'road book'. Before long, however, his friend Neal Cassady (Dean Moriarty in *On the Road*) had tracked him down and encouraged him to join him on a trip to Mexico. This was to be Kerouac's first journey south of the border, and in the summer of that year he and Cassady crossed over at Nuevo Laredo, before driving non-stop, apart from a brief stop for drugs in Ciudad Victoria, along the Inter-American highway to Mexico City. Kerouac was to return to Mexico repeatedly throughout the 1950s (in May 1952, and again in 1955, 1956, 1957 and finally 1961). But it was this first visit which was later to form the basis of part four of *On the Road*, although such was the onslaught of the drugs Kerouac was to consume while in Mexico City that it was some time before he was to attempt any major work on the book.[46] Seven years later, however, when *On the Road* was finally published, plot, as far as one can be said to exist in Kerouac's novel, had been replaced by movement, a hymn to the open road and the creed of a life lived free from obligation or resistance to one's desires. In such a world, freedom is equated with speed, with warmth, with sex, with light and with drugs, the majority of which appear to be located in the South, and so given the choice there was really only one direction in which to travel: 'Flashed past the mysterious white signs in the night somewhere in New Jersey that say SOUTH (with an arrow) and WEST with an arrow and took the south one. New Orleans! [...] We got out of the car for air and suddenly both of us were stoned with joy to realize that in the darkness all around us was fragrant green grass and the smell of fresh manure and warm waters. "We're in the South! We've left the winter!"'[47] The further south they travel, the more stoned they become, and by the time Dean and Sal have crossed the southern states and finally approach the border with Mexico, their understanding of what lies ahead begins to be expressed in an increasingly mystical fashion, the South expanding (in tandem with their own drug-fuelled consciousness) to encompass a vision not merely of the southern United States, or even Mexico itself, but of all the souths of the world, swelling to form one single unified belt of humanity stretching across Asia, Africa and the Pacific:

> And now we were ready for the last hundred and fifty miles to the magic border. We leapt into the car and off. [...] But everything changed when we crossed the mysterious bridge over the river and our wheels rolled

on official Mexican soil, though it wasn't anything but carway for border inspection. Just across the street Mexico began. We looked with wonder. To our amazement, it looked exactly like Mexico. [...] Behind us lay the whole of America and everything Dean and I had previously known about life, and life on the road. We had finally found the magic land at the end of the road and we never dreamed the extent of the magic. [...] I was alone in my eternity at the wheel, and the road ran straight as an arrow. Not like driving across Carolina, or Texas, or Arizona, or Illinois; but like driving across the world and into the places where we would finally learn ourselves among the Fellahin Indians of the world, the essential strain of the basic primitive, wailing humanity that stretches in a belt around the equatorial belly of the world from Malaya (the long fingernail of China) to India the great subcontinent to Arabia to Morocco to the selfsame deserts and jungles of Mexico and over the waves to Polynesia to mystic Siam of the Yellow Robe and on around, on around, so that you hear the same mournful wail by the rotted walls of Cádiz, Spain, that you hear 12,000 miles around in the depths of Benares the Capital of the World.[48]

The journey that *On the Road* describes is one without an end, each stop merely one further interval on a route which has no clear direction, destination or purpose beyond the onward movement it provides. Although Kerouac's novel inaugurated a new kind of travel narrative which celebrates the freedom of speed and movement, there is, of course, a well-trodden tradition within American literature which proclaims the joy of the open road. But for Thoreau, Emerson, Whitman, and, as we have seen, John Muir, this was a road which was to be walked rather than driven. Kerouac and the Beats certainly wouldn't have got far on foot, for theirs was an exploration of America's expanding network of interstate highways, and of those roads that would take them beyond America's frontiers: 'Think if you and I had a car like this what we could do', exclaims Dean Moriarty, 'Do you know there's a road that goes down Mexico and all the way to Panama? – and maybe all the way to the bottom of South America where the Indians are seven feet tall and eat cocaine on the mountainside? Yes! You and I, Sal, we'd dig the whole world with a car like this because, man, the road must eventually lead to the whole world. Ain't nowhere else it can go – right?'[49] The tradition which Kerouac's journey into Mexico invokes is that of John Reed and William Burroughs, the North American radicals who have looked for inspiration south of the border.[50] It is here that Sal and Dean finally encounter the 'magic land' to the south, an idealised if not imaginary world, in which the spiritual is privileged over the material, where the temporal imperatives of the North no longer apply, and where the poor are transformed into the *fellaheen*:

> In downtown Mexico City thousands of hipsters in floppy straw hats and long-lapeled jackets over bare chests padded along the main drag, some of them selling crucifixes and weed in the alleys, some of them kneeling in beat chapels next to Mexican burlesque shows in sheds. [...] We wandered in a frenzy and a dream. [...] Nothing stopped; the streets were alive all night. Beggars slept wrapped in advertising posters torn off fences. Whole families of them sat on the sidewalk, playing little flutes and chuckling in the night. Their bare feet stuck out, their dim candles burned, all Mexico was one vast bohemian camp. [...] This was the great and final wild uninhibited Fellahin-childlike city that we knew we would find at the end of the road.[51]

Mexico City offers a delirious, fever-ridden, drugged glimpse of the magic south that lies at the end of the road, a land that is more a symbol than a nation, and one which is defined by the spirit of its people. Of course, this spirit, like the country itself, is at least as much the product of literary invention as it is observable reality, for Kerouac, like so many of his countrymen, had formed a preconceived notion of Mexico long before he ever went there, an idealised vision underpinned by a Western philosophy.[52] The roots of this philosophy were to be found in *The Decline of the West* (1918–23), in which Oswald Spengler identifies a residue of humanity existing outside of time and history itself – both, for Spengler, constructs of Western civilisation – a primitive mass which will inherit the earth once the West has completed its inevitable course towards decline and dissolution. 'At the last', writes Spengler, 'only the primitive blood remains, alive, but robbed of its strongest and most promising elements. This residue is the *Fellah type*.'[53] As the West declines, so will the South that Kerouac affirms rise up in its place. The vagrants, bums and hoboes wandering the American Continent; the 'closeted homosexuals, stifled minorities, shunned drug addicts, each sapped of hope or support from the society that helped put them there'; these are the *fellah-people* addressed by Spengler and appropriated by Kerouac to form the characters which dominate his entire body of work, and the population which he was to portray so vividly in Mexico City.[54] *On the Road* ends, however, not in the *fellaheen* south, but with Sal's return north to New York and his reconciliation with Dean, and in the closing pages his thoughts turn once again to California and the journey west. But if amidst this ceaseless movement, *On the Road* can be said to have a principal direction, if not a clear destination, then that direction is down, and south across the border.

The idea of dropping out of society may have been an appealing one to many young Americans in the 1950s but Kerouac's depiction of the freedom to be won by turning one's back on everyday life did not convince everyone. John Updike recalls how on the novel's release in 1957, he resented its apparent instruction to cut loose from society, even before he had read it, questioning the idea that such an escape could ever prove as straightforward as Kerouac suggests: 'There was no painless dropping out of the Fifties' fraying but still tight social weave' he was later to claim.[55] Updike's response was to write a more realistic demonstration of the effects of such a drop-out upon those who are left behind. *Rabbit, Run* (1960), the first of his series of novels to feature the attempts of the then 26-year-old, Harry 'Rabbit' Angstrom, to escape the pressures and constraints of everyday life, sees another headlong rush southwards to freedom: 'He wants to go south, down, down the map into orange groves and smoking rivers and barefoot women. It seems simple enough, drive all night through the dawn through the morning through the noon park on a beach take off your shoes and fall asleep by the Gulf of Mexico.'[56] But freedom, argues Updike, is not so easy to acquire, and rather than experiencing the South as Kerouac might have done, reality for Angstrom proves rather more complex and the past more difficult to outrun: he gets lost, returns to his home town and, following a brief affair, he is finally reunited with his wife. But to question the realism of *On the Road* is, of course, to rather miss the point. For what has proved so endlessly appealing to the readership of Kerouac's novel, both in the US and elsewhere, both then and now, is neither the reality of life on the road, nor the reality of a life lived at odds with society's norms, but rather the idea of escape, an idea that has never lost its allure precisely because of the fact that it has never had much to do with the reality it exhorts one to turn one's back on.

In any case, by the 1960s *On the Road* had certainly done its job. Following the trail blazed by the Beats, a new wave of countercultural 'tourists' was soon to descend upon Mexico. The arrival of the hippies was to take place in much greater numbers and was to produce a much larger impact, as the nascent and home-grown countercultural movement, *La Onda*, which had developed in tandem with the Beats, was now boosted by the burgeoning ranks of the *jipis*, or *jipicetas*. Soon the Mexican youth, by now very much aware of the countercultural developments to their north, were watching their US counterparts, who were in turn looking south: 'Mexican youth observing American youth observing

Mexico', or the South observing the North observing the South.[57] Following in the footsteps, or rather tyre tracks, of Kerouac, Burroughs, Ginsberg and their cohorts, in addition to more mainstream traffic, the arrival of the hippies helped to ensure that throughout the 1960s Mexico remained a popular holiday destination. Ultimately, however, their successors were not to find in Mexico quite the unchecked fantasy that Kerouac had bequeathed them. By the 1970s, the realities of more regulated border control, along with the changing political, legal and economic climate of the North American continent were conspiring to curtail the southward (and northward) direction of countercultural movement.[58] With the hippies now part of a wider movement in the US demanding precisely those freedoms at home which the Beats had sought in Mexico, it was hoped that for those seeking an alternative way of life the flight south might soon no longer be necessary. Indeed, as the youth movement became a worldwide phenomenon, the Mexican authorities began to look upon their countercultural visitors from the North, as well as their compatriots at home, with rather less affection than before. But if the border crossing which Graham Greene had described so memorably was now to become a little less porous and a little more regimented, other borders and other journeys remained for those, like Muir and Kerouac, whose compass was set to the south. For by this time the connotation of the 'magic south' could more readily be applied to those regions lying much further down the Pan-American Highway, far beyond the confines of North America.

## *Sur*, Borges and 'The South'

In the northern hemisphere one may navigate by Polaris, the North Star, which lies almost directly above the North Pole (it's actually about one degree away); in the South one's orientation is less straightforward. The South does have its own astronomical equivalent, the Southern Cross, but this constellation of four stars is some 25 degrees from true south. According to one commentator, however, the constellation of the Southern Cross may be said not only to indicate the South astronomically, but also to offer a reflection of the very people it is supposed to guide. For in Argentina, the southernmost country of the Latin American continent, each of these four stars may be viewed as representative of one of the four groups which constitute its population: Europeans, porteños (the inhabitants of Buenos Aires), Indians and gauchos.[59] But as is so often the case, Argentine conceptions of their own country bear little allegiance to any cartographical convention, and although in strictly geographical terms this most southerly of countries incorporates both Patagonia and Tierra del Fuego to form the southernmost point of South America, the Argentine conception of the 'South' also includes the pampas, that vast expanse of grassland which extends not only to the south and west, but which also reaches to the north of Buenos Aires. For here, as elsewhere, the 'South' is an elastic term, applicable not only geographically, but also culturally, politically and historically:

> The South in Argentina is protean. [...] it functions as a signifier of a time and space that is incorporated into different cultural and political projects and ideologies from post-independence to the present day. It is present in the evocative mythologies of the gaucho, the Indian, the horse, and the vast expanse of land [...] Throughout its history, the South has been the physical and imaginative frontier that has enabled definitions of the nation. As the nation's discourse shifts to include or exclude different peoples and places, the South's boundaries are moved to accommodate it. These boundaries are temporal as much as they are spatial, and they demarcate the divisions not only between urban and rural, but also between modernity and the premodern past. The frontier of the South moves according to the locus of enunciation.[60]

Since the eighteenth century, when the first scientific travellers began to explore the region, the Argentine South has widely been regarded as the remnant of an older age, distinct from the remainder of the country both geographically and temporally, an empty zone existing somehow beyond the confines of historical time. In an all too familiar fashion, however, just as the term 'South' was to be defined according to the whims of those applying the term, so too was the term 'empty' to prove equally malleable. In 1879, the Argentine oligarchy and military were to launch a genocidal attack upon this empty quarter, eradicating the South's indigenous (and seemingly invisible) population in the so-called 'Conquest of the Desert', a grand but clearly misleading, if not contradictory, title for a campaign which succeeded in turning 'the representation of emptiness into a reality.'[61] For just as the government of the United States in the nineteenth century used the ideology of Manifest Destiny to project an image of America westwards from Washington, so too did the ruling powers in Buenos Aires employ a similar expansionist rhetoric in their competing claims for the South. But while the advance into the American West resulted in a similar subjugation of the indigenous population, it was an expansion which also led to the colonisation of the 'empty' space it produced. In Argentina, however, the conquest of the South was not so much a prelude to expansion and colonisation as a means of ensuring that such a process was indefinitely deferred, ensuring its continued emptiness for future generations.[62] It is this contrast, between this empty southern region, on the one hand, and Buenos Aires and the more heavily populated North, on the other, which has since informed so many of the country's literary representations; the myths of a romantic primitivism, or barbarism, with which the 'South' has been traditionally imbued – once again in a manner similar to that of the romantic but violent frontier spirit of the 'Wild West' – at odds, historically, with the presumption of more modern and 'civilised' values to be found in the North. This opposition within Argentina has been further reinforced by the distinction between the indigenous populations of the Latin American continent and the European nations which have colonised them, placing those who seek to write about the country from within in the curious, if not disorientating, situation of having to position themselves 'as both southern to Europe and northern to their own South.'[63]

It was from an awareness of such an ambiguity in Argentina's position, bound by its own 'primitive' South and yet equally southern to a Europe with which it aspired to compete on equal terms, that *Sur* magazine was born in 1931. This journal, the founding project of Victoria Ocampo, which was soon to become the most famous cultural enterprise in Latin America, took its title not only from the geographical position from which it was produced but from the position which its founders perceived themselves to stand culturally in relation to Europe. For despite the growth and prosperity Argentina had achieved in the early part of the twentieth century, it remained, in its own eyes, or at least in those of the Anglophile *criollo* ruling class, 'someone else's South.'[64] But rather than acting simply as a vehicle for the dissemination of European texts to an Argentine audience, *Sur* was also, initially at least, viewed as a means of displaying Argentina and Latin America's own distinct and home-grown cultural movement to a European readership, the magazine adopting the role of a bridge between the two continents and highlighting the best each had to offer. However, according to the historian of *Sur*, John King, the magazine was never able to truly establish a clear direction for itself, this despite the logo adorning the cover of the opening issue, which displayed an arrow pointing firmly southwards.[65] From the outset, the founders of *Sur* and its contributors seemed unable to isolate that distinct, unified 'South' with which they hoped the magazine would be associated, and rather than the competing claims of south and north (Europe) leading to a true exchange of ideas, it soon became apparent that the traffic was largely flowing in one direction only, and with one, very notable exception, none of the *Sur* writers were to command an enthusiastic response in Europe.[66]

The exception here is, of course, Jorge Luis Borges (1899–1986), although it wasn't until the 1960s that he began to achieve the recognition abroad that he was to enjoy subsequently. Today Latin American fiction is often described through the shorthand of magical realism, the literary genre most closely associated with writers such as Isabel Allende and Gabriel Garcia Márquez. This term, which posits the existence of magic and magical thinking within the confines of an otherwise rational world, was first used by the critic Angel Flores in 1955 in his influential essay 'Magical Realism in Spanish American Fiction', in which he was to identify Jorge Luis Borges as the progenitor of the movement. Borges himself was to make no such claims for his work, however, and today he is more widely regarded as an influence upon the movement and its practitioners rather than an exemplar of its ideas. But what is apparent throughout Borges' work is precisely that sense of the uncanny and the supernatural which is not only to be found in magical realism, but which has also been identified with the literary subgenre of the Southern Gothic, that dark and unsettling vision of the American South anticipated by Poe, but most closely associated with the work of William Faulkner, a writer whom Borges both admired and translated, and whose awareness and acknowledgement of his own 'southernness' Borges came to share.[67] Borges was frequently to articulate his fondness for the literature of the American South, remarking: 'The common phrase, "the deep South" is a good one. In Spanish it goes well too, if I say, *el hondo Sur*, it sounds as it should.'[68] For despite his lifelong affection for the English and European literature he had first discovered as a child, by the late 1930s, as he began to find his voice as a writer of fiction, so Borges made the conscious decision to turn away from the European literature which dominated Argentine culture in favour of that of North America. In doing so, Borges hoped to reverse 'the master/slave polarity of north and south in the literature of the Americas' by creating a new and distinctive Latin American, or southern voice, no longer subservient to, or imitative of, other global literatures.[69] Alongside his admiration for Faulkner, the other North American writer for whom Borges displayed a particular affection was Poe, with whom he felt a close kinship. Beyond the fact that, like Borges himself, Poe (Boston born, but a writer who strongly identified with the South) was a southern writer attempting to establish himself within a northern literary establishment, the two men also appear to have shared a similar family background, both having a military heritage towards which they felt an instinctive sense of obligation.[70] Poe's own considerable addition to the literature of the South (Polar, as well as American) will be discussed in the following chapter, but his influence upon Borges was crucial, allowing him to establish a sense of identity within a regional designation – the South – which many of his contemporaries were attempting to downplay or to escape altogether.

'No other writer is more Argentine than Borges,' the critic Beatriz Sarlo writes, 'especially in his exploration of how great literature can be written in a culturally marginal nation located in the extreme south.'[71] If, however, Borges can be seen as identifying himself with the south in wider terms – Argentina, Latin America, the Global South – so too was he fiercely, if not obsessively, loyal to the city in which he was to spend the great majority of his life, Buenos Aires. In fact, in Borges' case such a designation was as much local as it was global, for his was the 'Southside' of the city:

> a house on the Southside stands open until dawn,
> unfamiliar to me, and not to be seen again,
> [...] and graven streets on the Southside, one by one to
>     be savored,
> and a dark breeze in my face as I walk home[72]

Both here in 'Deathwatch on the Southside' as well as in his poem, 'The Southside', Borges recalls the streets of

Buenos Aires in which he grew up, an area which he (and his fellow porteños) regarded as distinctively different from the remainder of the city, and one which he was to return to repeatedly in his work.[73] But as his translator, Norman Thomas di Giovanni, makes clear, the *sur* which Borges refers to in these lines is neither a symbolic south, nor a representation of the wider Argentinian South, but rather a local and very specific area (and time) with its roots in his own childhood.[74] For Borges, the South represented the enchanted landscape of his earliest memories amongst the streets of the Southside. But beyond the context of his own family history, Borges also regarded Buenos Aires as a state of mind, a city in which fiction and reality intersect, a place in which spatial and temporal boundaries may become blurred and indistinct.[75] Nowhere was Borges to be more explicit in exploring his preoccupation with the city, the South, and his own place within it, than in the story which he was to regard as his best, 'El Sur' ('The South'), first published in *La Nación* on 8 February 1953.[76]

Borges was later to assert this story could be read in two ways, both as a straightforward narrative, but also in another way, less clearly articulated.[77] The direct narrative tells the story of Juan Dahlmann, the 'secretary of a municipal library' in Buenos Aires and the grandson of a heroic Argentine soldier. In February 1939, Dahlmann catches his head on a casement window and from the resulting injury he develops a fever. He soon finds himself incarcerated in a sanatorium and on his recovery he is sent south to his country home to recuperate. After a long and dreamlike train journey, Dahlmann finds himself in a strange station from where he walks to a nearby bar. Here, he finds himself the target of a group of strangers, whose insults soon provoke him into accepting their challenge to a fight. Unarmed, he is tossed a dagger by an old gaucho and as the story ends he walks outside ready to face his inevitable death. From this brief summary, it is immediately apparent that one 'other way' this story may be read is as an autobiographical account of Borges himself and his own preoccupations as a writer: he too was to work as a librarian; he too had a famous military ancestry; he too was to become seriously ill following a head injury he received in 1939. The oppositions that Borges draws here, between the city and the pampas, Europeans and the gauchos, the urban north and the rural south, and ultimately, the life of the mind and the life of action and violence, are those which he was to replay throughout his work. Indeed, Borges manages to compress almost his entire symbolic vocabulary into this brief work, creating a text which appears to summarise, albeit in miniature, an entire worldview. This is most clearly embodied in the character of Dahlmann himself, whose dual-ancestry, both European and Argentine, simply reflects such a division within Argentina itself, in which the European heritage of the 'educated' southerner is offset against that of the 'aboriginal' Argentine, represented by the gaucho. Here, the city of Buenos Aires, with its population of 'imitation' Europeans is contrasted with a south of 'authentic' Argentine values; but Borges' stories can rarely be taken at face value, and the contemporary Buenos Aires of 1939 he portrays is contrasted with an image of the South that is taken from the past, or rather from his own romanticised vision of the past: 'Dahlmann almost suspected that he was traveling not only into the South', writes Borges, 'but into the past.'[78] For Dahlmann's journey is one that takes him into a past (and a south) which no longer exists, or may never have existed, and the tensions and contradictions that his story exposes may be said to originate as much in Borges' own imagination, as they do in any wider conception of the Argentinian psyche.[79]

'Everyone knows', writes Borges, 'that the South begins on the other side of Avenida Rivadavia. Dahlmann had often said that that was no mere saying, that by crossing Rivadavia one entered an older and more stable world.'[80] But if Dahlmann (and Borges) are clear where the South begins, what is much less clear is where this south ends, or rather how it ends. For Dahlmann, the journey south appears to end with his death, and in this respect Borges' story joins those of other writers in whose work the protagonist is drawn irresistibly but fatally southwards.[81] The end that Borges chooses for Dahlmann, the fight against the knife-wielding gaucho, is certainly the most romantic, the most idealised and the most replayed, of all the many fictional deaths in Argentine literature. It is also a death that Borges himself idealised, and which he appears, unlikely as it may seem, to have wished for himself.[82] The south that Borges creates is one in which the notion of courage and physical bravery holds a value and esteem that is no longer present elsewhere, for in this unchanging landscape, the timeless South, the spirit of the gaucho lives on:

> On the floor, curled against the bar, lay an old man, as motionless as an object. The many years had worn him away and polished him, as a stone is worn smooth by running water or a saying is polished by generations of humankind. He was small, dark, and dried up, and he seemed to be outside time, in a sort of eternity. Dahlmann was warmed by the rightness of the man's hairband, the baize poncho he wore, his gaucho trousers, and the boots made out of the skin of a horse's leg, and he said to himself, recalling futile arguments with people from districts in the North, or from Entre Ríos, that only in the South did gauchos like that exist anymore. [...] From out of the corner, the motionless old gaucho in whom Dahlmann had seen a symbol of the South (the South that belonged to him) tossed him a dagger – it came to rest at Dahlmann's feet. It was as though the South itself had decided that Dahlmann should accept the challenge.[83]

In accepting this duel with an unknown stranger, Dahlmann's motives at first appear incomprehensible to the reader. But within the strange logic of Borges' tale, it is not Dahlmann who chooses to fight, but rather it is the South itself, symbolised by the aged gaucho, which has chosen for him. For while he is perceived by his persecutors to be an outsider, a northerner from the city, Dahlmann believes himself to be a southerner returning to his ancestral home, and in choosing (or rather in having been chosen for) death, Dahlmann is simply affirming to himself his rightful place in the South. But in a final confirmation that this south is one firmly rooted within Borges' imagination, or within his childhood memory, the motif of the aged gaucho tossing Dahlmann a dagger with which to perform his allotted sacrificial role, closely resembles an episode in which the young Borges was himself handed a dagger by his father, who urged him to stand up to the bullies who were tormenting him at school.[84] Unsurprisingly, this memory of his father's intervention, with its implicit suggestion that he live up to the deeds of his illustrious forbears, was one which was to haunt Borges (and his work) for the rest of his life. Of course, this interpretation of 'The South' is no more definitive than any other, but having affirmed the idea that Dahlmann is somehow reliving Borges' own childhood, it only requires the reader to take one further short step for the narrative to move beyond the realm of memory into that of a dream. For while Borges' story may begin in a recognisable time and place – Buenos Aires in 1939 – as soon as Dahlmann moves south of the Avenida Rivadavia, these spatial and temporal coordinates begin to fade, and as his train takes him southwards so his perception of the surrounding countryside becomes increasingly dreamlike. This, then, may be the final reading of Borges story, and one which ends not with Dahlmann's death but with his awakening, as he, like Borges himself, now recovered from his illness, wakes to find himself in a Buenos Aires hospital.

In 2002, almost fifty years after the publication of 'El Sur', and in a curious coda to Borges' preoccupation with the South, an Australian writer named Guy Rundle revealed that Borges, unbeknownst to his many biographers, was once a visitor to Melbourne in Southern Australia. According to Rundle, Borges arrived on 16 May 1938, exploring the city for ten days, giving a lecture and spending much of his time in the State Library, 'a place he found awe-inspiring, even overwhelming.'[85] Referring to notes found in 'a recently discovered notebook', Rundle records Borges' impressions of Melbourne, with its 'wide Victorian streets and languorous gardens, the tang of rusting air from the wide verandas, the stately trams, the pompous stone buildings shaded by palms.' In fact Borges appears to have taken rather a liking to Melbourne, a city he found to be reminiscent of Buenos Aires, 'albeit more staid.' Melbourne, writes Rundle, 'had the sort of timelessness that [Borges] associated with all southern places. "Cita metafisica" he called them, transcendental cities in which the eternal was open at every moment'.[86] The title of Borges' lecture, we are told, was 'The Author's Fictions', an apt title as it turns out, for Rundle's article was also a work of fiction. Borges was otherwise engaged in 1938, at home in Buenos Aires, mourning the death of his father. The motivation behind this literary hoax remains unclear, yet in its playful elaboration upon the theme of 'southernness', one cannot help but think that it is one which Borges himself would have appreciated. Rundle was later to declare that he had wanted 'to describe a Melbourne that had perhaps never existed: a forgotten city, as imagined by a great artist, Borges.'[87]

## Notes

1. Faulkner, p. 174.
2. Kerouac, pp. 241–2.
3. Tindall, p. 2.
4. Benjamin Schwarz writes (1997):

   Readers' urge to know about the South and writers' compulsion to explain it have engendered a vast subfield of American letters over the past century and a half. Even leaving aside the southern novelists, poets, and storywriters, since the 1850s not five years have passed without a major work seeking to explore, explain, justify, or condemn a region that the historian David Potter called "a kind of sphinx on the American land." [...] Since it is almost impossible to see the region through fresh eyes, for a long time it has been difficult to find fresh perception in anything written about the South, or even in one's own impressions, for that matter.

5. Davidson, p. 10.
6. O'Brien, p. 3.
7. Marshall, Introduction, p. 2.
8. WJ Cash, 'The Mind of the South' (1941), in Ayers & Mittendorf, pp. 75–76.
9. O'Brien writes (pp. 5–6):

The idea of the South was strengthened, ironically, by the destruction of its political expression, the Confederacy. The war left welding memories and compelling economic realities. [...] One South might be dead, but another was to take its place. The New South was born, which was somehow to be compatible with the Old South while supporting movements that the ancient regime had perished to resist. The New South helped to make permanent the very idea of a South.

10. O'Brien, p. xi.
11. O'Brien, p. 226.
12. Muir, quoted by Badè, Introduction, Muir, *A Thousand-Mile Walk*, pp. xix-xxi.
13. Branch, Introduction, Muir, *John Muir's Last Journey*, p. xxix.
14. Muir, quoted by Branch, Introduction, Muir, *John Muir's Last Journey*, p. xxix.
15. Hunt, pp. 54–55.
16. In his book *Walkers* (p. 122), Miles Jebb disputes the title of Muir's book, claiming that 'the name given to his walk is misleading: it was around 800 miles and done in two sections with a sea passage in between.'
17. Muir, *A Thousand-Mile Walk*, pp. 1–2.
18. Hunt, p. 60.
19. Hunt, p. 62.
20. Muir, *A Thousand-Mile Walk*, pp. 6, 55 & 63.
21. Muir, *A Thousand-Mile Walk*, p. 93.
22. Smith, p. 35.
23. Smith, p. 35.

24. Smith writes (p. 36): 'Muir was almost perfectly fitted to be a witness of the situation in the South after the Civil War. He was a good observer, and he probably had as much sympathy for the South as anyone in the North.'
25. Muir, *A Thousand-Mile Walk*, p. 84.
26. Smith, p. 44.
27. Letter to David Gilyre Muir, 13 December 1867, quoted in Hunt, p. 145.
28. Muir, *A Thousand-Mile Walk*, p. 169.
29. Muir, *A Thousand-Mile Walk*, p. 169.
30. Muir, *John Muir's Last Journey*, Correspondence, 26 January 1911 – 12 August 1911, p. 15.
31. Branch, Introduction, *John Muir's Last Journey*, p. xxiii.
32. Badè, Introduction, Muir, *A Thousand-Mile Walk*, pp. xxiv–xxvi.
33. Branch, Introduction, Muir, *John Muir's Last Journey*, p. xxxiii.
34. Branch, Introduction, Muir, *John Muir's Last Journey*, p. xlvii.
35. Cocks, pp. 1–2. Describing the impact of 'tropicality' on race, Cocks writes (p. 4):

By the nineteenth century tropicality had become a critical element in the consolidation of racial difference. [...] In this way of thinking, tropical places produced dark-skinned, lazy, passionate people and temperate zones pale-skinned, hard-working, cool-headed ones. The scientific and medical understanding of humanity held that the environment and human social relations were mutually and closely implicated. A people's natural setting could explain differences not simply of colour but also of social organization, family form, gender roles, sexual morals and practices, religion, and capacity for self-rule.

36. Cocks, p. 2.
37. Cocks, p. 3.
38. Cocks, p. 5.
39. Cocks writes (p. 17): 'These invalid hegiras laid the foundations for what would soon become a booming tourist industry in Florida and Southern California, and to a lesser extent in the Caribbean and Mexico.'
40. Cocks, p. 13.
41. Cocks, p. 13.
42. Greene, p. 11.
43. Gunn, p. 187.

44. Zolov, p. 252.
45. Gunn, p. 218.
46. Charters, Introduction, Kerouac, p. xv-xvi.
47. Kerouac, pp. 121–125.
48. Kerouac, pp. 249–255. Kerouac's description of Benares as the spiritual 'Capital of the World' is one which is echoed in the work of Jorge Luis Borges, who was to share his belief that the city is somehow analogous with other cities of the South, and in Borges' case, Buenos Aires: 'Borges often evoked the name of Benares', writes Robin Fiddian, 'the ancient center of many faiths that stands on the bank of the Ganges, doing so as early as 1921 in a short prose piece and then again in a poem dated 1923. [...] Unnoticed by critics until recently, Benares serves in both texts as a spatial analogue for the Argentine capital and even nestles within the name, "BuENosAiRES."' See Fiddian, p. 100.
49. Kerouac, p. 209.
50. Adams, p. 58.
51. Kerouac, p. 275.
52. Jorge García-Robles writes (p. 126):

Kerouac turned to 'the magic land' to the south essentially to escape the suffocation of his own country. [...] Kerouac was desperate to find a spiritual climate that could release him from himself. This he easily achieved, inclined as he was to imagine a Mexico that only existed in his neurons. In short, Jack made a Mexico to the measure of his inner chimeras and boiled it down to a fiction that helped him survive at the time.

53. Spengler, *The Decline of the West, Vol II: Perspectives in World History*, Knopf, 1928, p. 105, quoted in Maher Jr., p. 160.
54. Maher Jr., p. 160.
55. Updike, 'Afterword by the Author' (1995), p. 268.
56. Updike, p. 23.
57. Zolov, p. 255.
58. Adams, p. 65.
59. Jagoe, p. 86.
60. Jagoe, pp. 12–13.
61. Jagoe, p. 14.
62. Jagoe writes (p. 14): 'The process of emptying that had taken place in the late nineteenth century did not lead to colonization

and expansion, but rather to a construction of the South as a resource on reserve. It was an investment for the future, available for whatever national needs might arise.'

63. Jagoe, p. 16.
64. Jagoe, p. 129.
65. King, pp. 46–47.
66. King, p. 200.
67. Irwin writes (p. 169–171):

[Borges's] sense of his own southernness – was probably mediated and reinforced by the work of another author from the American South who was Borges's contemporary, William Faulkner. Borges was a fan of Faulkner's work, and between 1937 and 1939 he reviewed three of his books – *The Unvanquished*, *Absalom, Absalom!*, and *The Wild Palms* – and in 1941 published a Spanish translation (done in collaboration with his mother) of the last of these. [...] One can sense Borges already assimilating Faulkner's South, with its "equestrian wars," to his own south and to the image of his grandfather's death on horseback during one of the Argentine civil wars. [...] And in a sense Borges's self-definition as a writer depended upon his ultimately convincing himself [...] that he didn't hate the South.

68. Borges quoted in Byrne (2015).
69. Irwin, p. 163.
70. For an account of Poe and Borges' similar family histories and its impact on their work see Byrne (2015).
71. Sarlo, p. 3.
72. Borges, 'Deathwatch on the Southside' in *Selected Poems*, pp. 69–71.
73. Borges, 'The Southside' in *Selected Poems*, pp. 271.
74. di Giovanni, in Borges, *Selected Poems*, Introduction, p. xxii. Elsewhere, di Giovanni writes (p. 66–7):

The south as an emblem of the Argentine past – and by this Borges did not mean Patagonia; he meant both the south side of Buenos Aires and the south of the Province of Buenos Aires – and the mystique of this south were very much Borges's dearly-held private views. This south that he turned into myth represented his childhood, a link with his forebears and what seemed to him [...] the less abysmal days of a pre-Peronist Argentina.

75. Describing Borges' perception of Buenos Aires, Jagoe writes (p. 131):

His spatial and temporal mappings of the specific topography of Buenos Aires position the places where modernity meets earlier moments, and where "civilisation" is confronted with "the South" [...] The time is not present, but it is measured rather by a nostalgia for a past that never existed. It is no-man's-time, just as the space in which these illusions are shared is a no-man's-land, the indeterminate and shifting edge where the city ends and the South begins. [...] This image of the city is founded on a romantic construction of the South.

76. Bell-Villada writes (p. 78): 'From its first appearance in print Borges has repeatedly maintained – in prologues, essays, and interviews – that this story is his best. It is certainly his personal favorite, for it exalts bravery, something that, Borges told an interviewer, means a great deal to him since he is not particularly courageous himself.'
77. Irwin, p. 171.
78. Borges, 'The South', p. 150.
79. Waisman asks (p. 149):

But does Dahlmann really have as much choice as he believes? In other words, does Dahlmann choose the South, or does the South choose him? Can we say for sure what is Argentine and what is European about his choice, about his personal South? [...] The tensions and contradictions that Dahlmann enacts in the text suggest that the local and the foreign are in fact inseparable; that it is not North versus South, but rather North and South, which defines the Argentine.

80. Borges, 'The South', p. 148.
81. Irwin writes (p. 173):

And here again we see the influence of Poe, for in several of his best-known stories Poe figuratively represents the act of writing as an exploratory journey into terra incognita, into some new realm of the human imagination where virtually every aspect of the act of writing is metaphorized, the exploratory journey is specifically a journey to the south [...] Like the journeys of Arthur Gordon Pym and the narrator of "MS. Found in a Bottle," Juan Dahlmann's trip to the south turns out to be fatal.

82. Di Giovanni writes (p. 67): 'Many times Borges expressed to me his longing for an end exactly like the one we expect for Dahlmann. Alas, when death finally came to him, Borges died of cancer, weak, frail, bedridden, and – perhaps most poignant of all – in Geneva, far from his idealized *sur*. What he had written in "The South", then, was a scenario of his own ideal end.'
83. Borges, 'The South', pp. 151–2.
84. Williamson, p. 46.
85. Rundle (2002). For a discussion of Rundle's hoax, see Byrne (2015).
86. Rundle (2002).
87. Byrne (2015). In the light of Rundle's hoax, one further point of reference here is the work of the Far South Project, a loosely affiliated collective of authors, artists, filmmakers and musicians from Argentina, Uruguay, Wales, Ireland and elsewhere, who have come together to, in their own words, 'blur the line between truth and misinformation.' Built, ostensibly at least, around the search for a 'missing' Uruguayan theatre director named Gerardo Fischer, the Far South Project uses a blend of multimedia, text and images to record 'sightings' of Fischer as he moves across the globe. In 2011, under the heteronym of David Enrique Spellman, *Far South* was published, a novel set in the Argentine south which tells the story of Fischer's disappearance. See The Far South Project at www.far-south.org and David Enrique Spellman, *Far South* (2011).

*'Endurance' in the ice* by James Francis Hurley (1915) NATIONAL MARITIME MUSEUM

# 4

# The Polar South

*'We all have our own White South.'*

Ernest Shackleton.[1]

*I like to think of the subconscious as being very much like Antarctica. It was only really approached and explored in the late 19th century. It's very difficult and expensive to visit, and even then we're unsure of its long-term value or if it was worth the visit. It only seems to create worry and trouble: ozone holes; Oedipus complexes.*

Douglas Coupland.[2]

'Great God! This is an awful place'.[3] Scott's famous entry in his journal, written in 1912, serves as an accurate summary not only of his own attitude towards the Antarctic, but also of historical perceptions towards the southernmost continent, this despite, or perhaps precisely because of, the fact that this region was for so long to remain almost entirely uncharted and unvisited. Even in the realms of polar mythology, the Antarctic appears to attract wholly negative associations, evoking tales of desolation and horror, isolation and madness. Nor can such prejudices be dismissed simply as the result of fear and ignorance. For even in the twentieth century, with the South Pole long since discovered and the territory now mapped, the feeling has endured that this is a region of malign indifference to human life, lacking in all the charms of its northern counterpart:

It is upon the northern parts of this earth that the civilizations that have persisted have grown up, then extending themselves colonially southward. History, like South America and Africa, tapers southward. There are no ruins of temples, pyramids, obelisks, in Australia, Argentina, South Africa. Preponderantly peninsulas are southward droops. As if by design, or as if concordantly with an accentuation of lands and peoples in the north, the sun shines about a week longer in the north, each year, than in the south. The coldness in the less important Antarctic regions is more intense than in the Arctic, and here there is no vegetation like the grasses and flowers of the Arctic, in the summertime. Life withers southward. Musk oxen, bears, wolves, foxes, lemmings in the Far North – but there are only amphibious mammals in the Antarctic. Fields of Arctic poppies in the Arctic summertime – but summer in the Antarctic is grey with straggling lichens. If this earth be top-shaped as some of the geodesists think, it is a bloom that is stemmed with desolation.[4]

Written in 1941, Charles Fort's comments indicate a broader antipathy to the South in general, of which the Antarctic is merely its most extreme manifestation. But the reasons behind such an outlook are not hard to find, for whilst the Antarctic has the unspoilt beauty of a pristine wilderness, such beauty is more than outweighed by the sheer hardship of its environment: apart from being the highest continent, as well as the driest, it is also the coldest and the windiest. Indeed, if it is a place of mythology and romanticism, it is also one of superlatives and brutal statistics: it covers one tenth of the earth's land surface and is bigger than Europe and the United States combined; it contains 90 per cent of the planet's ice, which is at its deepest more than 15,000 feet thick; for much of the year it is in perpetual darkness or daylight; and, if this were not enough, aside from the endless ice fields it is also a home to both volcanoes and the towering Transantarctic mountain chain.[5]

These facts are impressive, certainly, but the single feature of Antarctica which resonates, above all else, in the popular imagination, is its emptiness. For as we shall see, perhaps the most striking difference between the poles, and the one which is most commonly overlooked when they are habitually elided into a single polar entity, is the fact that unlike the Arctic region, which has more than four million inhabitants, the Antarctic has no indigenous population; it is a place with no human history, beyond that imported from elsewhere. It has been argued that, due to the fact that direction is suspended at the poles, the points of the compass momentarily rendered meaningless, these two locations are 'places outside place.'[6] But if it is true that the terrestrial poles are, in this sense, placeless, then the Antarctic may also be said to lie largely outside human history, a region which exists not only outside of place but also outside of time. 'One of the very strongest imaginative themes' writes Francis Spufford, to result from 'the different phases of the twentieth-century encounter with Antarctica' is 'the sense of the southern continent as a repository of lost time.'[7] As Spufford explains, one of Antarctica's most disorientating characteristics is that it appears to be subject to two quite different scales of time, with little middle ground to differentiate them: on the one hand, the aeons of geological time through which the continent has continued oblivious to human existence, and on the other, the recent, and by comparison, negligible, scale of human history to set against it. By this way of thinking, of course, the human history of Antarctica, only begins to come into its own at the end of the nineteenth century, while in imaginative terms the continent 'is a product of the twentieth-century, contemporary with jazz, or the internal combustion engine, or [...] the Freudian unconscious. Twentieth-century science has defined it; twentieth-century cultural preoccupations have played out in the perception of it; twentieth-century social changes have worked through in the ways that human presence in it has been manifested.'[8]

Yet if the physical history of human interaction with the Antarctic is a relatively recent one, the role that the region has played in the human imagination has been much more prolonged. Precisely because the continent has been seen historically as an empty space, so it has been, like a blank sheet of paper, repeatedly written across by those wishing to outline their utopian dreams, nightmarish visions, or fantastical theories. In this sense, as we shall see, the history of polar exploration may be considered as little more than a footnote to the history of polar fantasy, the discoveries of Cook, Scott and Byrd continually replayed and refashioned by writers such as Coleridge, Poe and Lovecraft. In fact, so enduring has this imaginative impulse proven, that despite the surge in scientific evidence to result from modern polar exploration, it has done little to stem or even interrupt the flow of such fantastic visions. And even today, a century after the discovery of the South Pole, the polar refuge that the Antarctic has become remains home not only to its multinational scientific community but also to residual currents of more esoteric and outlandish thought.

## Arctic and Antarctic

In his brief introductory guide to Antarctica, the author, Klaus Dodds, inserts a short section entitled 'The Antarctic is *not* the Arctic', in order to remind those who might think otherwise that the two polar regions are distinct from one another, rather than forming two outposts of the same (cold and white) polar landmass. That such a reminder should prove necessary is at least in part a consequence of the fact that in the UK there is a tendency to study 'cold places' comparatively. In the 1920s, for example, the creation of the Scott Polar Research Institute at the University of Cambridge led to precisely this methodology, one which, as Dodds points out, would be likely to arouse scepticism, if not outright hostility, in those parts of the world, such as Canada, where the study of the populated Arctic regions are unlikely ever to be merged with an uninhabited southern continent.[9]

That the South Pole should have assumed such a position may also result from the fact that both etymologically and geographically, the region has been defined historically through its relationship to the North. Thus the word, 'Antarctic' owes its origins to the Ancient Greek word for the North Pole, *Arktos* (the bear), its opposite being termed simply as the 'Anti-Arctic', *Antarktikos*. In the imagination, then, the Antarctic becomes a southern outpost of the Arctic, rather than a region in its own right, a continent whose characteristics have come to be defined by those found at the other end of the earth. 'All the ways of thinking about Antarctica', writes Peter Davidson, 'are taken from ideas of the far north, raising the question that there may be places – mountain ranges as well as the South Pole – that are thought of as honorary norths.'[10] According to Davidson, this process, by which the regions of the polar south were subsumed by the north as 'honorary' territories, reached its apotheosis in the nineteenth century, as a part of the wider colonial expansion of the European powers, and resulted in not just Antarctica, but the Himalayas and, indeed, 'everywhere above the snowline', becoming thought of as, by extension, "norths."[11] This northern land grab came at the expense of a region that had historically been viewed as the negative counterpart to the more positively endowed north. The medieval analogy which equated the earth with that of the human body, placed the head at the north, leaving the far south in a highly unfortunate position. While in the late nineteenth century, against the backdrop of the appropriation of the south by the colonial north, Madame Blavatsky was to express a similar sentiment: 'The two poles are the right and left ends of our globe – the right being the North Pole – or the head and feet of the earth. Every beneficent (astral and cosmic) action comes from the North; every lethal influence from the South Pole.'[12] Historically, then, the South appears to have been characterised in two ways, either as an indistinct proxy of the North, or as the polar negative, defined only in opposition to its northern equivalent. The result of this is that the Antarctic finds itself in the curious position of being portrayed, often simultaneously, as having both purely negative characteristics and having no distinct characteristics at all. 'It is always the Arctic', writes Joscelyn Godwin, 'that is imagined as the location of the endless springtime and the cradle of noble races. The Antarctic, on the other hand, is negative: it evokes tales of gloom and destruction, and is populated by primordial horrors [...] If the Arctic Ocean is still imaginable as open to the world within, from which the Aurora Borealis streams in all its wonder and beauty, any hole at the South Pole is firmly shut with a lid of ice three miles thick.'[13]

It should be remembered, however, that such a relentlessly bad press betrays a certain northern chauvinism, with such perceptions originating in mythologies and histories penned for the large part in the European north. Behind such mythological representations, the Antarctic and the Arctic remain fundamentally different kinds of places. The former is a vast continental landmass covered by ice, and surrounded by ocean, while the latter is itself an ocean, covered by ice, and surrounded by land. While much of the Antarctic is several kilometres above sea level, the Arctic sits on an ocean basin and is therefore much warmer. While the north is relatively close to major centres of population and has its own indigenous population, the south is much more distant from its surrounding populations and was unknown to humans until a couple of centuries ago. Economically and politically also, these two regions remain distinct: the north is heavily exploited for resource development; the south, thus far, is not. And finally, while the north remains the subject of competing territorial claims, the Antarctic is owned by nobody, and the international community does not recognise the seven claimant states (Argentina, Australia, Chile, France, New Zealand, Norway, and the UK).[14] In short, we have two wholly distinct polar regions whose differences have often been obscured by myth and speculation generated almost entirely in the North, the majority of which pre-dates the discovery of the Antarctic by at least several centuries. Surprising as it may seem, however, some of the most startling of these myths are of a much more recent origin.

## Antarctic Mythology

'There is no clear definition possible of what the myth of Antarctica is', writes Joscelyn Godwin, 'but the continent is as mythopoeic as any place on earth.'[15] The myths that Godwin is describing here, however, are not principally those of the ancient world but rather those which have originated in the twentieth century, and which have by now come to assume a reassuringly familiar feel: 'extra-terrestrial visitations, secret technology, the eternal war of good and evil, and the coming New Age.'[16] I shall be examining these myths in greater detail later in this chapter, but perhaps one should not be wholly surprised by such beliefs, when one considers that the Antarctic has been generating similarly outlandish ideas for more than two thousand years.

The notion that some kind of land must exist at the bottom of the world has long been suspected, if only for the reason, as the Greeks believed, that such a continent was necessary to provide a counterweight to the lands of the north, and to stop the globe toppling off its axis. Once such a supposition was in place, it was then possible for an assortment of poets, philosophers and dreamers to fill in the blanks and to provide us with the details of who might inhabit such a place. All roads here lead us back to Aristotle, who is generally cited as the origin for the first description of the polar regions.[17] In his *Meteorology* (ca. 330 BC), Aristotle speculates that the earth is a sphere divided into northern and southern zones which mirror each other. Both hemispheres are comprised of habitable temperate belts bounded by a fiery band at the equator and two uninhabited frozen wastes at the poles – *Arktikos* to the north and *Antarktikos* to the south.[18] Aristotle claims that this unknown southern continent may be capable of sustaining life but (unlike many of his successors) he never speculates upon an Antarctic civilisation. The Stoic Strabo (ca. 64–18 AD) is more forthcoming, however, arguing that the south must be inhabited by creatures precisely the opposite of those to be found in the north. Therefore, just as the sun rises in the south and sets in the north, so must the people of the south plant their footsteps in exactly the opposite direction to their counterparts in the north, a theory of opposing worlds which resulted in geographers naming this southern region the 'Antipodes,' 'with the feet opposite,' or 'Antichthon' meaning 'counterworld.'[19]

As Eric G Wilson notes in his book *The Spiritual History of Ice: Romanticism, Science and the Imagination*, this classical dichotomy between north and south, in which the latter is viewed simply as an inversion of the former, has had profound consequences for our understanding of the south, which persisted at least until Cook finally crossed the Antarctic Circle in the eighteenth century. For in contrasting the unknown south with the temperate world of the *oikoumene*, or known world, the southern hemisphere inevitably came to be viewed as 'the dark other, the alien planet – the antihuman, the monstrous.'[20] Geographers familiar with moderate tracts of the northern polar regions, having received reports from explorers such as Pytheas (ca. 300 BC) on the Arctic Ice, would understandably use such factual accounts, however incomplete, as the basis for their speculations concerning those regions south of the equator of which little was known. As a result, these early geographical projections of the south reflected the fears, anxieties and prejudices of their northern creators, whose maps were shaped accordingly and which, concludes Wilson, is likely to explain why Antarctic exploration was to fall so far behind that being undertaken in the north. Thus, by the fifteenth century, when European geographers were first beginning to establish an accurate outline of the Arctic Circle, 'the bottom of the world remained a blank expanse or a precinct of freaks.'[21]

According to the OED, the first known English usage of the adjective 'Antarctic' occurs in Geoffrey Chaucer's *Treatise on the Astrolabe* (c. 1391).[22] By the time of the medieval and early Renaissance maps, however, which were the first to incorporate this unknown region, the newly termed 'Antarctic' was still just that, a term, a hypothetical landmass whose contours were wholly dependent upon the imagination of the mapmaker. In the majority of such maps, the Antarctic is indeed monstrous – monstrously overblown, a continent which having so clearly filled the imagination of the mapmakers, comes to fill a vast portion of their maps too, expanding to fill much of the southern hemisphere and subsuming within it those areas occupied on current maps by both Australia and the Antarctic.[23] In fact, while both the northern and southern extremities were later to become associated most powerfully with precise points on such maps – the poles – to medieval geographers it was the wider landmasses within which they were situated that were of greater interest. The term 'Pole' (Greek *polos*, axis or sky; Latin *polus*), was originally an astronomical term applied to the entire axis of the celestial sphere, which only later became identified with the two fixed points around which the stars seemed to revolve. It was not until the sixteenth century that this usage evolved to signify the point at which the axis came into contact with the surface of the earth, and the term was later extended to include each of the two opposite points on the surface of a magnet, which aligns itself north–south.[24]

Of all the numerous visions which have been imagined

by poets and philosophers, novelists and filmmakers to represent the mysterious polar south, perhaps none have been as colourful or exotic as those produced by the mapmakers and geographers of the medieval age. This was an era of monsters, giants and demons, and nowhere are these figures more populous than in the largest known surviving such map, the Hereford *Mappa Mundi* attributed to Richard of Holdingham, created in c. 1285 and still on display today in Hereford Cathedral:

> The strip bordering the southernmost arc of the map is replete with no less than eleven Antarctic monsters. Among these are the Blemyae, with eyes and mouths on their breasts; the Himantopodes, who crawl on the ground with four legs; the Sciopods, a one-legged species notable for holding their single foot above their heads as an umbrella; and the Philli, who test the chastity of their wives by exposing babies to serpents (the 'legitimate' infants are left unbitten while the 'bastards' are instantly killed). These species are part of a group of fourteen monstrous peoples living along the South Pole, which includes, in addition to those mentioned, men with the heads of dogs, a horde which consumes serpents, and a species that suffers from such a small mouth that it must suck food through a reed.[25]

The medieval tradition of peopling the unknown regions of the south with fantastical creatures culminates in the *Travels* (ca. 1370) of Sir John Mandeville, in which he reiterates the classical belief that the south is an inversion of the polar north. Mandeville's southern continent contains the necessary complement of 'giants, horrible and foul'; 'men of figure without heads'; 'dwarfs with no mouths'; 'folk whose ears hang down to their knees'; beings that 'are both men and women.'[26] But within this medieval freak show of disjointed nature, he contrasts the horrors on display with a world of wonders too, creating a European fantasy of the polar south that is, unlike so many of the classical and medieval depictions of the southern hemisphere, not simply a nightmarish vision but one which contains both positive and negative aspects. For just as the polar south has historically been assigned the role of the world's (or rather Europe's) unconscious, acting as a repository for many of its deepest fears and unspoken anxieties, so too has it been the source of more benign speculations. Unsurprisingly, perhaps, this region has not acquired the level of utopian longing directed towards the more favoured climes of the South Pacific, but neither has it been viewed solely as the desolate wilderness that, in reality, it is. In fact, some classical geographers have chosen to identify the south not with hell but with paradise, a positive interpretation that reveals the dichotomy between these two opposing traditions of polar thought, which have tended to be attracted to (or repelled by) their corresponding poles – north, positive; south, negative. In those instances, admittedly rare, in which this polarity has been reversed, the south has come to be seen as a sanctuary, free from the failings of human society in the north, a view which has outlived the classical and medieval imagery depicted above, resurfacing sporadically until the eighteenth century when geographers once again looked southward in search of utopia.

## The Aristocrats of the South

Even now the Antarctic is to the rest of the earth as the Abode of the Gods was to the ancient Chaldees, a precipitous and mammoth land lying far beyond the seas which encircled man's habitation, and nothing is more striking about the exploration of the Southern polar regions than its absence, for when King Alfred reigned in England the Vikings were navigating the ice-fields of the North; yet when Wellington fought the battle of Waterloo there was still an undiscovered continent in the South.[27]

When Apsley Cherry-Garrard wrote these lines in *The Worst Journey in the World* (1922), perhaps the greatest of all the many narratives of polar exploration, he was expressing a sentiment that had remained largely undiminished since the voyages of Cook 150 years earlier. 'Cook, Ross and Scott,' proclaims Cherry-Garrard, 'these are the aristocrats of the South.'[28] Cherry-Garrard was himself a member of Scott's *Terra Nova* Expedition of 1910–13, of which his book is an account, and as such he writes from within the context of the so-called Heroic Age of polar exploration (1898–1916), the period which culminated in the successful discovery of the South Pole, a period forever associated in the public imagination with the names of Scott and Amundsen, Shackleton and Mawson. In fact, so heroic has our recollection of this age become, so inextricably linked with national identity and colonial ambition, and imbued with such emotional resonance, that these few years of Antarctic exploration have almost entirely eclipsed the accomplishments of both their forebears and their successors, freezing their achievements (and failures) and distorting our perception of the admittedly short human history of the Antarctic.[29] For in reality, the history of polar exploration in the south spans a far greater period, of which the achievements of the Heroic Age were but a brief part. And just as this is a period which may best be understood through the contrast between the pinnacle of polar discovery on the one hand, and the less distinct hinterland which surrounds it on the other; so too can polar history itself and the manner in which it is recounted also be viewed in contrasting ways, the objective exactitude of geographical fact offset by the less readily observable impact of our wider cultural and emotional response:

Polar history, as it is usually written, is technical history. It recounts a sequence of expeditions. [...] The different explorers form a chain of discovery. They map the fringes of the world, learn the proper techniques of ice-navigation and sledge-travel. Their achievement is measured easily by the distance they leave untravelled to the two poles: a sort of geographical determinism informs this history, causing judgements of failure and success to spring from, not hindsight, but an eerily perfect rationality. [...] But there is a second kind of polar history, largely uncharted; an intangible history of assumptions, responses to landscape, cultural fascinations, aesthetic attraction to the cold regions.[30]

Of course, amidst the precision of polar science, it is easy to overlook the fact that while the terrestrial poles are indeed precise points on the globe marking the axis of the earth's rotation, and therefore possess a certain concrete reality, so too are they both highly abstract and undetectable by the human senses alone (unlike their celestial counterparts which are, at least, visible to the naked eye.) This being the case, might one not question the motivation behind the search for the poles? As the history of polar exploration makes abundantly clear, those willing to risk their lives in search of the poles were nothing if not highly motivated. But beyond the need to test oneself against the harshest of environments; to establish the truth of scientific hypotheses; to map the unknown corners of the globe; such motivation is, as always, inseparable from its wider historical context, in this case the competing claims of territorial expansion, global power and colonial ambition.[31]

On 17 January 1773, at 11.15 am, the *Resolution* crossed the Antarctic Circle, 'the first and only Ship that ever cross'd that line.'[32] Faced with a seemingly impenetrable wall of ice, however, Cook and his crew were forced to turn back. On 20 December 1773, his ships once again crossed the circle, this time coming within some seventy nautical miles of the Antarctic coastline before once more being forced back by the ice. In January of the following year, 1774, he made one further foray into the circle, this time reaching the farthest point south achieved in the eighteenth century. Still, however, he was unable to sight land. In his report, *A Voyage towards the South Pole*, published in 1777, Cook defended his decision to turn back, stating his belief that the ice must extend all the way to the Pole:

> I will not say it was impossible anywhere to get in among this Ice, but I will assert that the bare attempting of it would be a very dangerous enterprise and what I believe no man in my situation would have thought of. I whose ambition leads me not only farther than any other man has been before me, but as far as I think it possible for man to go, was not sorry at meeting with this interruption, as it in some measure relieved us from the dangers and hardships, inseparable with the Navigation of the Southern Polar regions.[33]

'I can be bold to say', Cook was to conclude, 'that no man will ever venture farther than I have done and that the lands which may lie to the South will never be explored.'[34] Having failed to reach the pole, Cook claimed that it was not possible to do so, and in addition, perhaps as a disincentive to those who might be tempted to try, he was also to suggest that the South Pole was not even worth discovering. Far from being the paradise that many had wished for, it was simply a frozen wasteland whose discovery would bring little renown, and 'the world would not be benefited by it.'[35] In the final phase of his second voyage in 1775, Cook did have the consolation of discovering the island of South Georgia which he promptly claimed for the Crown, naming it after King George III. But it was seemingly little more than a rocky outcrop of no conceivable future purpose, and Cook returned to England convinced that no one would be back.

Cook had been despatched across the globe in search of *terra australis*, the 'Great South Land', a continent which it was hoped would rival the Americas for its wealth. Having scoured the oceans in vain, however, he had disproved its existence, although after penetrating the polar ice he had come close to discovering the land which he believed existed further to the south. Although he had fulfilled his commission from the Admiralty, Cook remained sceptical of the value of what was to be found in the far south. The results of his voyages, in which he had twice circumnavigated the South Pole, had been predominantly negative, and had only confirmed the absence of the temperate lands he had hoped to discover. The distinctive shapes of the icebergs he encountered led him to believe that they had formed at the edge of a great landmass close at hand, yet the discoveries of South Georgia and the South Sandwich Islands offered an underwhelming glimpse of the probable nature of such a continent: an uninhabitable polar wasteland.[36] Little did Cook realise that the very lands which he had dismissed as worthless, would in fact become the source of great wealth; and rather than being their first and last visitor, as he imagined, his voyages would in fact act as a catalyst for a further two centuries of polar exploration. Indeed, within only decades of Cook's landfall on South Georgia, the first whaling ships had arrived on the islands in search of the bountiful supply of fur seals, and such was the demand for their furs and oil that the seal population was soon hunted near to extinction. But just as Cook was unable to foresee the economic potential of the far south, so too he was unable to predict the impact his travels would have on the public imagination at home; and while the accounts of his Tahitian experiences were, as we have seen, hugely popular with his English audience, so his polar adventures were to find their own similarly enthusiastic supporters. While South Georgia could hardly hope to compete with the islands of the South Seas in supplying the romantic imagery that the public craved, stories of stormy oceans afloat with massive icebergs provided their own particular appeal to set against the more exotic imagery of Tahiti, and polar exploration soon came to command its own place within the English imagination. Indeed, the contrast between Cook's journeys from the temperate paradise of Polynesia, on the one hand, with the unforgiving cold of the polar regions, on the other, 'delivered a thrill comparable to the idea of a blizzard in July.'[37] For just as the more rugged, and hitherto neglected, landscapes of rural Britain were beginning to be viewed in a new light by the poets and artists who sought to capture their stark beauty, so the idea of a desolate southern continent provoked similar emotions in the readership of Cook's journals. Of particular fascination was the inversion of the seasons between the northern and southern hemispheres, through which the cold of the polar winter could be pleasantly contrasted with the warmth of the English summer. This inversion was reinforced by a climatic imbalance which meant that in the southern half of the world the tropics extended further to the south than did their corresponding zone to the north, the transition from temperate weather to the sub-polar cold taking place much more abruptly in southern latitudes. Hence, the frozen interior of South Georgia, at 54 degrees south could be happily contrasted with its direct counterpart at 54 degrees north, 'amidst the comfortable hotels of Harrogate, in the West Riding of Yorkshire, where glaciers were scarce.'[38] Imagination alone, however, was not enough to dictate the course of future Antarctic exploration; it was instead economic imperatives that guided polar exploration throughout the nineteenth century. Sightings of land were recorded by whaling vessels in the Antarctic as early as the 1820s but it was the British naval expedition of 1839–43, led by James Clark Ross and the ships *Erebus* and *Terror* which made the first Antarctic landfall. But as seal numbers were swiftly depleted following the first boom in the early years of the century, so attention switched again towards the north, and the South Pole was largely overlooked for the next fifty years. By the close of the century, however, as political and economic realities once again began to favour the south, the Antarctic began that brief period of its human history through which it has since come to be defined.

'At the opening of the twentieth century', Spufford

records, 'tiny gangs of human beings, all male, arrived on
the margins of an unmapped space about the size of the
continental United States, built themselves wooden cabins
to live in, and set off inwards into the unknown. Ordinary-
sized people when they were at home, they expanded,
in their own conceptions of themselves, to match the
giant scale of the landscape.'[39] These extraordinary men
(the first female to arrive was the US explorer, Jackie
Ronne, in 1941) came from across the globe and as well
as Scott and Shackleton, included the Anglo-Australian
Douglas Mawson, Norwegian Roald Amundsen, German
Wilhelm Filchner, and the Japanese, Nobu Shirase. Often
poorly equipped, and unprepared for the hostility of the
environment they were about to encounter, these men set
their sights upon an invisible point on the map which, as it
turned out, happened to be located in the midst of an ice
plateau some 10,000 feet high, ringed by mountains, and
subject to the harshest climatic conditions on the planet.
In fact, so inaccessible was the place they were attempting
to reach that the pull that the South Pole was able to exert
over these men can only be understood in terms of that fatal
attraction which has long since lured men south: 'I think it
came to me during my first voyage', wrote Shackleton, 'I
felt strangely drawn towards the mysterious south. [...] It
was a simple dream. I seemed to vow to myself that some
day I would go to the region of ice and snow and go on and
on till I came to one of the poles of the earth, the end of the
axis upon which this great ball turns.'[40]

The story of polar exploration in the Heroic Age has long
since crossed over from the realm of history into that of
myth, a process in which only the dates of the expeditions
themselves remain unaltered: Scott's *Discovery* expedition,
1901–4; Shackleton in *Nimrod*, 1907–9; Scott in *Terra Nova*,
1910–13; Shackleton in *Endurance*, 1914–16.[41] Scott's heroic
failure, in particular, has by now come to resemble many
of the characteristics of the Antarctic itself, appearing to
be frozen in time and to have been submerged beneath the

ever expanding weight of history that has formed above it. In his journal entry for 18 January 1912, the day following that fateful moment at which he and his companions finally reached the South Pole only to find a Norwegian flag marking the spot, (Amundsen having arrived some 33 days previously) Scott writes poignantly, 'Well, we have turned our back now on the goal of our ambition and must face our 800 miles of solid dragging – and good-bye to most of the day-dreams!'[42] And there is indeed something dreamlike, or rather nightmarish, surrounding both Scott's and the other tales of polar exploration from this period, a sense of madness or horror barely contained within the precise and matter-of-fact accounts in which they are recorded. The facts of Scott's expedition have since been endlessly reworked, the subject of numerous books, films, and historical revisions, all of which attempt to claim him for a new historical context, while his own Edwardian England recedes further into the past.

The Heroic Age of polar exploration came to an abrupt end with the outbreak of the First World War, the final entry belonging to Shackleton, who was to embark on the Imperial Trans-Antarctica Expedition in 1914 just as war in Europe was being declared. Shackleton's attempt to lead his men across the Antarctic continent from the Weddell Sea to the Ross Sea ended after his ship, the aptly-named *Endurance*, became trapped by the polar ice, and from this point on, the expedition became famous as a great escape. Having been stranded on the ice along with his 28-man crew, after the *Endurance* was crushed by the ice in the winter of 1915, Shackleton and five of his men eventually navigated their way over 800 nautical miles in an open boat to the Norwegian whaling community on South Georgia, reaching safety in 1917 before the remainder of their party were rescued without loss of life. No further such journeys were to be attempted until the 1950s, on land at least; but this interlude did see the introduction of aircraft to the Antarctic, culminating in November 1929 with Admiral Richard Byrd becoming the first man to fly over the Pole:

'There was nothing new to mark that scene', he was to remark, 'only a white desolation and solitude disturbed by the sound of our engines.'[43]

In travelling to the Pole and back, Byrd, who had performed the same feat over the North Pole in 1926, managed to complete the route that had taken Amundsen an entire season to cover, in only two days, radically enlarging the scale through which the Antarctic would in future be apprehended.[44] Having established the famous base, Little America, during the Antarctic expedition of 1928–30, Byrd returned repeatedly, leading a second expedition there in 1933–35, and a third in 1939–40. But as the Second World War broke out, Antarctica became the subject of less welcome intervention from the North, and in 1939 a German expedition to the Weddell Sea claimed a swathe of the interior by employing the time-saving technique of overflying the desired territory while sprinkling thousands of little metal swastikas onto the surface below.[45] Returning once again in 1946–7, Byrd this time mapped more than a million square miles of the continent as well as flying over the South Pole for a second time. 'I'd like to see that land beyond the Pole', he said in 1947, 'that area beyond the Pole is the Great Unknown.'[46] For despite his exhaustive polar explorations, Byrd, who made a final visit to the Pole in 1956, seemed unable to overcome the sense of awe that the continent was to inspire in him. Indeed it was precisely this ability to maintain such a sense of wonder, just at the moment that he and others were opening up the continent to scientific scrutiny, which has since led to Byrd being placed in some very curious company. For his seemingly innocuous remarks above have since been seized upon by advocates of a theory which has its roots in a medieval conception of the world, namely that the earth is hollow, with openings at the poles. Such a worldview has, remarkably, persisted throughout the twentieth century, and this despite the evidence of those such as Byrd himself who have visited the poles yet reported the existence of no such openings. But before turning to the bizarre and strangely prolonged history of this belief and its surprisingly numerous adherents, it may be wise here to contrast the tales of heroism and steadfast belief outlined above with the more sceptical tone of Henry David Thoreau, who, in response to the 'Polar Mania' that briefly gripped the West in the first half of the nineteenth century, not only questioned the ultimate value of such adventurism, but also hinted at the unexpected nature of where it all might lead:

> What was the meaning of that South-Sea Exploring Expedition, with all its parade and expense, but an indirect recognition of the fact that there are continents and seas in the moral world to which every man is an isthmus or an inlet, yet unexplored by him, but that it is easier to sail many thousands of miles through cold and storm and cannibals, in a government ship, with five hundred men and boys to assist one, than it is to explore the private sea, the Atlantic and Pacific Ocean of one's being alone [...] It is not worth the while to go round the world to count the cats in Zanzibar. Yet do this even till you can do better, and you may perhaps find some "Symmes Hole" by which to get at the inside at last.[47]

## Hollow Earth

The peculiar theory of the hollow earth appears to originate in the seventeenth century in the work of the Jesuit polymath, Athanasius Kircher (1602–1680). In his *Mundus Subterraneus*, or 'Treatise on the Subterranean World' (1665), Kircher speculates upon the nature of the poles, claiming that as the two previous centuries had seen the exploration of almost the entire globe, apart from the polar regions, it was unlikely that they would ever be explored, his arguments instead relying upon a combination of logic and analogy. For Kircher held an essentially animistic conception of the earth, reasoning that just as the human or animal body was

182

dependent upon the passage of nourishment, in addition to the recently discovered idea of the circulation of the blood, so too the planet itself was organised on a similar basis, requiring an interior passage through which such motion might take place.[48] Thus in order to keep the oceans circulating and to prevent them from becoming putrid, or like the polar seas, frozen, so the poles must be open at both ends: 'After [the seas] have been absorbed at the North Pole, they are cooked in the earth's interior by the subterranean fires which [...] permeate the earth's body and occasionally break out in volcanoes. The elements in sea–water are extracted by this process, to be used for the generation of metals. The undigested remains are then expelled at the nether end, the South Pole.'[49] Drawing upon medieval geography in support of his thesis, Kircher proclaimed the North Pole to be the site of a giant whirlpool through which the world's oceans were ceaselessly drawn; icy water entering at the North Pole is then filtered and warmed by fires deep within the earth before emerging at the South Pole. Kircher's ideas were later to be echoed by the theologian Thomas Burnet, in his *Sacred Theory of the Earth* (1681). But the first attempt to construct a 'scientific' theory of the hollow earth can be attributed to Sir Edmund Halley. In 1692, Halley published in the *Philosophical Transactions* of the Royal Society 'the hypothesis of an earth of three closed concentric hollow spheres with a hot spherical core at the centre.'[50] Halley was then able to use the movements of these hollow spheres to explain the observed variations in the earth's magnetic poles. By the eighteenth century such theories had begun to give way to fictional portrayals, and in the first of many such examples to employ hollow earth imagery, an anonymous French novella of 1721, *A Voyage from Pole to Pole by Way of the Centre of the Earth*, describes how a ship is blown to the North Pole by a storm, only to be sucked into a giant whirlpool before being discharged intact into the Antarctic Ocean.[51]

In the absence of any expedition through which these unlikely scenarios might be disproved, throughout the eighteenth century the poles remained the source of increasingly far-fetched accounts, often presented as the narratives of sailors who had survived extraordinary voyages. Such accounts had a wide readership, drawn, then as now, to thrilling tales of exotic adventures, but few of these took what they read to be true, and of those that did fewer still were willing to proclaim the fact. One such exception was a man named John Cleves Symmes (1780–1829). Born in New Jersey, Symmes enlisted in the US army and reached the rank of Captain. On being discharged in 1816 he became a supplier to the troops and a trader in St. Louis. There is little in this brief biographical outline to indicate what was to happen next.[52] For without warning, on 10 April 1818, Symmes released a circular to every learned society in the US and Europe, and to an assortment of distinguished individuals. Addressed 'To all the World', it states:

> I declare the earth is hollow and habitable within; containing a number of solid concentric spheres, one within the other, and that it is open at the poles twelve or sixteen degrees. I pledge my life in support of this truth, and am ready to explore the hollow, if the world will support and aid me in the undertaking.[53]

Symmes has been described as being 'of middle stature, and tolerably proportioned; with scarcely any thing in his exterior to characterise the secret operations of his mind, except an abstraction, which, from attentive inspection, is found seated on a slightly contracted brow; and the glances of a bright blue eye, that often seems fixed on something beyond immediate surrounding objects.'[54] Symmes' distracted air was understandable given that despite his persistent attempts to direct the world's attention to the true nature of the planet they inhabited, no one seemed at all interested in what he had to say, while those who did take notice were to dismiss his beliefs as those of a madman. In the America of the 1820s and 1830s, 'Symmes' hole!' was to become a common jeer directed towards anything fake or outlandish, but despite the wholly predictable response of the majority of the public to his astonishing ideas, Symmes gradually began to acquire a small and surprisingly influential following.[55] Symmes' theory is difficult to summarise, not least because it tends to change continually in order to incorporate any new piece of 'evidence' which might emerge. His principal claim, however, was that the earth was a hollow shell, pierced by vast circular holes at each pole: 4000 miles across at the North, 6000 at the South. Such were the scale of these holes that to sail around the outer surface of the inner rim into the concave ocean within was a journey of some 1500 miles, a distance so large that it effectively concealed the shallow change of direction inwards, thus explaining why sailors had hitherto failed to notice its existence.[56]

While Halley had proposed the idea of a hollow earth, he failed to mention the existence of large holes at the poles; and although Kircher had taken from medieval geography the location of a great vortex at each of the poles, these hardly corresponded to the vast openings that Symmes envisaged. So the question which remains is who could possibly be the source of Symmes' outrageous claims? The Swiss mathematician, Leonhard Euler, (1707-1783) and the Scottish physicist, Sir John Leslie, (1706-1832) have both since been identified as possible candidates, but the fact remains that the most likely source of Symmes' theories was his own highly fertile imagination.[57] Yet despite his theory being essentially home-grown, Symmes and his supporters corralled an impressive array of evidence in support of the existence of these polar openings, much of which was drawn (retrospectively, and without the support of the individuals themselves) from the first-hand accounts of earlier polar voyages. In this way, Symmes was able to 'explain' the migratory habits of birds and animals which move northward at the onset of winter, only to reappear in the spring, having, as he suggests, wintered within the earth's warm interior. He also insisted that the ring of polar ice which had hitherto proved impassable to Antarctic voyages, was not the rim of an impenetrable ice-bound continent, as Cook had suspected, but merely a protective zone of polar ice which once traversed gave way to a warmer, ice-free polar sea within. In this part of his theory, he was to draw on the anecdotal support of many polar explorers who had encountered ice-free conditions at the poles, amongst them the British explorer, James Weddell on his third Antarctic Voyage of 1822–24.[58]

In 1819 Symmes moved to Newport, Kentucky and soon after he began to petition Congress to launch an expedition which he proposed to undertake to the Arctic in order to confirm the existence of the polar opening. His application to the US Senate in 1822 received a startling 25 votes in support, and always a man willing to keep his options open, he was later granted permission by the Russian government to set off on a proposed expedition from Siberia. He was never to embark on such an expedition, however, for in addition to publishing an endless series of papers promoting his theories, Symmes also conducted a punishing series of lecture tours across the United States, the strain of which led to ill health. He died in Cincinnati, aged 49, on 29 May 1829 and was buried beneath a monument depicting a hollow globe, erected by his son Americus. His theories were to survive him, however, and it was an enthusiasm for Symmes' ideas which was largely responsible for the US Exploring Expedition of 1838–1840, led by Charles Wilkes, which first determined the dimensions of the Antarctic continent.[59]

'In scope and influence', writes Francis Spufford, 'Symmesianism was an almost entirely American madness.'[60] Yet whilst the influence of Symmes' ideas has since remained largely confined within the borders of the United States, his ideas have proved both remarkably resilient and largely impervious to the scientific revelations of polar exploration. Perhaps the field in which the influence of Symmes' theories has proved most enduring, however, is that of literature, and the genre of utopian fiction in particular. For it is

here, in a realm in which the truth of Symmes' ideas is of
little consequence, that writers have been able to explore
and develop his ideas, with the result that long after both
poles have been discovered and their surrounding regions
exhaustively mapped and studied, hollow earth fictions
continue to appear. The original text in this tradition, and
one which has since been identified as the first American
utopian fiction, is a novel called *Symzonia: A Voyage of
Discovery*, which was first published in 1820 and attributed
to a Captain Adam Seaborn. In a manner which to some
extent replicates the divisions provoked by Symmes' theories
themselves, the identity of the author of this work has itself
been disputed, with some critics claiming that Seaborn
is Symmes himself, and others ridiculing this idea.[61] In
either case, *Symzonia* is certainly a novel which perfectly
encapsulates Symmes' theories, albeit one in which the praise
lavished upon Symmes himself may often read as parody:
'That profound philosopher, John Cleves Symmes', invokes
Seaborn; while the community which Seaborn and his
crew discover in the earth's interior is immediately named
*Symzonia*, 'out of gratitude to Capt. Symmes for his sublime
theory.'[62] The novel may be read as a straightforward tale of
Symzonian wish-fulfilment, but it is rather more than that.
For *Symzonia* also established an enduring template for such
fictional polar narratives, in which the discovery of a strange
land is followed by a series of adventures, culminating in an
escape home to ridicule and disbelief.[63] It is in this manner,
then, that the novel describes Seaborn's journey south,
ostensibly on a sealing voyage, albeit in a specially reinforced
steamboat equipped with slanted paddlewheels able to churn
through ice. Finding the waters of the Southern Ocean to be
pleasantly temperate, Seaborn and his crew continue south
through the increasing heat before finally finding their way
through the polar chasm and into the interior of the earth.
Here they encounter a society strongly resembling that of a
nineteenth-century pastoral community in the US, although
it is one whose inhabitants, the Internals, are all albinos. As

we shall see later in this chapter, this particular aspect of *Symzonia*, with its implicit comment on the racial politics of the American South, was to prove highly influential on other representations of the Antarctic. In *Symzonia*, however, it is not only questions of race which are addressed but also economic concerns, for in this ideal society deep within the earth, taxation is light and individuals who accumulate more than they require voluntarily donate the excess to their neighbours, an arrangement which, as one critic notes, has yet to be fully replicated within contemporary American society.[64]

If *Symzonia* was to prove Symmes' literary testament, his most significant contribution to polar exploration was to come through the efforts of his most notable convert, Jeremiah Reynolds (1799–1858). Reynolds first met Symmes, twenty years his senior, in 1824 and so taken was he with his theories that he left his job to join him on his lecture tour. Neither gullible nor deferential, Reynolds was an entrepreneur and natural promoter who was to persuade Symmes to embark on a more ambitious series of lectures across the US. Alert to the possibility of using Symmes' growing influence to further his own plans to lead a national polar expedition, Reynolds soon began to downplay the more outlandish elements of Symmes' theories, including that of Symmes Holes, instead placing his own emphasis upon the national prestige to be gained through polar discovery. This divergence eventually resulted in Symmes and Reynolds parting company, but by 1826 Reynolds' polar ambitions were attracting the attention of Congress and the wider scientific community, and by expressing his ambitions through the rhetoric of patriotism and national pride, he was able to secure their support. The Antarctic had first been sighted only a few years before in 1820, with America attributing the honour, in defiance of the competing claims of Britain and Russia, to the sealer Nathanial B Palmer, the 21-year-old commander of the sloop, *Hero*.[65] But Reynolds' focus had been drawn to the continent as a possible new source for the four million barrels of whale oil produced annually by New England. Eventually, after prolonged political wrangling, Reynolds finally set sail in October 1829 as a member of an expedition bound for the South. Unfortunately for him and his crew, however, this 1829 expedition proved an unmitigated disaster. After sailing southwards and sighting what they believed to be land, they found themselves faced with none of the more welcoming surroundings that Symmes (and Reynolds himself) had so tirelessly promoted; and instead of temperate, open seas, they found, like Cook before them, only impenetrable ice. They were forced to turn back, and on the return journey the crew mutinied, setting Reynolds ashore in Chile, and turning to piracy as a more profitable alternative. Reynolds, as seemingly imperturbable as ever, went on to explore the country over the next three years before continuing his travels and later establishing his reputation as a writer through an account of his experiences.

It was largely through the efforts of Symmes and Reynolds, that the idea of the hollow earth first became inextricably linked with the then equally mysterious nature of the polar regions. Because of the fact that thus far nobody had actually been to the poles – or inside them – Symmes and his followers were able to give their imaginations free rein, filling the blank space they had at their disposal with their visions of warm seas and alien races. As we have seen, they were by no means the first to speculate upon what the polar explorers of the future might find. But in tandem with the tentative advance of polar exploration in the early years of the nineteenth century, it was speculations such as these, dominated by representations of Antarctica, then the least known and most inaccessible place on earth, which were soon to coalesce into a new literary genre, the Polar Gothic.

## The Polar Gothic: Coleridge, Poe and Lovecraft

In her recent overview of the literature of the polar south, *Antarctica in Fiction: Imaginative Narratives of the Far South*

(2012), the author, Elizabeth Leane, surveys the entire history of what she describes variously as the Antarctic Gothic, the Far Southern Gothic and the Polar Gothic, exploring the myriad attempts to give substance to the 'nothingness' that is this continent's abiding feature:

> The speculations of Greek philosophers; the superstitions of medieval sailors; the fantastic voyages of the seventeenth and eighteenth centuries; the far southern utopias of the nineteenth century; the unlikely theories of John Cleves Symmes; the gothic and nautical romances of Edgar Allan Poe and James Fenimore Cooper – for anyone familiar with Antarctic literature, these traditions can be found lurking subtextually in the latest polar airport novel (and the occasional mainstream movie). What joins them all is the urge to fill in the blanks, to speculate.[66]

Regarded from a literary perspective, Antarctica has traditionally been judged as 'unwritable.' 'This Antarctica', Leane emphasises, 'is ground, not figure – it is nothingness, and nothingness cannot, by definition, be depicted.'[67] The depiction of Antarctica as a blank slate is itself by no means new; but if, as Leane suggests, the Antarctic is truly 'unwritable', then it is equally true, as her lengthy survey confirms, that it is a continent which has inspired an enormous number of literary representations. Nor does this number appear to be diminishing. Another critic has calculated that, since 2006 alone, more than 40 novels in English have been published with an Antarctic theme, with aliens being the most common subject: 'a mysterious relic of possibly alien origin'; 'aliens hiding in the ice or crashing into Antarctica'; 'leaving behind alien technology in Antarctica'; and 'Earth's governments allowing refugee aliens to have Antarctica.'[68] But despite a seemingly ubiquitous role, science fiction is only one genre amongst many to have chosen the Antarctic as a backdrop, and while the thriller predominates, there is also 'Antarctic category romance, Antarctic chick-lit, Antarctic cyberpunk – even an Antarctic sitcom', alongside hundreds of novels and short stories, poems, plays and films. 'There is hardly a popular genre that cannot boast an Antarctic title', Leane concludes, 'The "cultural turn" in Antarctic studies has begun.'[69]

Just as our perception of the Antarctic is such that it is often merged with its northern counterpart within an indivisible polar world, so too the literary productions inspired by the polar south are often seen merely as a footnote to the larger body of work associated with the north.[70] In this way, the literature of the Antarctic can risk losing that which is distinctive to it, and which most strongly identifies it as a region in its own right. As the lesser known and less inhabited region, the Antarctic remains most powerfully identified as a wilderness, a place defined through its distance from human civilisation; and it is precisely this remoteness from any trace of the human that has resulted in it being characterised as, above all, a gothic setting. For in addition to its sublime landscape, perhaps the most sublime of all landscapes, in as far as the icy grandeur it possesses is so utterly divorced from any human concern; so too its position, from a northern perspective at least, as literally an underworld, allows it to become a repository for our deepest unconscious fears and desires:

> The Western worldview in which the Arctic rests on the top of the planet and the Antarctic clings, spider-like, to its bottom brings an asymmetry to polar psychotopography. At least since Freud, parallels between mental and physical landscapes have frequently assumed a depth model of the psyche, with the darker, less accessible aspects of ourselves – the id, in Freud's terms – imagined as sitting somehow 'below the surface'. This means that the metaphorical southern journey is not simply a journey inwards but also downwards, a journey that penetrates the darkest, deepest regions of the unconscious.[71]

As we have seen, this identification of the Antarctic with the underworld of our darkest imaginings has a history which pre-dates Freud, finding support within polar mythology which has long since situated the monstrous and the infernal in the far south. But in the second half of the eighteenth century, as the Romantics took up the idea of the sublime and began to make the fictional experiments out of which the gothic would soon emerge, the Antarctic began to be viewed as a location which displayed all the necessary attributes required for this new genre. Not only had the far south become a gothic setting, but the journey south was itself to undergo a similar transformation, becoming as much an inward journey as an outward one, with fictional protagonists returning home, if at all, utterly transformed by their experiences. And as the narratives of early polar exploration began to filter back to Europe and the West, a new villain was to emerge, the pole itself. No longer merely the site for the exploration of the gothic imagination, the Antarctic had itself become a part of the story, a cruelly indifferent and immensely powerful adversary which the hero of the piece must face up to and overcome. In this light, then, the factual accounts of the polar explorers could themselves be seen to take on the nature of gothic melodrama, contributing to the urge for others to take up the challenge and explore these polar landscapes.[72]

## Coleridge and *The Rime of the Ancient Mariner* (1798)

> And now there came both mist and snow,
> And it grew wondrous cold:
> And ice, mast-high, came floating by,
> As green as emerald.
> And through the drifts the snowy clifts
> Did send a dismal sheen:
> Nor shapes of men nor beasts we ken –
> The ice was all between.

The ice was here, the ice was there,
The ice was all around:
It cracked and growled, and roared and howled,
Like noises in a swound![73]

First published in 1798 in *Lyrical Ballads* and revised in 1800, Coleridge's *The Rime of the Ancient Mariner* is one of the first literary attempts to depict Antarctica as a distinct location, rather than simply another manifestation of the unknown *terra australis*; as such it remains the foremost influence on subsequent representations of the polar south. This despite the fact that less than half of the poem's opening part actually takes place in the far south, and many of the poem's most famous scenes and most striking imagery are set elsewhere.[74] Coleridge read widely amongst the travel narratives of early polar voyages, most notably those describing the northern polar regions which then dominated such accounts. But having read Cook's narration of his own journey south, Coleridge became attracted by the geographical isolation of the southern ocean, transposing his reading on the Arctic to the polar south and fusing these accounts with those of Cook's to form an image of the region more realistic than the fantastical depictions of earlier tales. Establishing a pattern for future writers to follow, Coleridge's vision of Antarctica introduced many of the most enduring themes and images which were to be replayed over the following two centuries, from the whirlpool and the polar spirit, to the icebergs of the southern ocean and, most notably, the figure of the lone survivor cursed to repeat his tale.[75] What really distinguishes Coleridge's vision, however, from the fantasies which come both before and after, is its sense of both inaccessibility and isolation; the *Ancient Mariner* captures the prevailing characteristic of Antarctica, its absence. Gone are the lost civilisations and curious inhabitants which peopled the utopian tales of the South Seas, and in its place is an empty landscape of ice and snow, a monotonous whiteness that extends in every direction.[76]

Coleridge's poem displays all the motifs of the gothic, from the clash between man and an impersonal environment on the one hand, to a series of gruesome and supernatural occurrences on the other. But the poem is concerned as much with the inner realm as that of the outer, and these landscapes of ice and snow find their reflection in the mariner's own spiritual and psychological isolation. Even after he escapes homeward he remains trapped in a frozen hell of his own creation. In this sense, one may see how the Antarctic setting extends throughout the poem, an environment from which the mariner is unable to escape. Sent deep into the Antarctic Circle, the mariner is haunted by a nightmare of monstrous ice from which he cannot wake, a curse which he brings upon himself and his crew through one of the most famous errors of judgement in all literature. In killing the albatross, the mariner knowingly commits the crime for which he receives a hellish punishment: forced by the polar spirit to relate his tale, he is condemned to repeat eternally his mistake and its consequences. Coleridge's albatross has since been described as 'one of the most over-determined creatures in all of English literature', and its death at the hands of the mariner has been ascribed a seemingly endless series of allegorical meanings, from the violence of colonial expansion, to an assault on ecological purity.[77] In whatever manner one chooses to interpret these events, however, a similar punishment was not forthcoming for Cook and his crew when they committed the same crime twenty years earlier. For as Cook records in his *Journals*, however powerful the symbolism of the albatross, it was not sufficient to outweigh the pangs of hunger: 'The next day, having several hours calm, we put a boat in the water, and shot some albatrosses and peterels, which, at this time, were highly acceptable.'[78]

Coleridge's Antarctic is a region which the mariner is destined never to leave, an Antarctic of the mind which permeates the entire poem. For by setting his *Rime* in the remote South, Coleridge allows the journey to become a tale of psychic transformation, an archetypal sea journey from the populous north to the empty and unknown south, from consciousness to unconsciousness, and home again.[79] In this way, Coleridge was able to create a blueprint for his many literary imitators to follow, establishing the journey south as one which ventures into the depths of isolation and madness.

## Poe and *The Narrative of Arthur Gordon Pym* (1838)

In January 1837, as editor of the *Southern Literary Messenger* in Virginia, Edgar Allan Poe was to write an enthusiastic review of Jeremiah Reynolds' address to Congress in April the previous year, in which Reynolds had spoken for more than three hours outlining the reasons why Congress should underwrite his plans to embark on an expedition to the South Seas. Reynolds had been vociferously promoting his plans for more than a decade, arguing that such an expedition was vital for American national prestige, and Poe had become an ardent supporter of his position. Reynolds' petition proved successful and the American Exploring Expedition was authorised in 1836, although protracted delays meant that it was not until August 1838 that it finally set sail under the command of Charles Wilkes. It was, therefore, against a backdrop of mounting public excitement and widespread coverage in the newspapers that Poe was to release, in serial form, a novel capitalising on these events, a novel disguised as a factual account of an earlier journey undertaken in 1827–28, purporting to be the journal of one Arthur Gordon Pym of Nantucket. This was not the first instance of Poe producing a fictional account of a maritime voyage to the South. His first significant success as a writer, the short story 'MS Found in a Bottle' (1833), had itself portrayed such a voyage. Clearly alert not only to the ideas of Jeremiah Reynolds, but also to those of his one-time mentor, John Cleves Symmes, Poe's tale describes a ship, caught up in the current produced by a polar vortex, as it rushes headlong towards the South Pole. Here, having gone farther south than any of their predecessors, the crew are pleasantly surprised to find themselves, as Symmes forecast, in an ice-free environment. Quite what the narrator discovers when he reaches the pole, however, is destined to remain forever undisclosed; for it appears that the mystery of the southern pole can only finally be understood through death itself:

> As I imagined, the ship proves to be in a current – if that appellation can properly be given to a tide which, howling and shrieking by the white ice, thunders on to the southward with a velocity like the headlong dashing of a cataract. [...] It is evident that we are hurrying onwards to some exciting knowledge – some never-to-be-imparted secret, whose attainment is destruction. Perhaps this current leads us to the southern pole itself. It must be confessed that a supposition apparently so wild has every probability in its favour.[80]

Clearly intrigued by such imagery, Poe was to revisit this scenario some years later, this time at the North Pole, in his 'A Descent into the Maelström' (1841). Here, once again, his narrator experiences at first hand the truth of hollow earth ideas: 'Kircher and others imagine', he writes, 'that in the centre of the channel of the Maelström is an abyss penetrating the globe, and issuing in some very remote part.'[81] There is little evidence to support the view that Poe himself believed in such theories, but he was certainly aware of the currency they held with his readership, and it was in his only full-length novel, *The Narrative of Arthur Gordon Pym*, that he was to explore these ideas in detail.

'Writers of fictions about Antarctica', one commentator notes, 'seem anxious for their work to be mistaken for fact.'[82] Nowhere is this more true than in the case of Poe, who appears to have gone to extraordinary lengths to give his novel the trappings of verisimilitude. At the time at which he was writing, the first landfall had taken place on Antarctica but its interior was yet to be explored. Under pressure to complete his novel and to cash in while the public's enthusiasm for this subject was at its peak, Poe borrowed, plagiarised and stole from as many of the extant accounts of South Sea voyages as he could find in order to buttress his account. Cook was one source, as was Benjamin Morrell's *Narrative of Four Voyages* (1832), while Coleridge's *Ancient Mariner* and Defoe's *Robinson Crusoe* (1719) were both consulted. Reynolds was also to prove particularly useful, with both his *Voyage of the Potomac* (1835) and his address to Congress ransacked for convincing detail, the latter supplying almost the whole of chapter sixteen.[83] But it was *Symzonia* which was, above all others, to provide the unacknowledged basis for Pym's tale, this novel so clearly supplying the template for Poe's *Narrative* that one scholar was later to suggest that it might just as easily have been called *Pymzonia*.[84] Of course, the reason that Poe undertook such extensive 'research', drawing upon such a disparate array of sources, was that his *Narrative* was an attempt to convince his audience that it was his own creation, Arthur Gordon Pym, who was the first explorer to reach the South Pole. In short, Poe was perpetrating a hoax, an attempt to persuade his audience that what they were reading was not fiction presented as fact, but quite the opposite. Indeed, in the preface to *Pym*, Poe forestalls his reader's objections to the authenticity of his tale with the acknowledgement that his poor recollection of events may result in his version being mistaken for fiction.[85]

Like Coleridge's *Rime*, with which Poe's novel has much in common, the majority of *Pym* takes place outside of the Antarctic. But the ultimate destination of the book is always southwards, and it is here that the meaning of the novel, in as far as one can be clearly ascertained, is to be found. While Coleridge places his Antarctic scene within the opening section of the poem, the remainder dealing with its horrific aftermath, Poe's account is essentially a one-way journey, which begins, in conventional fashion, with Pym stowing away aboard a whaling ship, the *Grampus*. The story quickly casts off the familiar feel of the maritime tale, however, in favour of a series of nightmarish adventures, as a combination of mutiny, shipwreck and finally cannibalism see the crew gradually dispatched until only Pym, and his compatriot Dirk Peters, remain. In fact, it is not until relatively late in the story that Pym, having been rescued by the *Jane Guy*, finally sets 'sail for the southward, with the resolution of penetrating in that course as far as possible.' This final stage of his narrative is delayed still further by a lengthy factual account in which Poe adds Pym's voyage to those of his forebears, amongst them Cook, Kreutzenstern, Weddell, Morrell and Briscoe, in a history lesson spanning the period 1772 to 1832, and it is not until the reader has endured this unwieldy interlude that Pym finally penetrates the polar circle:

> We had now advanced to the southward more than eight degrees farther than any previous navigators, and the sea still lay perfectly open before us. We found too, that the variation uniformly decreased as we proceeded, and, what was still more surprising, that the temperature of the air, and latterly of the water, became milder. [...] So tempting an opportunity of solving the great problem in regard to an Antarctic continent had never yet been afforded to man [...] I must still be allowed to feel some degree of gratification at having been instrumental, however remotely, in opening to the eye of science one of the most intensely exciting secrets which has ever engrossed its attention.[86]

It is from this point onward that Poe's story, having begun as an account of maritime exploration before giving way to gothic horror, finally transforms itself into full-blown Symmesian fantasy. Having successfully navigated their way through the southern ocean, only to find themselves in an unexpectedly (or perhaps predictably) temperate climate, Poe and his companions finally reach the island of Tsalal, a land where everything and everyone is black and whose inhabitants, led by the treacherous chief Too-wit, bear a striking resemblance to the African-American slaves of the American South. Here further adventures ensue, before Pym and Peters, betrayed by the islanders and with their ship now destroyed, make their final escape south towards the Pole: 'We now found ourselves in the wide and desolate Antarctic Ocean, in a latitude exceeding eighty-four degrees in a frail canoe, and with no provision but the three turtles. [...] We resolved to steer bodily to the southward, where there was at least a probability of discovering other lands, and more than a probability of finding a still milder climate.'[87] What precisely Pym and Peters discover at the pole, however, remains unclear. For here Poe is at his most obscure, the ending to the novel an abrupt one, in which the protagonists race towards the polar vortex that awaits them, enveloped by a snow-like whiteness on every side: 'And now we rushed into the embraces of the cataract, where the chasm threw itself open to receive us. But there arose in our pathway a shrouded human figure, very far larger in its proportions than any dweller among men. And the hue of the skin of the figure was of the perfect whiteness of the snow.'[88]

Poe's conclusion to *Pym* has since encouraged any number of ingenious interpretations. With the whiteness of the Pole, and the ocean itself, which is a milky colour, along with its striking contrast to the wholly black environment they have left behind them in Tsalal, the most obvious of these is that Poe is simply replaying the racial divisions of his own time and place: the American South of the early nineteenth century. In this light, his description of a cruel and treacherous black race may be read as 'a Virginian fantasy of race-war and racial degradation [...] the worst Virginian fears about rebelling nigrahs personified.'[89] While elsewhere, and rather less obviously, *Pym* has been read as a Gnostic allegory, in which 'black Tsalal stands for matter in its most evil incarnation while the white pole signifies release from matter into the immaterial.'[90] Poe's mystical imagery has also led to more conventional biblical interpretations in which *Pym* becomes 'a tale of death and transfiguration' culminating in the hero encountering 'the radiant Christ of the book of Revelations.'[91] More improbable still, the shrouded human figure that towers over the polar chasm has even been identified as the shadow image of Pym himself, albeit one which he fails to recognise.[92] Or could it simply be, as many critics have suggested, that Poe simply decided to cut his losses and bring the book to a swift conclusion? He evidently had little affection for what was to be his only novel, describing it two years after its publication as 'a very silly book', an opinion evidently shared by the public – it was a commercial disaster.[93] But perhaps we are wrong to look too closely or too seriously for an explanation to Poe's novel, and should instead let the inconclusive ending stand as it is, a symbol of the Antarctic itself, a continent whose immensity and mystery render it beyond the capacity of art and literature to express meaningfully. Could it be that the region truly is 'unwritable' after all?

Apart from puzzling his readers, the indeterminacy of Poe's ending was also to set them a challenge, provoking them to come up with an alternative of their own, one which would conclusively 'complete' his story and perhaps finally capture the true nature of the far south.[94] In this sense, just as *Symzonia* had inspired Poe's novel, so *Pym* itself was to prove a catalyst to the newly emerging genre of science fiction, and to one writer of science fiction in particular. It was not until 1897, however, more than 50 years after *Pym* was first published that Jules Verne (1828–1905) was to reveal his conclusion to Poe's narrative in *Le Sphinx des Glaces* (The Sphinx of the Icy Regions). Reintroducing Pym's companion and sole survivor of their earlier adventures, Dirk Peters, Verne's novel follows him on a return journey to Antarctica in search of the missing Pym. Peters' party finally locate him, only to find him dead, his body pinioned to the magnetic mountain which marks the South Pole and which is shaped, inexplicably, in the form of a crouching Sphinx. Overcome by the fate of his former shipmate, Peters dies of a broken heart and the expedition returns home. In transforming the polar vortex which Pym discovers at the Pole from a watery chasm to a giant magnet, Verne's attempt to update Poe's novel fails dismally and rather than eclipsing the earlier tale it simply emphasises the elegance of Poe's ambiguous conclusion. Indeed, if an ending is to be found to surpass Poe's novel then it is not one to be found in fiction, but rather that which Poe was himself to supply through the equally bizarre culmination to his own life. Following the death of his wife, Virginia, in 1847, Poe was to descend into a vortex of his own, as his drinking spiralled out of control and his behaviour became increasingly erratic. The end came two years later in 1849, when having gone missing for a week he was found wandering the streets of Baltimore, delirious and disorientated. He was admitted to hospital where he died several days later. His last hours, however, have since been the subject of close scrutiny, for as one biographer was later to report, he appears to have gone to his death playing out in his mind the concluding act from Pym's own journey, his death and that of his creation converging in a final plunge into the abyss, complete with an indecipherable closing scene:

> On that last night, as the shadow fell across him, it must have been the horrors of shipwreck, of thirst, and of drifting away into unknown seas of darkness that troubled his last dreams, for, by some trick of his ruined brain, it was scenes of Arthur Gordon Pym that rose in his imagination, and the man who was connected most intimately with them.

> "Reynolds!" he called, "Reynolds! Oh, Reynolds!" The room sang with it. It echoed down the corridors hour after hour all that Saturday night. The last grains of sand uncovered themselves as he slipped away, during the Sunday morning of October 7, 1849. He was now too feeble to call out any more. It was three o'clock in the morning and the earth's shadow was still undisturbed by

dawn. He became quiet, and seemed to rest for a short time. Then, gently moving his head, he said, 'Lord help my poor soul.'[95]

## HP Lovecraft and *At the Mountains of Madness* (1931)

Rather than bringing the attempts of those wishing to follow in Poe's footsteps to an end, the discovery of the South Pole in 1911 simply inspired ever more imaginative solutions to the enigma of the Antarctic, with factual accounts of polar exploration continuing to find a place within fictional depictions of the continent. First published in *Astounding Science Fiction* in 1936, but written five years earlier, *At the Mountains of Madness* pays explicit homage to Poe's text, to which it is a sequel of sorts, as well as displaying the clear influence of William Clark Russell's tale of suspended animation, *The Frozen Pirate* (1887). But above all else, Lovecraft's depiction of a seemingly blank and empty continent whose frozen depths conceal and preserve a pre-human history, is one which originates within his own, highly eccentric, Cthulhu Mythos, the elaborate framework of ancient esoteric knowledge which underpins his work.[96] Like Coleridge and Poe before him, Lovecraft (1890–1937) was to use the features of isolation and emptiness that these writers had projected, and the facts which polar exploration had since so emphatically confirmed, to update Poe's narrative by demonstrating what Pym would have encountered at the Pole. Polar exploration had revealed the Antarctic to be something every bit as terrifying as fictional speculation had led us to believe, a horrifying absence wholly indifferent to human life and history. But what, asks Lovecraft, lies behind, or rather beneath, this blank and inhospitable landscape, and what is scientific exploration likely to uncover?

*At the Mountains of Madness* describes the fate of an Antarctic expedition which begins in September 1930 and which is led by the narrator, Dr William Dyer: 'We planned to cover as great an area as one Antarctic season – or longer, if absolutely necessary – would permit, operating mostly in the mountain-ranges and on the plateau south of Ross Sea; regions explored in varying degree by Shackleton, Amundsen, Scott and Byrd.'[97] From the outset, however, the expedition's scientific objectives appear to be offset by more literary concerns, as Dyer's colleague Danforth reveals: 'Danforth was a great reader of bizarre material, and had talked a good deal of Poe. I was interested myself because of the Antarctic scene of Poe's only long story – the disturbing and enigmatical *Arthur Gordon Pym*. [...] Danforth had hinted at queer notions about unsuspected and forbidden sources to which Poe may have had access when writing his *Arthur Gordon Pym* a century ago.'[98] Needless to say, Danforth's 'queer notions' are quickly confirmed, and when an advance party report the discovery of what appear to be previously unknown life forms at the base of a vast mountain range, Dyer and Danforth fly on to meet them, only to find the camp destroyed and the men dead or missing. For far from being the blank space that it appears, the Antarctic is in fact home to a long-dead civilisation, the malignant descendants of which lie buried beneath the ice:

At last we were truly entering the white, aeon-dead world of the ultimate south. [...] That seething, half-luminous cloud-background held ineffable suggestions of a vague, ethereal beyondness far more than terrestrially spatial; and gave appalling reminders of the utter remoteness, separateness, desolation, and aeon-long death of this untrodden and unfathomed austral world.[99]

Dyer and Danforth fly across the mountains where they discover the remains of an ancient city, the home to an alien civilisation whose original inhabitants they refer to as the 'Elder Things.' Long since abandoned, the alien architecture of this fantastic city is decorated with hieroglyphics which reveal the history of this lost race as it gradually declines. It is the survivors of this alien race which the expedition has inadvertently disturbed and which destroyed the camp. But these creatures, far more sophisticated than the human race, are not the true horror; for having come into conflict with a biologically engineered class of creatures called Shoggoths, which they had first created as slaves, the Elder Ones were ultimately defeated, and it is one of these shapeless, horrific entities which Dyer and Danforth encounter before escaping to safety. Now aware of the true danger that the Antarctic poses to future expeditions, the book closes with a warning to those who may try to follow them: 'It is absolutely necessary, for the peace and safety of mankind, that some of earth's dark, dead corners and unplumbed depths be let alone; lest sleeping abnormalities wake to resurgent life, and blasphemously surviving nightmares squirm and splash out of their black lairs to newer and wider conquests.'[100]

Perhaps more than any other writer who has taken the Antarctic as the backdrop to their fiction, Lovecraft digs deepest in unearthing those repressed anxieties buried beneath the ice. In *At the Mountains of Madness* this process is as much literal as metaphorical, his narrator being a geologist equipped with a futuristic drill able to plumb previously uncharted depths. Lovecraft's polar landscape is thus rendered psychic as well as geological, his explorers embarking on a journey deep into the human psyche, penetrating into the farthest depths of the unconscious. What they find there, however, is something deeply hostile to human reason, and as Lovecraft's warning would suggest, something that is better left undisturbed.[101] In this way, Lovecraft's novella acts as the progenitor to a new kind of Antarctic fiction, one which marks a further evolutionary stage, going beyond Coleridge and Poe in their own progression through the polar ice, to expose that which lies beneath: 'a medium that is seen to contain things long-buried, locked in cold storage, awaiting our unwitting excavations to unleash further possibilities of monstrous ambivalence.'[102]

Throughout his work, Lovecraft's characters act, often

rather incongruously, as a mouthpiece for many of their author's own concerns. In *At the Mountains of Madness*, for example, we find Dr Dyer expressing the view that 'all the continents are fragments of an original Antarctic land mass which cracked from centrifugal force and drifted apart over a technically viscous lower surface – an hypothesis suggested by such things as the complementary outlines of Africa and South America, and the way the great mountain chains are rolled and shoved up.'[103] Here, of course, as he acknowledges, Dyer is drawing upon contemporary theories of plate tectonics and continental drift which suggest that it was the great southern continent – in its original and cohesive form – which was gradually to give way to the globe we inhabit today. When Alfred Wegener (1880–1930) first proposed his theory of Continental Drift in 1915, he was seen as so out of step with orthodox geological beliefs that his views were simply dismissed out of hand. For rather than supporting the long-held belief in a rigid model of the earth, Wegener pictured the continents as plates floating over the softer body of the earth beneath, like pieces of shell on a hard-boiled egg.[104] Their movement was dictated by two forces created by the earth's rotation, *Polfluchtkraft* (pole-fleeing force) and *Westwanderung* (westward motion), and Wegener was forced to conclude that rather than occupying a permanently fixed position, the poles had in fact 'fled' from different places before arriving at their present locations. This theory of polar migration was reflected in Wegener's speculative maps of the ancient earth's continental formations which were quite different to those we see today. Thirty years after his death, Wegener's heretical ideas were reconsidered, and today they have become a part of accepted geological wisdom, which recognises his hypothesis that the present continents may be traced back to a single primordial source. This original landmass, into which our continents may all be fitted like a jigsaw, is named 'Pangea', and its shoreline separates it from the single primordial ocean, 'Panthalassa.' Having later fragmented into the first super-continents, these eventually

gave way to the continents which exist today.[105] According
to this schema, the ancient civilisation which Lovecraft
describes would have originally inhabited an Antarctica
which was then a part of the supercontinent of Gondwana;
over the course of the next 500 million years they would
have found themselves passing through equatorial latitudes
on their long migration southwards, as a richly forested
Antarctica eventually broke away to form its own continent
before becoming submerged beneath the ice sheet around
twenty million years ago.[106]

But Wegener is not the only theorist to find his ideas
expressed within the pages of Lovecraft's tale, for his views
are accompanied by those of another writer attempting
to record the shifting patterns of global upheaval, albeit
historically rather than geologically. For like Kerouac,
Lovecraft was also highly influenced by Spengler's *The
Decline of the West*, the first volume of which he first read
in translation in 1927. 'When discussing *At the Mountains of
Madness*', asserts China Miéville in his introduction to the
novel, 'the importance of Spengler's *The Decline of the West*
cannot be stressed too highly. [...] The very setting, that
enormous, impossible city, is utterly Spenglerian, recalling
the "civilisation" phase in his cycle, when culture passes
beyond its high point and its upheavals occur in burgeoning
metropolises.'[107] For in a return to the racial undertones to
be found in the works of Symmes and Poe, Lovecraft's novel
also portrays 'a dark city surrounded by country that has
been sucked so dry it is bone-white, bled of all color'; the
contrast between light and darkness once again conveying
the familiar aesthetic through which the Antarctic comes to
represent a threatened racial purity.[108] Lovecraft's abandoned
city is symbolic of a defeated race, a degenerate civilisation
finally overcome through the consequences of its own
decadence; a city whose story can be read, literally, as one
wanders through it: 'As the narrator navigates the vast stone
corridors, he literally walks through the architecturalization
of Spengler's cyclical history. In the bas-reliefs that he and

Danforth are able (however improbably) to decipher, we read a fantasticated representation of *The Decline of the West*.'[109] For just as Wegener's drifting continents were gradually to fragment around a migrating polar axis, so too it would seem, to Lovecraft at least, must the West face a similar fate, as it too drifts southwards towards inevitable decline, a 'decultured' *fellaheen* civilisation preserved beneath the ice.

Within the history of southern polar fiction exemplified by Coleridge and Poe, there is one further work which demands inclusion here, the remaining 'ur-text' to set alongside Lovecraft's within the 'buried polar alien' tradition.[110] John W Campbell's novella *Who Goes There?* was first published in *Astounding Science Fiction* in 1938 under the pseudonym of Don A Stuart, but it was to become more widely known through the three film adaptations it was later to inspire: Howard Hawks' *The Thing from Another World* (1951), which relocates the film to the Arctic; John Carpenter's *The Thing* (1982); and *The Thing* (2011), a prequel based upon Carpenter's film. Published only seven years after *At the Mountains of Madness*, but displaying none of the more mystical overtones of Lovecraft's tale, *Who Goes There?* is explicit in its awareness of the literary tradition in which it follows, at one point comparing its alien namesake to the Ancient Mariner's albatross. Like Lovecraft, Campbell is meticulous in his use of realistic detail, also drawing upon Byrd's account of his polar expeditions, and in this case using his renowned Antarctic station, 'Little America' as the basis for his fictional camp, 'Big Magnet'.[111] Whereas Lovecraft's novella, however, is a panoramic overview of the Antarctic, both geographically and temporally, Campbell's is the opposite, a claustrophobic tale largely confined to its cramped Antarctic base and set over the course of a few feverish days. In its story of the uncovering of a crashed alien spacecraft long since immersed in the ice, *Who Goes There?* explores the dangers of contagion and contamination posed by the discovery of an alien biology hostile to human life. An amorphous, unclassifiable entity, the 'Thing' unearthed from the ice has the capacity to mimic its host organism, a process which, if not contained, threatens to engulf not only the crew of the base but the wider world. Playing upon the claustrophobic conditions and inherent tensions of life upon a polar base, Campbell's story shows how such conditions can quickly give way to mistrust, paranoia and finally madness, as the presence of the 'Thing' exacerbates dormant hostilities amongst the crew and they begin to turn upon one another. In the finest traditions of the polar gothic, the crew of 'Big Magnet' gradually fall victim to this shapeless entity, until with only a few surviving members left to tell the tale, the 'Thing' is finally cornered and destroyed. Campbell's tale has none of the ambiguity or symbolism to be found in the work of his gothic predecessors, but in its depiction of a relentless adversary, malign, impersonal and formless, it reveals that what the 'Thing' comes to replicate most closely is the very environment in which it has been embedded for the previous twenty million years, the Antarctic itself:

> The Thing stands in metonymical and metaphorical relationship with the continent. The Thing is contiguous with Antarctica (it was buried in the ice for 20 million years) and also serves to symbolize Antarctica (it shares the same spatial characteristics). The alien is shapeless and shifting; the Antarctic, too, has no fixed shape or size, doubling its area from summer to winter, exceeding its own boundaries, constantly expelling material, fracturing, melting and reforming. Like the Thing, it is engulfing, threatening to swallow the unfortunate explorers who fall into its deep crevasses and to absorb them into itself. [...] But the Antarctic, despite being shapeless, is nevertheless autonomous: underneath the kilometres of ice is a large landmass, a separate continent. [...] Lastly, like the Thing, the Antarctic is undecidably both dead and alive – superficially frozen and lifeless, but actually moving, melting, growing, shrinking and fragmenting. The alien at the centre of Campbell's story can thus be read as an

embodiment of the continent itself. Antarctica is dis-placed in Campbell's story in a very literal sense: an undefinable, seemingly limitless place is transferred to the figure of a monster that shares its disturbing spatial qualities but can nevertheless be conquered and killed, defusing (at least temporarily) the anxieties it has aroused.[112]

In its concern with containment and the spread of contagion, *Who Goes There?* expresses an anxiety which was, in the following years, to become of growing concern. For in recent decades the Antarctic has increasingly come to be seen as an 'Antarctic Refuge', a continent apart which is to be kept under strict scientific supervision and free from the damaging military and economic imperatives which govern elsewhere. This was the logic underlying the Antarctic Treaty of 1961 under which the Antarctic was declared 'the continent for science and peace', and which forbids all military presence, except in support of scientific objectives, as well as suspending all mining, and any activity perceived as damaging to the environment. In 1991, under the Madrid Protocol, strict regulations were enforced on the bringing of foreign organisms into the Antarctic region; while human visitors are required to remove all waste they produce.[113] Today the borders of the Antarctic are policed more rigorously than ever in an attempt to ensure that its environmental integrity remains intact. What these measures have been unable to avert, however, is the incessant flow of highly questionable beliefs which the region continues to attract.

## The Antarctic as Refuge

The perception of the Antarctic as a refuge, free from the pernicious involvement of international powers seeking to further their own objectives, has allowed it to maintain what is perhaps the greatest of its natural resources, its emptiness. As we have seen, however, and as has been the case from the earliest speculative accounts of the continent to the present day, such a blank space permits, even encourages, our imaginations to overwrite this void, to fill in this last remaining 'empty' region of the globe. In this sense, then, the idea of a refuge is one which not merely provides an escape from the world as it is, but also from the world as it should or might be, a refuge from reality itself. And of all the many, often eccentric ideas that have sought sanctuary in the Antarctic, far from the centres of prevailing wisdom and out on the margins of human society, there is one in particular which has proven especially enduring.

Like many others who believed, or even hoped, that Hitler had escaped from Berlin at the end of the Second World War, the fascist occultist Miguel Serrano (1917–2009) was particularly fervent in his support of this claim. As we have seen, the Germans, like many of the western powers, had launched their own expeditions to the Antarctic in the early years of the twentieth century; but it was during their third such expedition, to Queen Maud Land in 1938–9, that they were to make some surprising discoveries, including 'a group of low-lying hills sprinkled with many lakes and completely free of ice and snow.' Resembling the hot springs of Iceland, this territory was claimed by the Germans for themselves (despite a prior claim by the Norwegians) and, marking it with swastika flags, they renamed it *Neuschwabenland* (New Swabia).[114] According to Serrano, it was in this newly acquired territory that the Germans were to first establish contact with the hollow earth and its secret cities, home to the first Hyperboreans who had taken refuge there following a cataclysmic event which had reversed the poles. It was here too that the Germans developed a secret base during the war, and naturally enough, this was also the place to which Adolf Hitler himself was to flee, in a *Vimana*, or flying saucer plane, in 1945, from where he was to direct the ongoing 'esoteric war.'[115] According to what is described as the earliest source of such a myth, Hitler's escape to the southern hemisphere can be traced to 'the unexpected surrender of a German submarine in early July 1945 at Mar del Plata, Argentina.

[…] Hitler and Eva Braun had disembarked here before being whisked away to the base built by the 1938–39 expedition.'[116] Two years later, in 1947, Admiral Byrd was once again in the Antarctic, this time with a senior command in the US Naval operation, Operation High Jump, which aimed to provide post-war employment for the navy as well as establishing an American presence in the region.[117] Or so it would seem. An alternative interpretation suggests that the American operation was in fact a cover for an expeditionary force of more than 10,000 men sent to the Antarctic to 'destroy the people of the German exodus, who had apparently reached a warm and habitable Antarctica through the hollow interior of the earth.'[118] The American mission was a failure, however, and having suffered a humiliating defeat, the American government hushed up the whole affair. According to the official maps of Byrd's many flights across the Antarctica, it would appear that he never actually visited Queen Maud Land, the supposed site of Hitler's Antarctic retreat. Far from disproving the conspiratorial thesis, however, this awkward omission can, of course, be explained: 'Byrd was scared away by the protective power demonstrated by the secret center, and after losing four planes, kept his distance.'[119] By the 1980s the notion of Hitler's post-war sojourn in the far south still lingered on, and was the subject of works such as WA Harbinson's *Genesis* (1980) and Jean Robin's *Opération Orth* (1989). In an apparent struggle to outdo one another in the sheer lunacy of their respective visions, Robin's book also offers a solution to the fate of Raoul Wallenberg, the Swedish diplomat and saviour of the Hungarian Jews, who, it turns out, is buried alongside Hitler himself, who died in 1953 and is enshrined in his subterranean base.[120]

One can only speculate as to the motivations behind such lavishly constructed fantasies, but perhaps it is precisely because of the absence of any military involvement or significant political upheaval in the region over the last 60 years that such extraordinary counterfactual accounts continue to find an audience. For despite the rise of Cold

211

War tensions in the 1950s, which resulted in the US and the Soviet Union expanding their territorial claims and establishing rival bases (the US South Pole base and McMurdo Station in 1956; USSR Vostok Station in 1957), the expected escalation in hostilities never materialised and the Antarctic Treaty of 1961 placed the region beyond the reach of such disputes. Instead, and rather more prosaically, scientific research has continued without disturbance, and the Antarctic has even become a fledgling tourist destination, with regular cruises having begun in 1966. In the intervening years, however, our entire perspective towards the Antarctic and its relationship to the rest of the planet has undergone a fundamental change, as emerging concerns over climate change have finally made apparent how environmental policies in the North and elsewhere can have unpredictable and destructive consequences for the not-so-distant South, actions whose effects will be multiplied catastrophically and which will in turn be revisited upon us all. Globalisation and our growing awareness of the interconnectedness of environmental ecosystems, mean that the Antarctic is no longer the place apart that it was once perceived to be, out of sight, if not out of mind:

> From the beginning, it had been crucial to its imaginative impact as a place that it was a place apart, locked away at the bottom of the world, beyond terrible seas patrolled by a ring of storms. It was an icy South far less continuous with the rest of the world than the icy North was. You could, if you had a mind to, hail a taxi in New York or Berlin, and be driven to the Arctic: but the Antarctic was on a separate map. Now the separateness, though not the uniqueness, was going away. First came the awareness that the industrial processes of the populated planet off to the north did, indeed, reach down and touch the ice. [...] Then, more troubling, came the realization that Antarctica could act back upon the rest of the planet. In the 1990s, it became plain that the Antarctic ice shelves,

by locking away vast tonnages of fresh water, effectively governed world sea levels. [...] Now, Antarctica no longer looked like a fortress of ice to be conquered. It was a fragile panel in the fabric of the planet. It no longer threatened to overwhelm tiny humans doing epic deeds in a harsh landscape. The balance of threat had reversed [...] What we think we see, in the far South, shifts with our own preoccupations, like the jumbled ice floes in Antarctica which have seemed to travellers to morph into very different architectures, depending on who was doing the looking, and when.[121]

Today the Antarctic is no longer perceived as an adversary to be overcome, but rather as a resource to be preserved. And just as Symmes was to identify his openings at the poles, the holes through which he believed one might visit the inhabited recesses of the earth, so we are now faced once again with new polar openings, this time within the earth's atmosphere, seemingly created through our own actions, and threatening life on our planet. There is undeniably a peculiar symmetry to be found between Symmes' proclamations, on the one hand (laughingly dismissed, it should be remembered, by the majority of his countrymen) and on the other, the holes in the ozone layer identified by the scientific community, the causes of which have provoked a similarly disputatious response. Could it really be true, as one commentator suggests, that quite apart from the scientific validity of such claims, the existence of such an opening also fulfils a deeper symbolic need within us? Do such holes perform the same function in our imaginations as they once did for our ancestors, an opening through which our imaginations can once again take flight? A hole in the head as much as one in the sky?[122] If so, then we really have come full circle, and however much we may attempt to comprehend the Antarctic through a purely scientific framework, such a perspective is continually undermined by the steady accretion of mythological debris under which the far South remains submerged.

# Notes

1.  Shackleton, quoted in Wheeler, p. 1.
2.  Douglas Coupland, 'Notes on Time', *The Happy Hypocrite* 1 (2008), p. 57, quoted in Spufford, 'The Uses of Antarctica', p. 17.
3.  Scott, 17 January 1912, p. 373.
4.  Fort, pp. 731–732.
5.  Wheeler, p. 7.
6.  Davidson, p. 13.
7.  Spufford, 'The Uses of Antarctica', p. 18.
8.  Spufford, 'The Uses of Antarctica', p. 17.
9.  Dodds, p. 21.
10. Davidson, p. 19.
11. Davidson, p. 48.
12. HP Blavatsky, *The Secret Doctrine* (1888), II, 400, quoted by John Sutherland in Shiel, Introduction, p. xxiv.
13. Godwin, p. 134.
14. Dodds, p. 22.
15. Godwin, p. 138.
16. Godwin, p. 138.
17. Such an attribution may be a misleading one, however, as the source which is often cited in support of this claim is the treatise translated as *On the Cosmos*, most likely a forgery of Aristotle's work and produced several hundred years later. See Leane, p. 26.
18. Wilson, p. 143.
19. Wilson, p. 145.
20. Wilson, p. 145.
21. Wilson, p. 146.
22. Leane, p. 26.
23. Leane, p. 27.
24. Nelson, p. 145.
25. Wilson, p. 149.
26. Sir John Mandeville, *Mandeville's Travels: Texts and Translations*, ed. by Malcolm Letts, 2 vols. London: Hakluyt Society, 1953, 1: 129, pp. 142–3, quoted in Wilson, p. 150.
27. Cherry-Garrard, Introduction, p. xlix.
28. Cherry-Garrard, Introduction, p. l.
29. Klaus Dodds writes (p. 47):

Strikingly, there remains vastly more media and indeed popular interest in tales of the physical endeavours of past European and North American explorers, usually during the 'race to the pole' era, than contemporary Antarctic discoveries. While we might admire the extraordinary bravery and tenacity of scores of explorers, scientists, and sealers, this tendency to focus on the heroic past has consequences. We tend to hear little about the way in which discovery and polar heritage is put to work by vested interests. Instead, histories of discovery are commercially exploited by tourist companies, politically exploited by governments, and intellectually exploited by authors and enthusiasts alike – tales of daring-do continue to sell.

30. Spufford, *I May Be Some Time*, p. 6.
31. Describing the terrestrial poles, Gyrus writes (p. 236):

They are not purely imaginary figments. However, to the concreteness that traditional peoples prioritise – that of sensual qualities, the realities of bodily encounter – the terrestrial poles are far more abstract than the celestial poles, which are at least subject to unaided observation. Why would anyone risk lives for a place that has no tangible value? The quests for the poles were marked by heroic and often tragic narratives [...] But beneath the overt motivations of science and adventure lay lingering traces of the old polar symbolism of power and transcendence. Geographic motives seem simple enough when considered antiseptically. But the act of tying up the loose ends of the cartographic grid – sealing off the totalising mapping project that European empires began when they reached the New World then circumnavigated the globe – is messily implicated in a mania for dominion.

32. Cook, quoted in Wilson, p. 161.
33. Cook, 'Sunday, 30 January 1774', p. 331.
34. Cook, quoted in Wilson, p. 162.
35. Cook, quoted in Wilson, p. 162.
36. Spufford, *I May be Some Time*, p. 43.
37. Spufford, *I May be Some Time*, p. 22.
38. Spufford, *I May be Some Time*, p. 23.
39. Spufford, ed., *Antarctica*, Introduction, p. 4.
40. Roland Huntford, *Shackleton*, New York: Atheneum, 1986, p. 24, quoted in Wilson, p. 142.
41. 'Although it is easy to list and date the major expeditions',

Spufford notes, 'they can seem to shed their identifying marks of period as we read about them. The guy ropes tying them to their time snap, and they float free, into a strange region of uncalendared events.' See Spufford, ed., *Antarctica*, pp. 2–3.

42. Scott, *Journals*, p. 378.
43. Byrd, quoted in Dodds, p. 36.
44. 'This made a considerable psychological difference', writes Spufford, 'A human being in Antarctica could now possess, imaginatively, a much wider spread of it than was visible through the eyeholes of any one knitted helmet. From ten thousand feet, you could begin to see how Antarctica worked; you could begin to see it as having a unity in which, paradoxically, humans played very little part.' See Spufford, ed., *Antarctica*, p. 9.
45. Spufford, ed., *Antarctica*, p. 9.
46. Standish, p. 276.
47. Henry David Thoreau, *Walden; or, Life in the Woods,* Boston: Ticknor and Fields, 1854, quoted in Standish, pp. 106–107.
48. Gyrus, p. 193.
49. Godwin, p. 107.
50. Godwin, p. 108.
51. Gyrus, p. 195.
52. Godwin writes (p. 112):

It is easy to laugh at Symmes and his holes. But researchers in the occult will recognize him as a familiar type: the man with a military background (or the daughter of one), sane and competent in worldly terms, who nurtures a secret belief, perhaps founded on a moment of inexplicable revelation, that is the antithesis of his outward persona. Some psychologists would say that the more disciplined the mask, the more repressed and fantastic might be the inner life of such a person. We might add how symbolically appropriate this particular theory is, concretizing, as it were, the subliminal contents of the mind, and crying out for their exploration!

53. Godwin, pp. 109–110.
54. Spufford, *I May be Some Time*, p. 64.
55. Spufford, *I May be Some Time*, p. 65.
56. Godwin, p. 111.
57. Standish, pp. 48–50.
58. It was these conditions which allowed Weddell to penetrate to

74 degrees, 15 minutes south, in the sea later named for him, beating Captain James Cook's 1774 record in the *Resolution* by more than three degrees. See Standish, p. 54.

59. Godwin, pp. 110–112.
60. Spufford, *I May be Some Time*, p. 71.
61. Victoria Nelson supports the idea that Symmes is the author (Nelson, p. 149), as does Standish, who asks: 'Can anyone doubt that Symmes wrote this?' (Standish, p.77). Spufford, on the other hand, does not (*I May be Some Time*, p. 72): 'Stingingly accurate about Symmesian self-deception, *Symzonia* has nonetheless been mistaken at times for pro-Symmes propaganda. (One twentieth-century critic assigns its writing to John Cleves himself, crediting him with a sense of the ridicule he certainly never possessed.) The only tribute *Symzonia* pays Symmes is a very American admiration for the author of an audacious hoax.'
62. Standish, p. 77.
63. Standish, p. 67.
64. Gyrus, p. 196.
65. In November 1820 Palmer sailed into Orleans Strait at about 63 degrees, 41 minutes south, to record the first sighting of the continent. The Russians meanwhile were to bestow the same honour upon Admiral Bellingshausen, the first man to circumnavigate Antarctica since Cook; while the British attributed the first sighting to Edward Bransfield and William Smith, who were on a mission to chart the South Shetland Isles. See Standish, p. 89.
66. Leane, p. 23. For a rather more concise alternative to Leane's account, see Rennison, 'The Poles in the Imagination' in his *A Short History of Polar Exploration*, pp. 115–122.
67. Leane, p. 1.
68. Kay, p. 93.
69. Leane, pp. 5–6.
70. Leane writes (pp. 15–16):

The south, as the farther-flung, less explored, less inhabited region, is inevitably – if inadvertently – treated as the poor cousin to the north. [...] Given the Arctic's long history of human inhabitation, it has produced a far older and more extensive body of imaginative work than the Antarctic, including rich indigenous literatures. If far southern fiction is folded in with its far northern counterpart, it risks becoming a postscript to or cartographically inverted version of it. The specificity of the Antarctic region can easily be lost, and it becomes simply a displaced Arctic.

71. Leane, pp. 55–56.
72. Spufford writes (*I May be Some Time*, pp. 37–38):

Like a Gothic villain (who ought not to have had the power to plot and manipulate, but did) the Antarctic landscape (which 'ought' to have admitted men to its fastnesses, but did not) in some sense took the initiative away from the heroes. Its sublime authority could not be gainsaid; and the explorers responded by identifying themselves with its sublimity, glorying in the place even as it thwarted or even hurt them. [...] It was a worthily impersonal adversary, whose force could be acknowledged without the shattering effect of submission to a human rival.

73. Coleridge, pp. 2–4.
74. Leane, p. 61.
75. Pyne, p. 163.
76. Wilson writes (pp. 169–170):

Yet, the mariner soon realizes that not even the medieval paradigm of the monstrous south can categorize the ice, for the Antarctic freeze is nothing – no discernible shape at all. Not the hellish opposite of Eden or the monstrous contrary of the humane, the ice is beyond pairs of opposites: not this or that, a monotonous whiteness that annihilates representations and individuals. Bereft of adjectives, similes, or synonyms, the Mariner is reduced to repetition: the ice is here, the ice is there, ice is all around.

77. Leane, p. 62.
78. Spufford, *I May be Some Time*, p. 46.
79. Nelson, p. 148.
80. Poe, 'MS Found in a Bottle', 179–189, p. 188.
81. Poe, 'A Descent into the Maelström', 223–239, p. 228.
82. Godwin, p. 130.
83. Leane, p. 63.
84. JO Bailey in his introduction to *Symzonia* (1965). See Nelson, p. 150.

85. Wilson, p. 193.

86. Poe, 'Pym', 1–178, pp. 129–130.

87. Poe, 'Pym', p. 170.

88. Poe, 'Pym', p. 175.

89. Spufford, *I May be Some Time*, p. 75.

90. Wilson, p. 207.

91. J Gerald Kennedy, Introduction, Poe, p. xii.

92. Wilson, p. 199.

93. Ackroyd, *Poe*, pp. 67–68.

94. Pyne describes Poe's tale as one which 'offered the kind of challenge to writers to explain Pym's fate.' 'It would demonstrate the superiority of the writer who accomplished it or the progress of a later age that could, unlike Poe's, actually penetrate Antarctica.' See Pyne, p. 165.

95. Hervey Allen, *Israfel: The Life and Times of Edgar Allan Poe*, New York: George H Doran, 1926, quoted in Standish, p. 110. Spufford describes Poe's death in similar terms (*I May be Some Time*, pp. 77–78):

The fact that Poe, delirious on his deathbed in a New York hospital in 1849, was heard to shout 'Reynolds! Reynolds!', never surfacing again to explain his calls for Symmes' protégé, has allowed his biographers to speculate that deep inside his head, Poe may then have been feeling himself passing helpless over the lip of a polar maelstrom, a traveller reaching the last of the space within the skull, whirling away. But the name of a man whom Poe had probably never met face to face, was only a sign for the long-imagined, now-arrived sensation.

96. Leane, p. 64.

97. Lovecraft, p. 4.

98. Lovecraft, pp. 7 & 93.

99. Lovecraft, pp. 9 & 28.

100. Lovecraft, p. 101.

101. Nelson, p. 152.

102. Gyrus, p. 201

103. Lovecraft, p. 66.

104. Godwin, p. 217.

105. Godwin, pp. 217–218.

106. Godwin writes (pp. 132–133):

Lovecraft's ancient civilization in Antarctica is placed so far back in time that those who wish can actually reconcile it with geology. I follow here the scientific account of Margaret Bradshaw, who writes that Antarctica, as part of the supercontinent of Gondwana, was probably in equatorial latitudes during the Cambrian Period (about 500 million years ago). By the beginning of the Permian Period (300 mya), Gondwana was polar, the South Pole migrating in the course of twenty million years from the region that would later become Africa/South America, across Antarctica, to Australia. In the Triassic Period (240–190 mya), Antarctica was richly forested and inhabited by reptiles. After that came the period of violent volcanic activity that eventually led to the breakup of Gondwana and the beginning of the continents' progress to their present situations. In the course of the Tertiary Period (65–1.5 mya), the major mountain chains were built on the continent, and the present ice-sheet was formed. The continent has been thoroughly glaciated for about twenty million years, so any later habitation is out of the question.

107.  Miéville, Introduction, Lovecraft, p. xx.
108.  Miéville, Introduction, Lovecraft, p. xxi.
109.  Miéville, Introduction, Lovecraft, p. xxi.
110.  Gyrus, p. 204.
111.  Both character names as well as some of the dialogue used in Campbell's narrative closely resemble those which are to be found in Byrd's own *Discovery: The Story of the Second Byrd Expedition* (1935). See Leane, p. 75.
112.  Leane, pp. 78–79.
113.  Leane, p. 83.
114.  Godwin, p. 126.
115.  Godwin, p. 127.
116.  Godwin cites Donald McKale's *The Hitler Survival Myth* (1981) as the source for this information. See Godwin, p. 127.
117.  McGhee, pp. 32–33.
118.  McGhee, p. 33.
119.  Godwin, p. 129.
120.  Godwin, p. 127.
121.  Spufford, ed., *Antarctica*, pp. 14–15.
122.  Victoria Nelson writes (pp. 160–161):

The fact that the notorious widening hole in the ozone layer over Antarctica, widely believed in our age to leave humans nakedly exposed to malign ultraviolet solar radii, is another perfect replication of Ptolemaic cosmology. Yes, there is a "real," empirically verifiable hole in the ozone layer, just as there is a "real" atmospheric polar vortex that aggravates it, but the polar hole – like holes in the head and black holes in the cosmos – is also a venerable construct of Western culture. [...] Just as the Symmes Hole functioned as a kind of global grotto for our immediate ancestors, its present-day equivalent the ozone hole, that provocative tear in the fabric of the "noosphere," functions as a space grotto in our imaginations. Popular storytelling has fed, and continues to feed, this symbolically rendered need.

Detail from *Panoramic view of London* by Wenceslaus Hollar (1647)

# 5

# South of the River

*'There is, in fact, something basically wrong about South London.'*
Harry Williams[1]

*'You never cross water without some psychic toll.'*
Iain Sinclair[2]

In her final novel, *Wise Children* (1991), Angela Carter begins by posing the reader a question: 'WHY is London like Budapest?' Her answer: 'Because it is two cities divided by a river.' 'If you're from the States', she continues, 'think of Manhattan. Then think of Brooklyn. See what I mean? Or, for a Parisian, it might be a question of rive gauche, rive droite. With London, it's the North and South divide.'[3] Carter's novel follows the fortunes of two sisters living south of the river, 'the side the tourist rarely sees, the bastard side of Old Father Thames.' But such distinctions as these, which have for so long governed our perceptions of the city, appear finally to be on the wane:

> Once upon a time, you could make a crude distinction, thus: the rich lived amidst pleasant verdure in the North speedily whisked to exclusive shopping by abundant public transport while the poor eked out miserable existences in the South in circumstances of urban deprivation condemned to wait for hours at windswept bus-stops while sounds of marital violence, breaking glass and drunken

song echoed around and it was cold and dark and smelled of fish and chips. But you can't trust things to stay the same. There's been a diaspora of the affluent, they jumped into their diesel Saabs and dispersed throughout the city.[4]

Finally, then, we come to my own south, south London, where I have lived, on and off, for almost twenty years. During this period the city has undergone a remarkable transformation, as Carter's novel anticipates, for the south London that she portrays in her novel is one which is already giving way to a region which is much less distinct, as the process of gentrification refashions the city into the one we inhabit today. But despite these changes the city is still home to recognisably different quarters; its division along the cardinal axis of north and south, east and west, is still sufficient to provide us with a thumbnail sketch of the city as a whole, one which, curiously enough, appears to replicate similar divisions to be found elsewhere across the globe.

Prevailing winds in the northern hemisphere are largely westerly, with the result that cities have tended to expand historically in a westerly direction, with poorer areas downwind in the east, and wealthier areas in the west escaping the worst of the pollution. In London the west and north have long since been associated with the centres of wealth and power; the east has been heavily industrialised; while the south has been a place apart, poor, disreputable and indistinct. In this respect, then, London may be said somewhat to reflect global conditions, with broad concentrations of wealth and power in the North at odds with the poverty and lack of political representation to be found in the South. And just as the global south has historically been seen as peripheral, an indistinct region in which all the traditional indicators of wealth and power are largely absent; so too has south London long been characterised as a region without a clear identity, a suburban space which enjoys none of the advantages to be found in the city to its north, and one which can only be defined through reference to its northern boundary, the river. Of course, one should not take this analogy too far – as a generalisation it offers some clear parallels without approaching the complexity of the global picture, or for that matter, south London itself. But if we are to recognise London in this way, as representative, however loosely, of wider global disparities, then we should also acknowledge the ongoing process through which economic forces have transformed the topography of the city in recent decades. For just as the centre of London, as in other cities, is hollowed out, homogenised and gradually depopulated, so previously suburban districts take on many of the characteristics formerly to be found only in the centre, dissolving many of the distinctions which previously supported the division between centre and suburb, north and south.[5]

Throughout their history, suburban areas of the city, exemplified by south London, have come to be seen in two ways: on the one hand, as demonstrating a clear absence of identity, both historically and topographically, rendering them examples of space, rather than place, rootless, devoid of historical depth and cultural significance; on the other hand, and perhaps as an over-compensatory response, these suburban spaces have also been seen as concealing something rather more interesting, a hidden life that exists behind the nondescript exterior of quiet conformity, a remarkable, even magical, way of life apparent only to those who know how to look. Seen in this light, what at first might be regarded as rather an abrupt transition from the Antarctic wastes of the previous chapter to the suburban streets of south London, may actually be viewed quite differently. For these two souths appear to display some unlikely affinities, south London having been habitually characterised through precisely that lack of distinctiveness which has so often been used to describe the southern polar regions. Thus when one critic describes south London as 'an area which remains chronically underhistoricised', one is immediately reminded of similar remarks directed towards the polar south, itself another blank space in chronic need of overwriting.[6] The suburb, like the wilderness with which it is often equated, is virgin territory which resists every attempt to historicise it; and as a result, those writers who have taken south London as the setting for their fiction have, like the writers of the Polar Gothic before them, frequently attempted to enchant or romanticise this seemingly inert, deadly space. As we have seen throughout this account, each example of a southern city, region or continent has its own history, literature and mythology, both distinct in itself but also held in common with its southern counterparts, and as we turn briefly to south London and its own store of such imagery and symbolism, we can see once again the degree to which this seemingly benighted and much disparaged south may encapsulate many of the characteristics, both positive and negative, magical and mundane, to be found elsewhere in this book.

The inexorable transformation of south London from little more than 'a poor and disreputable appendage' to the city proper, to the city it was to become in its own right, began with the construction of Westminster Bridge in 1750 and the completion of Blackfriars Bridge nineteen years later.[7] Up until this point London south of the river remained relatively unknown to other Londoners, except through its dubious reputation as a source of entertainment and pleasure. Otherwise it consisted of little more than Southwark, the riverside industry around Deptford, and the enclaves of Greenwich and Woolwich.[8] Improved access, however, was gradually to make south London an affordable, even an attractive, place to live, and within 150 years it had become home to more than two million people. Yet this largely unchecked and unplanned southern expansion was unable to eradicate the urban discrimination against which south London has always struggled; and in tandem with the growing tide of workers who began to stream southwards in the late eighteenth century, came the arrival of a less welcome population of the city's outcasts. For just as the early eighteenth century had seen the south become a repository for London's 'stink industries' banished from the north, so too it was to become the site of many of the city's prisons and asylums, as well as institutions for its female orphans. In the first decade of the nineteenth century, the completion of three toll bridges at Southwark, Waterloo and Vauxhall led the way for the building programmes on which south London was created in its present form; but it was the erection of the notorious Bethlem hospital in Lambeth in 1815 which was to reinforce south London's reputation as a poor relation to the north. 'London', writes Peter Ackroyd, 'was consigning all its difficult or problematic citizens to the South. [...] It was, in every sense, a dumping ground. [...] But the prospect of dirt, or dilapidation, did not materially affect the growth of London in that direction; like the beetle which lives upon dung, the 'offensive' smells and sounds might even arouse its powers into further expenditures of energy.'[9]

It was against this backdrop of unparalleled growth and its often unappealing consequences that London's greatest mythologist, William Blake (1757–1827) invoked his vision of the 'four-fold London eternal', a city reimagined as the New Jerusalem. Blake's life was largely coterminous with the developments outlined above, and in his work he stands as a witness to London's physical and spiritual transformation. In his impossibly complex mythology, London and Jerusalem are overlaid to form the city of the imagination, Golgonooza. According to Blake's schema, governed by its repeated four-fold divisions or symmetries, the cardinal points represent not only parts of the human body, but also the four-fold division of Eternal Man into the four Zoas, each of which adopts an aspect of the human personality. In this manner, the south is symbolised by the warlike Urizen, the intellect – a negative symbol in Blake's system in perpetual conflict with the imagination, situated in the north – as well as representing the seat of the intellect, the head, in a reversal of the more commonly ascribed bodily designation of north and south. One can easily lose oneself within Blake's imaginative universe, but, thankfully, while his symbolism is often oblique, the topography of his visionary city is mapped out with great precision:

> From Golgonooza the spiritual Four-fold London eternal
> In immense labours & sorrows, ever building, ever falling,
> Thro Albions four Forests which overspread all the Earth,
> From London Stone to Blackheath east: to Hounslow west:
> To Finchley north: to Norwood south: and the weights
> Of Enitharmons Loom play lulling cadences on the winds of Albion
> From Caithness in the north, to Lizard-point & Dover in the south[10]

Blake's *Milton* (1804–1810), sees the poet travel to Lambeth in south London – 'the Bride, the Lamb's Wife' – but according to the coordinates he outlines in this poem, it is further south in Norwood that we reach the southern perimeter of his eternal London. In the early nineteenth century, Norwood was recently enclosed common land, largely unpopulated, and at seven miles south of the City, too far south for all but the wealthier commuter. In the following decades, however, and following the opening of South Norwood station in 1839, it was to be rapidly transformed into the suburban corner of south London it is today. One would now search in vain for any evidence of the eternal in this location, but one of the great pleasures of reading Blake's poetry is to connect his vision of the city with that of our own, and Norwood in the south appears no less incongruous here, to the modern ear at least, than does its northern counterpart, Finchley. Nor should it surprise us that Norwood should be assigned such a role, if we are to consider the significance that many parts of south London held for Blake, most famously amongst them Peckham Rye, where as a young boy he experienced a vision of an angel in a tree.

If Blake depicts a bucolic and unspoiled countryside threatened with extinction, then his vision is one that finds persistent echoes in later accounts of south London, many of which appear to offer a condemnation of the present alongside a wistful remembrance of the past. Walter Besant, for example, writing in 1899, laments not only the loss of natural beauty, but also, in what was later to become a frequent complaint, the shallow and historically detached nature of what was to replace it: 'It is difficult, now that the whole country south of London has been covered with villas, roads, streets, and shops, to understand how wonderful for loveliness it was until the builder seized upon it. [...] We have destroyed the beauty of South London: we have also made its historical associations impossible.'[11] Besant's *South London* is a lengthy book and one in which the reader struggles to find anything positive to recommend its subject. For here, as has so often been the case elsewhere, is an image of the south defined wholly through comparison with its neighbour to the north, a region characterised not only through an absence of historical depth, but by an absence of almost everything one might expect to locate in a city:

In South London there are two millions of people. It is therefore one of the great cities of the world. It stands upon an area about twelve miles long and five or six broad – but its limits cannot be laid down even approximately. It is a city without a municipality, without a centre, without a civic history; it has no newspapers, magazines or journals; it has no university; it has no colleges, apart from medicine; it has no intellectual, artistic, scientific, musical, literary centre – unless the Crystal Palace can be considered as a centre; its residents have no local patriotism or enthusiasm – one cannot imagine a man proud of New Cross; it has no theatres, except of a very popular or humble kind; it has no clubs, it has no public buildings, it has no West End. It is argued that although it has none of these things, yet it has them all by right of being a part of London.

That is, in a sense, true. The theatres, concerts, picture galleries of the West End are accessible to the South. [...] Yet one feels there must surely be some disadvantage in being separated from the literary and artistic circles whose members, it must be confessed, reside for the most part in North London.[12]

Through its identification as a place apart, with its poverty and dilapidation, its suburban sprawl and apparent lack of recognisable landmarks, south London has often been associated with east London, with which it shares many similarities. But while the East End gains from its proximity to the City, the south has always been isolated by the Thames which severs many of its links with the remainder of the city.[13] Thus however great the transformation which may take place in south London, such changes appear unable to transcend the insuperable geographical reality of its northern boundary. Writing in 1911, a London reporter claims that to cross over London Bridge is to cross 'that natural dividing line of peoples'; and in drawing attention to this remark some 90 years later, Peter Ackroyd suggests that it demonstrates 'an almost atavistic reverence for the natural boundary of the river which changes the essence of the territory on either bank.'[14] Indeed, Ackroyd goes much further, arguing that if we can regard London as representative of the wider world (which he does), then it is legitimate to regard this division between north and south as indicative of deeper evolutionary differences between these two riparian communities:

If London contains the world, then there is a world of meaning here. The distinction between the 'northern' and 'southern' races is of ancient date, the North being considered more ascetic and more robust than the effete and sensual South. It was a distinction emphasised by Darwin who, in the context of that theory of natural selection which he developed in London, declared that 'northern forms were enabled to beat the less powerful southern forms.' The 'southern forms' may be weaker because they come from too attenuated an origin, perhaps stretching back to the great tracts of mesolithic and neolithic time. Those noisome smells may in part include the odour of ancient history. And what of their pleasures? According to the London reporter of 1911, 'even the dramatic tastes of the people "over the water" are now supposed to be primitive; and "transpontine" is the adjective applied to melodrama that is too crude for the superior taste of northern London.'[15]

The idea that the Thames might be acting not only as the dividing line through the city but as an evolutionary barrier between two races of Londoners is such a fantastic notion that I turned to Darwin's *On the Origin of Species* in search of Ackroyd's source. A little disappointingly, I found that the passage to which Ackroyd refers compares specific forms of plant life, rather than opposing breeds of Londoner.[16] Nevertheless, it remains an enticing notion and one which simply underscores the divisive role the river plays in determining our sense of the city and its inhabitants.

Indeed, while London is subject to unceasing change on both sides of the river, the role of the Thames in maintaining the separation of the two communities on its banks may well be the only feature of the city to remain constant. Thus in post-war London we hear the familiar lament that the Thames 'has cleft a mighty city into two separate and distinct communities', with equally familiar consequences for those left stranded on the wrong side of this divide: 'The southerners are "foreigners" still, and their threadbare town is almost unknown to the vast majority of visitors to London.'[17] Written in 1949, Harry Williams' *South London* is truly a successor to Besant's downbeat assessment of south London's many ailments, at times surpassing Besant in its damning indictment of what is to be found along the Thames' southern shore. So comprehensive are these failings, in fact, that Williams struggles to identify an overriding cause, although he appears to share Besant's belief that the essential difficulty is that everything one might hope to find in the south, lies, unfortunately, to the north:

> Once, long ago, the seeds of a fair and lovely city were sown on the southern shore of the River Thames. The jungle of weeds which has choked their growth in modern times is a reflection both upon our taste and our common sense. It would seem that lack of foresight and absence of aesthetic standards of beauty have become part of the national character, particularly during the past three centuries. There was ugliness, squalor and misery in Elizabethan England, but there was also splendour, colourfulness, joyousness and gaiety on every hand. These words, as applied to the South London of our time, are without meaning. Progress has stopped our mouths with dust. [...] There is, in fact, something basically wrong about South London. Across "the water" as the denizens of Bermondsey call the Thames, vigorous life is still to be found. Law, Government, Finance, Insurance, Shipping, Entertainment, Art Galleries, Museums, historical pageantry, these things are almost the monopoly of the northern bank. [...] The search for the soul of South London in a desert of bricks and mortar has been an argosy with an ever-receding fleece, for the small successes have but pointed the way to the romance of a mighty city without ever reaching a goal. [...] The tapestry of more than a hundred square miles of teeming human life may be explored, but it retains its secret. No man living knows South London. [...] For, despite the fact that, as a town, it is barely one hundred and fifty years old, it is already moribund. It is a monument to mediocrity, bad taste, and lack of quality.[18]

Once again, this passage describes the south in familiar ways: the image of a desert is invoked, a wilderness of bricks and mortar to set aside other similarly barren southern wastelands; it is unknowable too, an alien space that withholds its secrets from the would-be explorer, its endless terrain too vast to comprehend; devoid of colour and individuality, aesthetically bankrupt, this south is strangely indistinct and homogeneous, lacking the intellectual vigour, the creative energy and the historical depth to be found in the north. In Darwin's terms, its evolutionary progress has been stunted, its growth 'choked' by a 'jungle of weeds'; within the context of natural selection it has clearly been exposed as the weaker form, inferior to its northern competitor. Yet is it not possible, even likely, that within such a vast expanse of 'teeming human life' the picture is somewhat more varied than Williams acknowledges? What is the secret that is retained beneath this moribund exterior?

Literary responses to suburban London, of which the south has been described as the 'consummate' example, have long since looked to answer these questions, with writers such as Charles Dickens, Arthur Machen and GK Chesterton, all having sought to illuminate this neglected space, revealing the bizarre and fantastic reality which may well lie hidden beneath the outward uniformity.[19] And just as we have seen the emergence of the Gothic elsewhere as an attempt to challenge perceptions of conformity and to imbue other conceptions of the south with a sense of the magical and the otherworldly, so too the suburban Gothic has performed a similar function in enchanting the overlooked expanses of south London. In recent years, as London has once again undergone an extraordinary metamorphosis, a new generation of writers has sought to capture these changes. But amongst this chorus of literary voices who now speaks for the south?[20] One such writer, as we have seen, is Angela Carter, her magical evocations of Lambeth amongst the few to capture the distinct mood of south London life; another is JG Ballard whose *The Drowned World* (1962) was to establish a southwards trajectory he was later to pursue in *The Unlimited Dream Company* (1979), an equally exotic, Blakean reimagining of his home-town, Shepperton. Other well established London writers, such as Iain Sinclair and the native south Londoner, Michael Moorcock, now more commonly associated with the east and west of the city respectively, have seemed somehow resistant to south London's peculiar microclimate, not least because of the difficulties they seem to have encountered in crossing the river: 'I was walking with Moorcock one time', Sinclair recalls, 'when we came, from the north, unexpectedly, mid-conversation, upon Westminster Bridge. He froze. I had a car parked on the other side in Lambeth. I'd have to fetch it and return to pick him up. He would not cross the Thames; it was a kind of death.'[21] Other writers who may previously have been averse to south London's charms, however, now appear to be recalibrating their sense of the south. Jonathan Raban, for example, the author of *Soft City* (1974), has formerly described the ways in which the would-be Londoner establishes their own territory: 'Its boundaries, originally arrived at by chance and usage, grow more not less real the longer I live in London. I have friends who live in Clapham, only three miles away, but to visit them is a definite journey, for it involves crossing the river. I can, though, drop in on friends in Islington, twice as far away as Clapham, since it is within what I feel to be my own territory.'[22] More than 30 years later, however, and from the perspective of Seattle where he now lives, Raban has acknowledged the changes that London has undergone in the intervening period; for in a trend replicated in cities across the globe, rising rents have seen the diversity once encountered only in the centre now transplanted to the suburbs, in an inversion of the historic pattern of London's growth:

> South of the river, I was lost, navigating by the London A-Z on cautious excursions to Clapham, Catford, Brixton and Battersea, each place intimately associated with a friend who, so far as I was concerned, might as well have chosen to live in Sevenoaks or Guildford. But all of London north of the Thames felt like home to me. […]

Nowadays, as a visitor to London, I still recognise the city I used to live in but in postal districts far from my old haunts. [....] If I were to move to London now, I'd go south – a long way south – of the river; in driving time at least, halfway to Brighton.[23]

Like Raban, must we too recalibrate our notion of the south, of where it begins and ends, and of what we are to find there? Just as Wegener was to postulate in his theory of polar migration, could it be that here too the south is on the move? For it seems that south London, for so long the poor relation to the north, is finally casting off its reputation for depressing anonymity in favour of the social diversity and cultural complexity previously to be found on the opposite side of the river. Writing at the turn of the new Millennium, with a call of 'Resurgam!' Peter Ackroyd proclaimed a new era of hope and prosperity for London as it once again looked to the future, the evidence for which he was to locate principally to the south of the river:

South London has been underdeveloped, in past centuries, but this neglect has allowed it effortlessly to reinvent itself. The point can be made by looking at the stretch of the Thames where much redevelopment is taking place. On the northern bank the streets and lanes are filled to bursting with business premises, so that no further alteration in its commercial aspect or direction is possible without more destruction. The relatively undeveloped tracts south of the Thames are in contrast available for a spirited and imaginative transformation. [...] The northern bank of the Thames, to use a contemporary expression, has been 'privatised'. To the south, however, there is interchange and animation; from the new Tate Modern to the Globe [...] The ancient hospitality and freedom of the South are emerging once more; in the twenty-first century it will become one of the most vigorous and varied, not to say popular, centres of London life. So the South Bank has been able triumphantly to reassert its past. [...] It is part of London's power. Where the past exists, the future may flourish.[24]

The south, then, if Ackroyd's prediction is to be believed, is the future of London; and it will reassert itself over the course of this century. The north bank, by contrast, overdeveloped to the point of saturation, 'privatised' and off-limits to much of its own population, is in no position to renew itself in a similar fashion. This is, for those of us south of the river, an attractive image, not least because of the suggestion that a historical imbalance between north and south may at last begin to be rectified. And if it were to happen here, one might well ask, would we not be justified in believing that such changes could also be effected elsewhere?

## Notes

1.  Williams, p. 2.
2.  Sinclair, *London Overground*, p. 4.
3.  Carter, *Wise Children*, p. 1.
4.  Carter, *Wise Children*, p. 1. Carter describes the city in similar terms in 'D'You mean South?' (1977; pp. 177–180) in which she paints a vivid portrait of the 'transpontine' south London of her childhood:

    It was not so much poverty and squalor and petty criminality that I remember best of south London in the 1950s but the seedy respectability of soiled net curtains and well-attended dancing classes, classical and tap, held in bay-windowed front rooms. [...] We are always on the defensive. We rarely look you straight in the eye. Shiftiness is the prevalent mode of demeanour. And we are always complaining, in a characteristic querulous whine. For us born-and-bred south Londoners, sun is always the herald of rain. Things are always less good than they were; or, we prophesy with relish, not as bad as they're going to be. We exhibit many of the more unattractive personality traits of the colonialized. We lugubriously enjoy the area's reputation for violence. [...] Things are clearly looking up. But something is wrong. [...] Anyway, if you just stand still, social mobility will catch up with you anywhere, these days.

5. Ged Pope writes (2008): 'The capital's centuries old centrifugal expansionism is now at an end. [...] While the metropolis is hollowed, expelled, turned inside out, the former suburbs accelerate, and expand, their logic of purely functionalised homogeneity, so that now neither recognisable urban core nor peripheral suburb can be truly identified or located.'
6. The sociologist, Garry Robson, quoted in Campkin, p. 20.
7. Ackroyd, *London*, p. 689.
8. Porter, p. 222.
9. Ackroyd, *London*, p. 692.
10. Blake, 'Milton' in *The Complete Poems*, pp. 521–522.
11. Besant, pp. 307 & 315.
12. Besant, pp. 319–320.
13. Ackroyd writes (*London*, p. 694):

The East End offered a more intense kind of community than the South; it possessed more open markets, for example, and more music halls. In the South, also, there was less contact with the rest of London. By sheer proximity the East End could share some of the energy and animation of the old City; it had, after all, existed against its walls for many centuries. But the great swathe of the river had always isolated the South, lending it a more desolate quality. It is reflected in those comments about south London which render it a distinct and alien place.

14. Ackroyd, *London*, pp. 694–5.
15. Ackroyd, *London*, p. 695.
16. Darwin's exact words are as follows (p. 324):

It is a remarkable fact [...] that many more identical plants and allied forms have apparently migrated from the north to the south, than in a reversed direction. We see, however, a few southern vegetable forms on the mountains of Borneo and Abyssinia. I suspect that this preponderant migration from north to south is due to the greater extent of land in the north, and to the northern forms having existed in their own homes in greater numbers, and having consequently been advanced through natural selection and competition to a higher stage of perfection or dominating power, than the southern forms. And thus, when they became commingled during the Glacial period, the northern forms were enabled to beat the less powerful southern forms.

17. Williams, p. 48.
18. Williams, pp. 1–3.
19. Pope writes (2008): 'South London is the consummate suburb. [...] Like the "real" south London itself, suburban writing is nowhere and everywhere, both ignored and ubiquitous. [...] The idea that respectable suburban appearances are hiding something bizarre or horrible is surely explicable by a desire for revelation, for meaning: the feeling that the suburb is so banal and ugly that *something* must be going on.'
20. In *Lights Out for the Territory*, Iain Sinclair supplies his own answer to this question (p. 142): 'We are all welcome to divide London according to our own anthologies: JG Ballard at Shepperton (the reservoirs, airport perimeter roads, empty film studios); Michael Moorcock at Notting Hill (visited by Jack Trevor Story); Angela Carter – south of the river, Battersea to Brixton, where she hands over to the poet Allen Fisher; Eric Mottram at Herne Hill, communing with the ghost of Ruskin.'
21. Sinclair, *London Overground*, p. 109.
22. Raban, *Soft City*, p. 192.
23. Raban, 'My Own Private Metropolis' (2008).
24. Ackroyd, *London*, pp. 696–7.

# Bibliography

Ackroyd, Peter, *London: The Biography*, London: Chatto & Windus, 2000

—, *Poe: A Life Cut Short*, London: Vintage, 2009

Arcara, Stefania, *Constructing the South: Sicily, Southern Italy and the Mediterranean in British Culture, 1773–1926*, University of Warwick, 1998, PhD thesis, wrap.warwick.ac.uk/36389/1/WRAP_THESIS_Arcara_1998.pdf

Adams, Rachel, 'Hipsters and jipitecas: Literary Countercultures on Both Sides of the Border', in *American Literary History*, 16(1) 2004, 58–84, at racheladams.net/articles/Hipsters.pdf

Aldrich, Robert, *France and the South Pacific since 1940*, London: Macmillan, 1993

Auden, WH, *The Complete Works of WH Auden, Prose: Volume II, 1939–1948*, Princeton University Press, 2002

Ayers, Edward, I & Mittendorf, Bradley, C, *The Oxford Book of the American South: Testimony, Memory and Fiction*, Oxford; OUP, 1997

Ballard, JG., *Cocaine Nights*, London: Harper Collins, 1996

—, *The Drowned World* (1962), London: Gollancz, 1999

—, *Super-Cannes*, London: Flamingo, 2000

—, *The Atrocity Exhibition* (1969), London: Fourth Estate, 2014

Bell-Villada, Gene H, *Borges and his Fiction: A Guide to his Mind and Art*, Chapel Hill: University of North Carolina Press, 1981

Bertram, Ernst, *Nietzsche: Attempt at a Mythology*, ed. and trans. by Robert E Norton, Champaign, IL: University of Illinois, 2009

Besant, Walter, *South London*, London: Chatto & Windus, 1899

Blake, William, *The Complete Poems*, ed. by Alicia Ostriker, London: Penguin, 1977

Bloom, Nicholas Dagen, ed., *Adventures into Mexico: American Tourism Beyond the Border*, Lanham, MD: Rowman & Littlefield, 2006

Borges, Jorge Luis, *Selected Poems, 1923–1967*, ed. by Norman Thomas di Giovanni, London: Penguin, 1972

—, 'The South' (1953) in *Fictions*, trans. by Andrew Hurley, London: Penguin, 2000, 146–153

Bruce, Susan, ed., *Three Early Modern Utopias*, Oxford: Oxford University Press, 1999

Buzard, James, *The Beaten Track: European Tourism, Literature, and the Ways to 'Culture', 1800–1918*, Oxford: OUP, 1993

Byrne, Madeleine, 'Jorge Luis Borges and the South' (2015) at http://madeleinebyrne.com/blog/2015/5/7/jorge-luis-borges-and-the-south

Campbell, John W., *Who Goes There?* (1938), London: Gollancz, 2011

Campkin, Ben, *Remaking London: Decline and Regeneration in Urban Culture*, London: I.B.Tauris, 2013

Carey, John, ed., *The Faber Book of Utopias*, London: Faber, 1999

Carter, Angela, *Wise Children*, London: Chatto & Windus, 1991

—, 'D'you Mean South?' (1977) in *Shaking a Leg: Collected Journalism and Writings*, London: Chatto & Windus, 1997, 177–180.

Che'êng-ên, Wu, *Monkey* (1942), trans. by Arthur Waley, London: Penguin, 2006

Cherry-Garrard, Apsley, *The Worst Journey in the World* (1922), ed. by Sara Wheeler, London: Vintage, 2003

Cocks, Catherine, *Tropical Whites: The Rise of the Tourist South in the Americas*, Philadelphia, PA: University of Pennsylvania Press, 2013

Cohen, David, *Chasing the Sun: The Epic Story of the Star that*

*Gives us Light*, London: Simon & Schuster, 2011

Coleridge, Samuel Taylor, *The Rime of the Ancient Mariner* (1817), ed. by Marina Warner, London: Vintage, 2004

Conrad, Peter, *Islands: A Trip Through Time and Space*, London: Thames & Hudson, 2009

Cook, James, *The Journals of Captain Cook*, ed. by Philip Edwards, London: Penguin, 1999

Coverley, Merlin, *Utopia*, Harpenden: Pocket Essentials, 2008

—, *The Art of Wandering: The Writer as Walker*, Harpenden: Oldcastle Books, 2012

Crane, Ralph; Leane, Elizabeth; Williams, Mark, eds., *Imagining Antarctica: Cultural Perspectives on the Southern Continent*, Hobart: University of Tasmania, 2011

Damon, S Foster, *A Blake Dictionary: The Ideas and Symbols of William Blake*, London: Thames & Hudson, 1973

Davenport-Hines, Rupert, *Auden*, London: Heinemann, 1995

Davidson, Peter, *The Idea of North*, London: Reaktion Books, 2005

Darwin, Charles, *On the Origin of Species* (1859), ed. by William Bynum, London: Penguin, 2009

Day, David, *Antarctica: A Biography*, Oxford: OUP, 2013

De la Mare, Walter, *Desert Islands* (1930), London: Faber, 1988

Di Giovanni, Norman Thomas, *The Lesson of the Master: On Borges and his Work*, London: Continuum, 2003

Dodds, Klaus, *Antarctica: A Very Short Introduction*, Oxford: OUP, 2012

Evans, Julian, *Transit of Venus: Travels in the Pacific*, London: Minerva, 1993

—, 'Transit of Venus: a celestial wonder watched from the shores of the South Pacific', *Daily Telegraph*, 11 June 2012, at http://www.telegraph.co.uk/travel/destinations/australiaandpacific/frenchpolynesia/9324797/Transit-of-Venus-a-celestial-wonder-watched-from-the-shores-of-the-South-Pacific.html

Faulkner, William, *Absalom, Absalom!* (1936), London: Vintage, 1995

Fiddian, Robin, 'Post-colonial Borges', in *The Cambridge Companion to Jorge Luis Borges*, ed. by Edwin Williamson, New York: Cambridge University Press, 2013, 96–109

Fort, Charles, *The Books of Charles Fort*, New York: Henry Holt, 1941

Fussell, Paul, *Abroad: British Literary Travelling Between the Wars*, Oxford: OUP, 1982

García-Robles, Jorge, *At the End of the Road: Jack Kerouac in Mexico*, trans. by Daniel C Schechter, Minneapolis, MN: University of Minnesota Press, 2014

Gauguin, Paul, *Noa Noa: The Tahitian Journal* (1919), trans. by OF Theis, New York: Dover, 1985

Godwin, Joscelyn, *Arktos: Polar Myth in Science, Symbolism and Nazi Survival*, London: Thames & Hudson, 1993

Goethe, Johann Wolfgang von, *Italian Journey (1786–1788)*, trans. by Elizabeth Mayer & WH Auden, London: Penguin, 1982

—, *The Collected Works, Vol. 6: Italian Journey*, trans. by Robert R Heitner, with an introduction by Thomas P. Saine, Princeton, NJ: Princeton University Press, 1994

—, *The Flight to Italy: Diary and Selected Letters*, ed. and trans. by TJ Reed, Oxford: OUP, 1999

Gopnik, Adam, *Winter: Five Windows on the Season*, London: Quercus, 2012

Gramsci, Antonio, 'Some Aspects of the Southern Question' (1926) in *The Antonio Gramsci Reader: Selected Writings 1916–1935*, ed. by David Forgacs, trans. by Quintin Hoare, London: Lawrence & Wishart, 1988, 171–185

Greene, Graham, *The Lawless Roads* (1939), London: Vintage, 2002

Gunn, Drewey Wayne, *American and British Writers in Mexico, 1556–1973*, Austin, TX: University of Texas Press, 1974

Gyrus, *North: The Rise and the Fall of the Polar Cosmos*, London: Strange Attractor, 2014

Harman, Claire, *Robert Louis Stevenson: A Biography*, London:

Harper Collins, 2005

Holmes, Richard, *The Age of Wonder: How the Romantic Generation Discovered the Beauty and Terror of Science*, London; Harper Press, 2009

Hulme, Peter & Youngs, Tim, eds, *The Cambridge Companion to Travel Writing*, Cambridge: Cambridge University Press, 2002

Hunt, James B, *Restless Fires: Young John Muir's Thousand Mile Walk to the Gulf in 1867–68*, Macon, GA: Mercer University Press, 2012

Irwin, John T, *The Mystery to a Solution: Poe, Borges and the Analytic Detective Story*, Baltimore, MD: John Hopkins University Press, 1994

Jagoe, Eva-Lynn Alicia, *The End of the World as They Knew It: Writing Experiences of the Argentine South*, Lewisburg, PA: Bucknell University Press, 2008

James, Henry, *Italian Hours* (1909), ed. by John Auchard, London: Penguin, 1992

Jebb, Miles, *Walkers*, London: Constable, 1986

Kay, Laura, 'It was a Very Long Dark and Stormy Night: 'Bad' Antarctic Fiction from the Pulps to the Self-Published', in *Imagining Antarctica: Cultural Perspectives on the Southern Continent*, ed. by Ralph Crane, Elizabeth Leane, and Mark Williams, Hobart: University of Tasmania, 2011, 89–105

Kerouac, Jack, *On the Road* (1957), ed. by Ann Charters, London: Penguin, 2000

Kershaw, Alex, *Jack London: A Life*, London: Flamingo, 1998

King, John, *Sur: A Study of the Argentine Literary Journal and its Role in the Development of a Culture: 1931–1970*, Cambridge: Cambridge University Press, 1986

Kolb, Martina, *Nietzsche, Freud, Benn, and the Azure Spell of Liguria*, Toronto: University of Toronto Press, 2013

Lansdown, Richard, ed., *Strangers in the South: The Idea of the Pacific in Western Thought*, Honolulu, HI: University of Hawaii Press, 2006

Lawrence, DH, *Twilight in Italy and Other Essays* (1916), ed. by Paul Eggert, with an introduction by Stefania Michelucci,

London: Penguin, 1994

—, 'Sun' (1928) in *Selected Stories*, ed. by Louise Welsh, London; Penguin, 2007, 245–268

Leane, Elizabeth, *Antarctica in Fiction: Imaginative Narratives of the Far South*, Cambridge: Cambridge University Press, 2012

Lee, Laurie, *As I Walked Out One Midsummer Morning* (1969), London: Penguin, 1973

Leigh Fermor, Patrick, *A Time of Gifts* (1977), London: Hodder, 2004

Lewis, Norman, *Voices of the Old Sea*, London: Hamish Hamilton, 1984

—, *The Missionaries: God Against the Indians*, London: Vintage, 1998

Littlewood, Ian, *Sultry Climates: Travel and Sex Since the Grand Tour*, London: John Murray, 2001

London, Jack, *Tales of the Pacific* (1911) ed. by Andrew Sinclair, London: Penguin, 1989

Lovecraft, HP, *At the Mountains of Madness* (1931), ed. by China Miéville, New York: Random House, 2005

Maher, Paul Jr., *Jack Kerouac's American Journey: The Real-Life Odyssey of 'On the Road'*, Cambridge, MA: Thunder's Mouth Press, 2007

Marshall, Sara, ed. *America in Literature: The South*, New York: Scribner's, 1979

McGhee, Robert, *The Last Imaginary Place: A Human History of the Arctic World*, Oxford: OUP, 2006

Melberg, Arne, 'What did Nietzsche do on Capri?' (2007) at http://www.villasanmichele.eu/en/what_did_nietzsche

Melville, Herman, *Typee: A Peep at Polynesian Life* (1846), ed. by John Bryant, London: Penguin, 2000

—, *Omoo* (1847), ed. by Mary K. Bercaw Edwards, London: Penguin, 2007

—, *Moby Dick* (1851), ed. by Tony Tanner, Oxford: Oxford University Press, 2008

Michaels-Tonks, Jennifer, *DH Lawrence: The Polarity of North and South – Germany and Italy in his Prose Works*, Bonn:

Bouvier, 1976

Mighall, Robert, *Sunshine: One Man's Search for Happiness*, London: John Murray, 2008

Muir, John, *A Thousand-Mile Walk to the Gulf* (1916), ed. by Peter Jenkins with an introduction by William Frederic Badè, New York: Mariner Books, 1998

—, *John Muir's Last Journey: South to the Amazon and East to Africa. Unpublished Journals and Selected Correspondence*, ed. by Michael P Branch, Washington, DC: Shearwater Books, 2001

Murray, Kevin, 'Magicians of the South' (2002) at http://www.craftunbound.net/texts/magicians-of-the-south

—, 'Verticalism and its Underbelly' (2009) at http://ideaofsouth.net/verticalism/verticalism-and-its-underbelly

—, 'Where North Meets South' (2010) at http://kevinmurray.com.au/text/where-north-meets-south

Nelson, Victoria, *The Secret Life of Puppets*, Cambridge, MA: Harvard University Press, 2001

Nietzsche, Friedrich, *The Gay Science*, trans. by Walter Kaufmann, New York: Vintage, 1974

—, *Basic Writings of Nietzsche*, ed. and trans. by Walter Kaufmann, New York: The Modern Library, 2000

O'Brien, Michael, *The Idea of the American South: 1920–1941*, Baltimore, ML: John Hopkins University Press, 1979

Owen, Richard, *Lady Chatterley's Villa: DH Lawrence on the Italian Riviera*, London: Haus Publishing, 2014

Pemble, John, *The Mediterranean Passion: Victorians and Edwardians in the South*, Oxford: Clarendon Press, 1987

Poe, Edgar Allan, *The Narrative of Arthur Gordon Pym of Nantucket and Related Tales*, ed. by J Gerald Kennedy, Oxford: OUP, 1994

Pope, Ged, 'Deep in South London', *Literary London: Interdisciplinary Studies in the Representation of London*, Volume 6, Number 1 (March 2008) at http://www.literarylondon.org/london-journal/march2008/pope.html

Porter, Roy, *London: A Social History*, London: Hamish Hamilton, 1994

Prange, Martine, *Nietzsche, Wagner, Europe*, Berlin: De Gruyter, 2013

Pyne, Stephen, *The Ice: A Journey to Antarctica*, London: Arlington Books, 1987

Raban, Jonathan, 'My Own Private Metropolis', *Financial Times*, August 9, 2008 at http://www.ft.com/cms/s/0/247bc052-64dc-11dd-af61-0000779fd18c.html

—, *Soft City* (1974), London: Picador, 2008

Rennie, Neil, *Far-Fetched Facts: The Literature of Travel and the Idea of the South Seas*, London: Clarendon Press, 1998

Rennison, Nick, *A Short History of Polar Exploration*, Harpenden: Pocket Essentials, 2013

Ripa, Cesare, *Iconologia, or Moral Emblems*, illustrated by Isaac Fuller, London: Pierce Tempest, 1709 at https://archive.org/details/iconologiaormora00ripa

Rundle, Guy, 'A Surreal Visitor', in *The Age*, Melbourne, April 22, 2002 at http://www.theage.com.au/articles/2002/04/22/1019233309914.html

Ruskin, John, 'The Nature of the Gothic' (1853), in *Unto This Last and Other Writings*, ed. by Clive Wilmer, London: Penguin, 1997, 77–109

Sarlo, Beatriz, *Jorge Luis Borges: A Writer on the Edge*, Cambridge: Verso, 1993

Schwarz, Benjamin, 'The Idea of South' in *The Atlantic*, December1997,athttp://www.theatlantic.com/magazine/archive/1997/12/the-idea-of-the-south/377028/

Scott, Robert Falcon, *Journals: Captain Scott's Last Expedition* (1913) ed. by Max Jones, Oxford: OUP, 2008

Seaborn, Adam, *Symzonia: A Voyage of Discovery*, New York: J Seymour, 1820

Shackleton, Ernest, *South: The Endurance Expedition*, (1919) ed. by Fergus Fleming, London: Penguin, 2013

Sheldon, Glenn, *South of Our Selves: Mexico in the Poems of Williams, Kerouac, Corso, Ginsberg, Levertov, and Hayden*, Jefferson, NC: McFarland & Company, 2004

Shiel, MP, *The Purple Cloud* (1901), ed. by John Sutherland, London: Penguin, 2012

Sinclair, Iain, *Lights Out for the Territory*, London: Granta, 1997

—, *London Overground: A Day's Walk around the Ginger Line*, London: Hamish Hamilton, 2015

Smith, Herbert F, *John Muir*, New York: Twayne Publishers, 1965

Spellman, David Enrique, *Far South*, London: Serpent's Tail, 2011

Spengler, Oswald, *The Decline of the West: An Abridged Edition*, introduction by H. Stuart Hughes, Oxford: OUP, 1991

Spufford, Francis, *I May Be Some Time: Ice and the English Imagination*, London: Faber, 2003

—, ed., *Antarctica: An Anthology*, London; Granta, 2007

—, 'The Uses of Antarctica: Roles for the Southern Continent in Twentieth-Century Culture', in *Imagining Antarctica: Cultural Perspectives on the Southern Continent*, ed. by Ralph Crane, Elizabeth Leane, and Mark Williams, Hobart: University of Tasmania, 2011, 17–30

Standish, David, *Hollow Earth: The Long and Curious History of Imagining Strange Lands, Fantastical Creatures, Advanced Civilisations and Marvelous Machines Below the Earth's Surface*, Cambridge, MA: Da Capo Press, 2006

Stevenson, Robert Louis, 'Ordered South' (1874) in *Travels with a Donkey in the Cevennes and Selected Other Travel Writings*, ed. by Emma Letley, Oxford: Oxford University Press, 1992, 243–254

—, *In the South Seas* (1896), ed. by Neil Rennie, London: Penguin, 1998

—, *South Sea Tales*, ed. by Roslyn Jolly, Oxford: Oxford University Press, 2008

Tindall, George B, 'Mythology: A New Frontier in Southern History', in *Myth and Southern History, Vol. 1: The Old South*, ed. by Patrick Gerster & Nicholas Cords, Champaign, IL: University of Illinois, 1989, 1–17

Tremlett, Giles, *Ghosts of Spain: Travels through a Country's*

*Hidden Past*, London: Faber, 2007

Updike, John, *Rabbit, Run* (1960), London: Penguin, 2006

Waisman, Sergio Gabriel, *Borges and Translation: The Irreverence of the Periphery*, Lewisburg, PA: Bucknell University Press, 2005

Walker, Gabrielle, *Antarctica: An Intimate Portrait of the World's Most Mysterious Continent*, London: Bloomsbury, 2012

Weightman, John, 'The Solar Revolution: Reflections on a Theme in French Literature', *Encounter*, December 1970, 9–18.

Wheeler, Sara, *Terra Incognita: Travels in Antarctica*, London: Jonathan Cape, 1996

Williams, Harry, *South London*, London: Robert Hale, 1949

Williamson, Edwin, *Borges: A Life*, London: Penguin, 2005

Wilson, Eric G, *The Spiritual History of Ice: Romanticism, Science and the Imagination*, London: Palgrave Macmillan, 2009

Wortham, Christopher, 'Meanings of the South: From the *Mappaemundi* to Shakespeare's *Othello*', in *European Perceptions of Terra Australis*, ed. by Anne M Scott, Alfred Hiatt, Claire McIlroy and Christopher Wortham, Farnham: Ashgate, 2011, 61–81

Zolov, Eric, 'Discovering a Land "Mysterious and Obvious": The Renarrativizing of Postrevolutionary Mexico', in *Fragments of a Golden Age: The Politics of Culture in Mexico Since 1940*, ed. by Gilbert M Joseph, Anne Rubenstein & Eric Zolov, Durham, NC: Duke University Press, 2001, 234–272

Zweig, Stefan, *Hölderlin, Kleist, and Nietzsche: The Struggle with the Daemon*, Brunswick, NJ: Transaction Publishers, 2011

—, 'Flight into Immortality: The Discovery of the Pacific Ocean', (1940) in *Shooting Stars: Ten Historical Miniatures*, trans. by Anthea Bell, London: Pushkin Press, 2013, 11–38

## Websites:

The Idea of South
www.ideaofsouth.net

South is South
http://southissouth.wordpress.com

Roger Mills – Idea of South
www.eartrumpet.org/ios/

Far South Project
http://farsouthproject.tumblr.com/
http://www.far-south.org/

Southern Perspectives
http://www.southernperspectives.net/

Representations of Antarctica
http://www.antarctic-circle.org/fiction.htm

North: The Rise & Fall of the Polar Cosmos
http://polarcosmology.com/

# Index

# INDEX